ANGLISTISCHE FORSCHUNGEN
Band 474

Begründet von
Johannes Hoops

Herausgegeben von
Rüdiger Ahrens
Heinz Antor
Klaus Stierstorfer

JOSÉ M. YEBRA

The Traumatic Celebration of Beauty in Alan Hollinghurst's Fiction

Universitätsverlag
WINTER
Heidelberg

Bibliografische Information der Deutschen Nationalbibliothek

Die Deutsche Nationalbibliothek verzeichnet diese Publikation
in der Deutschen Nationalbibliografie;
detaillierte bibliografische Daten sind im Internet
über *http://dnb.d-nb.de* abrufbar.

This is an updated (including the analysis of Hollinghurst's latest novels)
and improved version of my PhD Thesis *Identity and Intertextuality in
Alan Hollinghurst's Fiction* (University of Zaragoza, June 2009).

The author gratefully acknowledges the support of the Spanish Ministry of
Economy, Industry and Competitiveness (MINECO) and the European Regional
Development Fund (DGI/ERDF) (code FFI2017-84258-P); the Government of
Aragón and the ERDF 2014–2020 programme "Building Europe from Aragón"
(code H03_20R), and IEDIS for the writing of this monograph.

UMSCHLAGBILD

The Analysis of Beauty, Plate 1, March 5, 1753, William Hogarth,
The Metropolitan Museum of Art, Harris Brisbane Dick Fund, 1932, 32.35(22)
https://www.metmuseum.org/art/collection/search/365314

ISBN 978-3-8253-4966-0

© 2022 Universitätsverlag Winter GmbH Heidelberg
Imprimé en Allemagne · Printed in Germany
Druck: Memminger MedienCentrum, 87700 Memmingen

Gedruckt auf umweltfreundlichem, chlorfrei gebleichtem
und alterungsbeständigem Papier.

Den Verlag erreichen Sie im Internet unter:
www.winter-verlag.de

Contents

The Traumatic Celebration of Beauty in Alan Hollinghurst's Fiction[1]

Introduction: On juxtaposition, Narcissus and Echo

Drawing on Freud, Cathy Caruth makes reference to the story of Tancred and Clorinda to address the uncanny nature of trauma. After undergoing a catastrophic event, the traumatised is bound to re-experience it. This repetition, Caruth argues, escapes the wish or control of the victim, who is possessed "by a sort of fate."[2] A particularly moving example of traumatic haunting is the story of Tancred and Clorinda in Tasso's *Gerusalemme Liberata*.[3] It is a tragic love story, Tancred wounding his beloved Clorinda twice; first, in a duel, when she turns up in the armour of the enemy. Once dead, she blends with a tree in a magic forest. Tancred, a crusader, gets into the forest and slashes at the tree by chance. It is then that Clorinda's voice is heard again claiming she has been wounded for a second time by the one she loves. Tasso's story serves Freud and Caruth to conclude that "the repetition at the heart of the catastrophe [...] emerges as the unwitting reenactment of an event that one cannot simply leave behind."[4] There are two preliminary issues from Caruth's analysis I would like to focus on, namely repetition compulsion and the status of victim (who does not know) and perpetrator (who does know).

From the Latin re-petere, repetition is a coming back to beseech and ask for, but also to attack and strive after. That is the oxymoron of Tasso's story and of trauma as well. One comes back as a passive individual, a victim looking for comprehension and empathy. But one can also come back as a perpetrator looking for redemption out of guilt. In both cases, one is returned by events that haunt the traumatised. The idea of (unwillingly) returning to an unfathomable scenario constitutes a myth of origins that may help understand the logic of trauma: Freud's death drive, the return to Arcadia and Christian return to Paradise or the return of a new Jerusalem are some examples. Clorinda returns in the form of blood and a voice from a tall tree. Her wounding thus haunts the unwilling perpetrator, and hence victim, Tancred. However, what if Tancred is not wounding Clorinda by chance? What if, as a Christian king, he wounds Clorinda,

---

[1] This is an updated (including the analysis of Hollinghurst's latest novels) and improved version of my PhD Thesis *Identity and Intertextuality in Alan Hollinghurst* (University of Zaragoza, June 2009). The author gratefully acknowledges the support of the Spanish Ministry of Economy, Industry and Competitiveness (MINECO) and the European Regional Development Fund (DGI/ERDF) (code FFI2017-84258-P); the Government of Aragón and the ERDF 2014–2020 programme "Building Europe from Aragón" (code H03_20R), and IEDIS for the writing of this essay.
[2] Cathy Caruth: *Unclaimed Experience: Trauma, Narrative, and History*, Baltimore 1996, 1.
[3] Ibid., 1.
[4] Ibid., 2.

consciously or unconsciously, to control her otherness? A white originally raised by
Africans, and warrior of the Saracen army who converts to Christianity before being
killed by Tancred, Clorinda is doubly saved, doubly returned to her Western whiteness.
Obviously, as Amy Novak argues, this aspect has not been overlooked by postcolonial
theorists.[5] Caruth has been accused of privileging whites' 'accident' or 'event'-based
traumata rather than the insidiousness "that involve[s] everyday, repeated forms of
traumatising violence, such as sexism, racism, and colonialism."[6] Is Clorinda's death
triggered by an unwilling event (e.g. Tancred wounds by chance) or by a culturally-
driven insidious racism that repeats itself (e.g. Tancred wounds by compulsion)? This
ambivalence, which I endorse, is problematic in Ruth Leys's view. For her, Tancred can
never be a victim as long as he is the perpetrator of an event whose sole victim is
Clorinda. Many postcolonial critics have "seconded Leys's critique of the apparent
collapse of distinction between perpetrators and victims."[7] This reasoning, though
irrefutable at first glance, can be read otherwise. Rothberg breaks the knot arguing it is a
category error that leads Leys, Novak and others to reject Caruth's interpretation of the
myth. Thus, he lucidly claims: "The categories of victim and perpetrator derive from
either a legal or moral discourse, but the concept of trauma derives from a diagnostic
realm that lies beyond guilt and innocence, good and evil."[8] Trauma narratives can
interfere with "legal and political judgments;" and hence, they should not "be a category
that confirms moral value."[9] This said, is the status of trauma also exclusively
diagnostic in the case of literary trauma narratives? Or has literature an ontology of its
own, the legitimacy to re-categorise trauma-related individuals in aesthetic, ethical and
political terms?

Ovid's myth of nymph Echo and hunter Narcissus draws on Tancred and Clorinda's
in more senses than one, but, thanks to its homoerotic undertones, it serves better the
purposes of this book. Like Clorinda, Echo is doubly wounded. First, she is cursed by
Juno because the once noisy nymph covers Zeus's affairs. Hence, she is deprived of the
use of speech, "except to babble and repeat the words."[10] She is wounded to death when
Narcissus, the man she is in love with, despises her: "He flies from her and as he leaves
her says, 'Take off your hands! You shall not fold your arms around me. Better death
than *such a one* should ever caress me!.'"[11] Unable to speak, but to repeat what others
say, the nymph can only answer "caress me" as both a cursed repetition and a desperate
beseech. Like Clorinda, Echo fades away, for "nothing remains except her bones and
voice."[12] The trauma of repetition also impinges on Narcissus, though in a different
fashion. It is here that Ovid's story departs from Tasso's again. Narcissus's mother,
Liriope, takes him to prophet Tiresias who forecasts the youth's future in a then
unknowable riddle: "If he but fails to recognize himself, a long life he may have,

---

[5]   In Michael Rothberg: *Multidirectional Memory: Remembering the Holocaust in the Age of
      Decolonization*, Stanford 2009, 89.
[6]   Ibid.
[7]   Ibid.
[8]   Ibid., 90.
[9]   Ibid.
[10] Ovid: *The Metamorphoses*, http://anthony.sogang.ac.kr/Classics/OvidEchoNarcissus.htm,
      511-12.
[11] Ibid., 556-558, my italics.
[12] Ibid., 569.

beneath the sun."[13] The riddle unfolds when Narcissus sees himself reflected on a pool and falls in love with his own reflection. Unable to recognize himself, his own image rejecting him, he can only bemoan his fate: "Oh, ye aisled wood was ever man in love more fatally than I?."[14] Indeed, the homoerotic undertones of Narcissus self-love are in line with "the 'old story' of fatal gay love.[15] Although fatal gay love usually ends up in murder rather than suicide, Narcissus's suicide is due to the excess of sameness classically attributed to homosexuality. Allan Johnson reads Narcissus's crisis as "his inability to situate his love within any known models of sexuality." [16] Although homosexuality is a well-defined model, Hollinghurst's heroes' homoeroticism is de-normalised to be regulated in untertextual terms. Narcissus's self-love is a case in point when he cries: "I am tortured by a strange desire."[17] The uncanny of loving (rather than identifying with) the same, as Narcissus claims, was pathologised by medical and psychoanalytic discourses. The myth helps power to construct its discourses of coercion, Narcissus's being a powerful one. His self-love triggers (and is owing to) a traumatic dissociation that threatens with erasing his identity: "No more my shade deceives me, I perceive 'Tis I in thee I love myself, the flame arises in my breast and burns my heart —what shall I do?[18] His desire for his beauty only increases when he rents "his garment from the upper edge," and "his naked breast, all white as marble,"[19] comes into view. Yet, self-love runs parallel to self-hatred. Unable to cope with his strange desire, Narcissus can only dissociate from himself beating his breast to blood. Dissociation does not heal, and the youth embraces himself to death. Before that happens, however, Echo comes back to give Narcissus's dissociation a new turn. Repeating his last words, Echo becomes Narcissus's relational other, which only confirms and spreads the impossibility of the other and his traumatic love and fate:

> 'Alas!' 'Alas!' her echoing voice returned; and as he struck his hands against his arms, she ever answered with her echoing sounds. And as he gazed upon the mirrored pool he said at last, 'Ah, youth beloved in vain!' 'In vain, in vain!' the spot returned his words; and when he breathed a sad 'farewell!' 'Farewell!' sighed Echo too.[20]

Johnson delves into narcissism as belatedness and as a trope of homosexuality, drawing on Edward Said's view that "lateness is the idea of surviving beyond what is acceptable and normal."[21] I go further, though. Like Clorinda's, Echo's repetition is not mere ventriloquism, but a call to cultural trauma that has been assimilated and transmitted to gays and through gay generations. It exposes what Gregory Woods has called 'the tragic queer.' Narcissus's tragedy has, however, a beautiful aftermath since "in his body's place a sweet flower grew, golden and white, the white around the gold."[22] Much before

---

13   Ibid., 493-494.
14   Ibid., 637-640.
15   Kevin Kopelson: *Love's Litany. The Writing of Modern Homoerotics*, Stanford 1994, 28.
16   Allan Johnson: *Alan Hollinghurst and the Vitality of Influence*. London 2014, 77.
17   Ovid: *Metamorphoses, 679*.
18   Ibid., 674-675.
19   Ibid., 701-702.
20   Ibid., 723-729.
21   Johnson: *Alan Hollinghurst, 66*.
22   Ovid: *Metamorphoses, 744-745*.

fin-de-siècle Decadentism, beauty constitutes the palimpsestic underside of the tragic
queer or, rather, the tragic queer as the underside of beauty. Beauty is repetition of
canonical lines. But repetition is in itself a coming back without end and hence, in a
rather Lacanian fashion, an act of anxious desire for the impossible. In other words,
repeating implies dissatisfaction. And what is more unsatisfactory and eventually
traumatic than desiring (dissociating from) oneself, coming back once and again?
Narcissus, Johnson argues, "becomes, at once, lover and beloved, master and pupil,
subject and object, and it is in this inability to rationalize such demand [...] that leads to
his lethal despair."[23] The tension between Narcissus's excess of sameness and traumatic
end, and the hero's beauty, which Echo spreads, makes up the discourse of
Hollinghurst's novels and characters' fates. Indeed, the present volume contends there
has been a progressive shift from the Narcissistic to the Echoic in Hollinghurst's fiction;
his early production mostly focused on self-centred heroes/narrators while the discourse
of his latest novels is more ambiguous and echoic, i.e. resounding with transgenerational echoes.

Michèle Mendelssohn and Dennis Flannery's edited volume *Alan Hollinghurst:
Writing under the Influence*[24] and Allan Johnson's monograph *Alan Hollinghurst and
the Vitality of Influence* analyse how the writer is tributary to a literary and artistic
tradition. In other words, they intend to explain Hollinghurst's visual and textual
universe as a repository of gay sensibilities along the twentieth century. The emphasis is
mostly in the process of connection and influence rather than in the effect. His novels
become thus a dialogic space rather than a final product. It seems to me that it is the
fluency in the in-fluence that matters. This influence is, however, not only a
textual/visual event. There is corporeality in the transference that often Mendelssohn,
Flannery and Johnson overlook. However, the connection between body and literary
sensibility is one of the main concerns of Mark Mathuray's edited volume *Sex and
Sensibility in the novels of Alan Hollinghurst*.[25] *The Traumatic Celebration of Beauty in
Hollinghurst's Fiction* breaks through the poetics of influence through an ambivalent
liminal discourse that embraces ethical, political and aesthetic concerns.

Alan Hollinghurst is one of the leading voices in the contemporary English literary
panorama; the best English novelist at the moment in Leo Tait's view.[26] Though not a
prolific writer —he has published just six novels so far in the span of thirty years— he
has received the attention and almost general acclaim by the critics. Hollinghurst has
reached this status of a gay writer he himself assumes (though he also transcends it),[27]
being 'out' and addressing "issues of homosexual desire and culture directly."[28] His
assumption of a gay narrative voice, which, according to Moss, he pioneered, does not
imply Hollinghurst does not aim at a universal readership.[29] Rather unexpectedly for an
'out' gay writer, he yearns for a pre-gay scenario claiming that the literature "of the

[23]   Johnson: *Alan Hollinghurst,* 74.
[24]   Michèle Mendelssohn and Dennis Flannery: *Alan Hollinghurst: Writing under the Influence*,
       Manchester 2016.
[25]   Mark Mathuray: *Sex and Sensibility in the novels of Alan Hollinghurst*, London 2017.
[26]   Tait, Leo: *The Stranger's Child* by Alan Hollinghurst review, 2011, https://bit.ly/3g4rnGM.
[27]   Stephen Moss: "I don't make moral judgments," 2004.
[28]   Mark Lilly: *Gay Men's Literature in the Twentieth Century*, London 1993, xv.
[29]   Alan Sinfield: *Gay and After*, London 1998, 112.

necessarily more discreet period prior to partial decriminalisation was obliged to be more mainstream and was therefore in some sense more universal in its appeal, less self-regarding and particularistic."[30] From this oxymoronic, often paradoxical, position, this book aims at analysing the (literary) discourses of homosexual representation recast by Hollinghurst in his six novels. My main contention is that, rather than being derivative texts, these novels adapt the same-sex literary tradition to the fluctuating panorama resulting from the AIDS crisis, new identity discourses and the current ethical turn. To do so, I will make reference to trauma theory, as a narcissistic rhetoric of coming back that echoes throughout Hollinghurst's fiction, and the rhetorics of transgression (for example, the Dionysian) and survival. Thus, the study starts with the delaying melancholia prevailing in his early fiction to later address the increasing ambiguity and relationality of his latest novels.

In view of Hollinghurst's controversial discourses (mainly) about sex and politics, as well as his aesthetic sensibility, Mark Mathuray claims there are two camps of critics in the writer's current scholarship. Although he acknowledges both groups overlap, the first "address directly and often problematise Hollinghurst's depictions of sex and same-sex desire and his representation of social regulative mechanisms of policing desire, and their significance for a contemporary politics of sexuality in his work. [...] The other group [...] usually address and celebrate his stylistic mastery and his English literary sensibility."[31] The first camp is mainly composed of gay activists committed to LGTBI politics[32] while the second, mostly literary critics, praises the writer's recasting of the English canon.[33] *The Traumatic Celebration of Beauty in Hollinghurst's Fiction* transits the liminal territory between both groups. The novelist's apparent lack of political and ethical commitment is probably related to his poetics of coming back, camp and oversexualisation. For some politically-committed groups, his literary style is too nostalgic, aesthetisised and celebratory to be effective. Like Ronald Firbank and Henry James, two of Hollinghurst's tutelary spirits, his novels are rejected by some queer criticism for being too gay, too nostalgic and too celebratory at the same time. Once again, camp is accused of being too decadent a discourse to be taken seriously. Drawing on the myth of Narcissus and Echo, his writing has been read as too self-committed (rather than committed to the other) as if somehow condemned to repeat itself (in line with gay tradition). This, which is a drawback for the first group, constitutes an asset for most reviewers. As Geoff Dyer argues and the volumes by Mendelssohn and Flannery and Johnson confirm, Hollinghurst's fiction proves "the inexhaustible vitality of the English novel."[34] It can be argued that his style is overshadowed by the AIDS trauma and a more structural trauma poetics, namely Woods's 'the tragic queer.' However, there is more to Hollinghurst than the tension between trauma and vacuous celebration. Trauma aesthetics is a potent metaphor and a potential galvanizer of change. And although his is not a politically-driven discourse, it is more ethically and politically committed than Mathuray's first camp of critics presume. Gay bodies and their aestheticisation matter, but also their political regulation and its ethical consequences.

---

[30] David Alderson and Linda Anderson (eds): *Territories of Desire in Queer Culture*, Manchester 2000, 29.

[31] Mathuray, *Sex*, 3.

[32] Ibid., 3.

[33] Ibid.

[34] Geoff Dyer: "The Secret Gardener," https://nym.ag/33jGGZ4, 2011.

The canon of gay 'sensibility' (or, rather, sensibilities) has been under a process of permanent re-construction. Thus, modern anthologies resurface early —frequently cryptic— representations of same-sex desire, explore their interaction with their gay hypertexts and call attention to new gay texts. Claude Summers's *Gay Literary Heritage*[35] and Gregory Woods's *The Gay Male Literary Tradition*[36] are two examples of the hardships of gay essentialists to canonise gay literature. Hollinghurst also addresses gay literary sensibility. However, unlike Summers and Woods, he is part of that sensibility, which makes the relation to it much more intricate and problematic. Hollinghurst's ambivalent discourse derives from his double status, as gay and writer. He feels politically committed to the gay liberation movement and the visibilisation of same-sex desire. Yet, he is aesthetically committed to a homoerotic literary tradition that underpins the movement but that also defies its politics of visibilisation. Yesteryear repression against homosexuals paradoxically furthered a poetics of indirection and sublimation in homosexual literature that Hollinghurst reclaims. *The Swimming-pool Library*[37] longs for the language of reticence of the closet, but simultaneously relies on the (homo-)sexual explicitness of post-Stonewall politics; the novel lives in the present but with an eye permanently looking backwards. In an interview, Hollinghurst himself explains that the novel "grew in part out of [...] the contrast between concealment and display."[38] That is, the novel juxtaposes the sublimation of old homoerotic texts and the overt sexuality of post-gay liberation literature. This juxtaposition has several purposes: first, it recalls how old homoerotic texts had to develop literary strategies to codify their 'true' messages and thereby escape a tacit (heterosexual) censorship. Second, it puts forward how this language of indirection and obliquity allegedly lost its *raison d'être* with the success of the gay liberation movement. Finally, in spite of the new political and social circumstances, old homoerotic texts and strategies are meaningful for the new generation of gay writers as a reserve of aesthetic possibilities and also to face new homophobic traumas, especially after the AIDS crisis. That is, the new generation of gay writers vindicates the tradition of the closet both for aesthetic illumination and survival.

In keeping with this, though the characters of *The Swimming-pool Library* live at the end of the twentieth century, they are still 'victims' of history and the different formulas of representing same-sex desire. When the past strikes back, Hollinghurst's characters must revise their roles and the world around them.[39] In fact, instead of denouncing his connivance with depoliticised aestheticism, as Mathuray's first group does, *The Traumatic Celebration of Beauty in Hollinghurst's Fiction* argues that coming back can be much more than an act of nostalgia. In 'troping' same-sex desire, new scenarios of political and ethical commitment open up. When saying is disguised as unsaying because it is unspeakable, as happens in trauma narratives, new ways of saying are hinted and promising lines of action come up. This logic, it seems to me, buttresses

---

[35]   Claude Summers: *The Gay and Lesbian Literary Heritage*, New York and London 2002.

[36]   Gregory Woods: *A History of Gay Literature. The Male Tradition*, New Haven and London 1998.

[37]   Alan Hollinghurst: *The Swimming-pool Library*, London 1998a.

[38]   Richard Canning: *Conversations with Gay Novelists. Gay Fiction Speaks*, New York 2001, 347.

[39]   Owen Keehnen: "A Talk with Alan Hollinghurst," http//www.Owen Keehnen Interviews 1995, 3.

Hollinghurst's fiction. What cannot be said in *The Swimming-pool Library*, despite its oversexualised discourse, is eventually uttered in *The Line of Beauty*.[40] And the repressive excess of his first novels turns excessive indirection and ambiguity in *The Stranger's Child*[41] and *The Sparsholt Affair*.[42] His apparent contradictions and ambivalence may be controversial both for conservatives and LGTBI activists alike. However, the novelist is firm to keep on his aesthetic and political allegiances.

Narcissus's beauty is also his curse and that of Echo's. Unlike Clorinda, who is wounded twice for unknown reasons, the myth of Narcissus is the trauma of the excess of the same, of beauty as repetition, of coming back to oneself. It is out of hubris and auto-referentiality that Narcissus demises. He ends up by dissolving into his own reflection, an act of duplication that Echo recalls after the logic of trauma. Tancred "does not hear the voice of Clorinda until the second wounding so trauma is not locatable in the simple violent or original event in the individual's past, but rather in the way that its unassimilated nature [...] returns to haunt the survivor later on."[43] Narcissus never really understands Echo's wounded voice. He dies and it is Echo, as victim, that survives haunted by his loss and compelled to spread her love for him. Caruth sees "the full force of trauma as operating belatedly."[44] Drawing on Freud's *Nachträglichkeit*, as deferred action, the traumatic event always happens too soon to be acknowledged. A period of latency is thus mandatory before the traumatic return takes place literally and unwillingly in the form of flashbacks, dreams or hallucinations.[45] Echo is traumatised with carrying Narcissus's impossible story, thus becoming "the symptom of a history [she] cannot entirely possess."[46] Narcissus's beauty is traumatic as Echo bears witness to in the form of repetition, as Narcissus's own face reflects itself.

The myth of Narcissus problematises the very concept of belatedness and elucidates the poetics of homoerotic traumatic narratives. Drawing on Barnaby, belatedness is, rather than "a temporal lag in the registering of an event [...], a formative condition of trauma."[47] In the lapse between Narcissus's words and Echo's loving repetitions is where their traumatic dénouement surfaces. In this case, moreover, "the subject does not just 'miss' the event but is in fact absent from it. Indeed, the event as constituted requires the subject's absence."[48] In this myth, whose absence is it? Narcissus's hubris and subsequent dissociation explains he is absent in his own presence. He somehow 'misses' the event he is the protagonist of, being only belatedly 'conscious' of his own demise. Echo is also absent, despite being a witness, because she can only belatedly recall what others say after Hera's curse. Same-sex desire has traditionally been made redundant for this very same reason. A male lover is but the reflection of the other, a belated replication of the same. This explains in part Woods's 'tragic queer' as a historic trope of homosexuals' 'anti-relational' experience and narratives. The historic

---

[40]   Alan Hollinghurst: *The Line of Beauty*, London 2004.
[41]   Alan Hollinghurst: *The Stranger's Child*, London 2011.
[42]   Alan Hollinghurst: *The Sparsholt Affair*. London 2017.
[43]   Caruth: *Unclaimed*, 4.
[44]   Andrew Barnaby: *Coming Too Late: Reflections on Freud and Belatedness*. New York 2017, 39.
[45]   Caruth: *Unclaimed*, 5.
[46]   Ibid.
[47]   Barnaby: *Coming*, 41.
[48]   Ibid.

trope turned insidious when, after the gay liberation movement rendered gayness a visible and identifiable identity, AIDS erupted. The disease became the event (though made up of many events) that condensed the tragic queer in the collective imagery. Beautiful young male bodies turned into rotten ones in a discourse where morality met medicine. The latency period of the virus itself became a powerful image of the belatedness of traumata. Like Narcissus and Echo, gays bore witness to their own dissolution as if they were absent from it. They could not cope with the events, and others constructed the discourses that they could barely recall. Drawing on the myth of Narcissus, gays are deemed a liminal status, victims yet survivors. They are always about to die due to their excess of self-same desire and worship of beauty, but they are also condemned to survive to mourn their own death. That is the iconography Hollinghurst recalls, constructs and reconstructs once and again. I do not mean that homosexuality itself triggers trauma. It is just the opposite. Same-sex desire has been constructed as a wound that, using Caruth's words, "cries out, [...] addresses us in the attempt to tell us of a reality or truth that is not otherwise available."[49] Homosexuality has been rendered an unspeakable 'truth' that Hollinghurst both endorses and contests, celebrates and mourns. The current volume follows a chronological order to outline Hollinghurst's evolution concerning the discourses of same-sex desire, with especial attention on the problematic articulation of celebration and trauma narratives.

Already in his unpublished doctoral thesis,[50] Hollinghurst showed a keen interest in aesthetics, particularly the discourses of indirection that homosexual writers used to sublimate same-sex desire within the literary canon. This piece of research is a fundamental source of inspiration for *The Swimming-pool Library*, as Hollinghurst admits in an interview with Charles Canning.[51] In his thesis, the novelist approached three canonical writers who had to 'trope' their works in order to make them publishable at the time when political circumstances still made homosexuality unspeakable. From within the closet, where these (and other turn-of-the-century) authors were forced to live and write, they re-produced their forefathers' homo-textual patterns in new forms, which is precisely what Hollinghurst is doing at the turn of the millennium. Indeed, the juxtaposition and tension between concealment in the works by Forster, Firbank and Hartley (among others) and display in post-liberation gay literature, lies at the heart of *The Swimming-pool Library*. The novelist himself confesses that he "was curious about how they [closeted homosexual writers] dealt with their homosexuality without openly writing about it."[52] As he further explains, the basic tenet around which all his novels develop is that gay experience and identity have an eminently textual character and, as such, they are accessible through literary representations. Homo-texts and Johnson's 'textual images' are thus the aftermath of homosexual bodies and lives, their belated representation that, paradoxically, is the only form for us to reach them. In Hollinghurst's novels, homosexuality results from the confrontation between gays' actual experiences and the way they are delayed, traumatised and 'troped'. For a long time, the closet was the site where homosexuality and its literature kept hidden and where gay writers learned how to speak cryptically.

[49]   Caruth: *Unclaimed*, 17.
[50]   Alan Hollinghurst: *The Creative Uses of Homosexuality in the Novels of Forster, Firbank and Hartley*, 1980.
[51]   Canning: *Conversations*, 347.
[52]   In Keehnen: "A Talk," 5.

Consequently, in Hollinghurst's view, the literature of the closet and its discourse of reticence is the genuine and best example of same-sex textuality. He goes still further when he argues that gay literature must necessarily use tropes to express sexual dissidence; that is, if there is a specific gay (literary) discourse, it is one that puts forward the (un)utterable character of homosexuality. Accordingly, the novelist connects the increasing explicitness in the literary production of Firbank or Forster with a lowering of their artistic standards.[53]

As Richard Canning points out: "In his thesis, Hollinghurst answered an unsolved question in the British gay literary canon: The division between gayness as a matter of content and as a literary style."[54] According to the novelist, a specific gay style is non-viable in a climate of homosexual liberation. Christopher Isherwood's *A Single Man* is a case in point[55] because it is too explicit and, therefore, fails aesthetically as a gay text.[56] The literary event must ignore gayness to make homosexuality aesthetically relevant. Philip Toynbee already addresses this paradox in his analysis of Forster's *Maurice*, as Hollinghurst recalls.[57] Hence, *Maurice* would be paradoxically *less homosexual* than novels such as *A Passage to India*. The first is overt and, therefore, it does not need any literary artefact to sublimate same-sex desire. In the second, the bond between the male protagonists reveals homoerotic undertones that stylistically recall the political restrictions and literary formulas born in the closet. With these ideas in mind, what can be said about Hollinghurst's first four novels? If they approach gayness explicitly and unapologetically, does it mean that they are not stylistically gay? By contrast, if gayness (particularly sexuality) is more vicariously addressed in his last two novels, does it imply Hollinghurst aims to regain so-called gay sensibility? Is he exploring new ways of representation of sexuality beyond gayness, as Joseph Ronan argues?[58] Or is it that, after having broken the taboo of overt sexuality, Hollinghurst seeks a wider audience and voice? Even if all these options are partially true, the writer has played with the juxtaposition between knowing and unknowing since the beginning. This ambivalence has taken different routes along his career, although the process is especially manifest in his last two novels.

After reading his thesis, Hollinghurst started working as an editor for *The Times Literary Supplement*. There, he acquired a vast knowledge of English and foreign (especially French) literature whose influence is present in all his novels. In 1982, he published *Confidential Chats with Boys*, a short collection of poems which follows the tradition of pastoral poetry in general and Housman's *The Shropshire Lad* in particular. Although Hollinghurst has not written poetry any more, he has repeatedly avowed the influence of Milton, Manley Hopkins and other poets on his prose. In his interview with Richard Canning, Hollinghurst mentions the literature he admires and that he considers a source of inspiration for his writing. Particularly, he shows a predilection for pastoral elegies from Renaissance poets like Milton to the Romantics. The atmosphere and tone

---

53 Hollinghurst: *Creative Uses*, 3-4.
54 Canning: *Conversations*, 347.
55 Ibid.
56 Hollinghurst: *Creative Uses*, 47.
57 Ibid.
58 Joseph Ronan: "Ostentatiously Discreet: bisexual camp in *The Stranger's Child.*" In Mendelssohn, Michèle and Dennis Flannery (eds.). *Alan Hollinghurst: Writing under the Influence*. Manchester 2016, 96-109.

of this poetry is recurrent in his novels, especially in *The Swimming-pool Library* and *The Folding Star*. In *The Stranger's Child* he turns his attention to first-world-war poetry as a historical and aesthetic frame of reference, though. Hollinghurst is the author of the introduction to Donald Mitchell's *Britten and Auden in the Thirties* (2000), a book on the personal and professional relationship between both artists. A musician and a poet, they joined their talents for the recital room during the nineteen thirties. The book also includes information extracted from Britten's diaries which bear witness to their collaboration. Britten is not the only foray of Hollinghurst into music, especially into opera. In fact, at least his first three novels make reference to operas that work as thematic and structural leitmotifs. The references to music and art in general not only confer coherence to the novels, they also help to sublimate same-sex desire. In *The Swimming-pool Library*, the protagonists attend a performance of Britten's *Billy Budd*, an episode strategically placed in the middle of the novel. More indirectly, *The Folding Star*[59] makes reference to Erich Korngold's opera *Die Tote Stadt* —in its turn an adaptation of the novel *Bruge la Morte*,[60] by the Belgian symbolist Georges Rodenbach— and Britten's *Death in Venice* —this one adapted from Thomas Mann's *Death in Venice*.[61] In the middle of *The Spell*[62] there is also an episode which establishes an intertextual connection with Shakespeare's *A Midsummer Night's Dream* and Britten's operatic adaptation of the play in 1960. Hollinghurst has also written reviews and introductory chapters to collections of his favourite authors. Among them, Ronald Firbank has been a constant reference both in his fiction and literary criticism. In fact, *The Swimming-pool Library* pays homage to and vindicates the half-forgotten modernist writer. As Hollinghurst himself has pointed out: "I think he is an important writer with far more depth than many people acknowledge and his reputation has never become firmly established as it should have done."[63] He has even edited and written the introduction to *Ronald Firbank, Three Novels*,[64] where he analyses and celebrates Firbanks's strategies to sublimate homosexuality. This interest in the modernist writer confirms the critical view that contemporary gay literature —and Hollinghurst's in particular— is tributary to the literature produced by homosexuals in the closet.

Between 1988 and 2017, Hollinghurst has published six novels in which he has explored a century of homosexual identity, its literature and its fight for social recognition. As the writer has pointed out, his first four novels form a cohesive sequence: "I do have a sense of having completed a quartet of books which, while not a tetralogy in any narrative sense, do cohere in a way."[65] The portrayal of contemporary gay life, particularly sexual promiscuity, and of gays' confrontation with a past of political repression and its problematic (frequently sublimated) representation are the pillars which support Hollinghurst's narrative series. Thus, the novels make up what could be called 'the sex tetralogy' or 'AIDS quartet'. His last two novels, *The*

---

[59]   Alan Hollinghurst: *The Folding Star*, London 1998b.
[60]   Georges Rodenbach: *Bruges-la-Morte*. London 2005.
[61]   Thomas Mann: *Death in Venice*, trans. H. T. Lowe-Porter, London 1975.
[62]   Alan Hollinghurst: *The Spell*, London 1999.
[63]   In Peter Burton: *Talking to* .... Exeter 1991, 49.
[64]   Alan Hollinghurst: Introduction to *Ronald Firbank. Three Novels,* London 2000.
[65]   Moss: "Moral judgments," 3.

Stranger's Child and *The Sparsholt Affair*, constitute a change of direction. As mentioned above, although gay life is still central, explicit sexuality virtually fades away from the scene. Moreover, the narcissistic repetition-compulsion of homosexual practices of prior novels has turned into a more ambiguous, echoic, discourse from *The Stranger's Child* onwards. Despite being a post-gay-liberation writer, he still uses some literary tropes and other devices of the closet to underline the trauma of gayness as compulsory and a permanent coming-back. He does it even in his most sexually explicit novels. First of all, the cyclical recurrence of fixed ideas helps Hollinghurst to make his production cohere both thematically and stylistically. Like Forster or Firbank before him, Hollinghurst's novels repeat an idea —particularly the traumatic end of adolescence and onset of adulthood— that sublimates same-sex desire, otherwise unapproachable. Through the cyclic repetition of this fixed idea, the writer establishes a thematic and structural pattern.[66] Another key artefact in Hollinghurst's representation of same-sex desire is the *tristesse* of the narrator's voice, which recalls past traumas and foreshadows tragedy. Such *tristesse* is his answer to homosexuals' cyclical downfalls throughout history, such as the difficult transition from gay liberation to AIDS in barely a decade; a trauma "impossible to negotiate at a psychic level."[67] The traumatic undertones that inform most —if not all— of Hollinghurst's fiction are recurrent not only in gay literature but also in gay history, as Edmund White notes:

> To have been oppressed in the fifties, freed in the sixties, exalted in the seventies, and wiped out in the eighties is a quick itinerary for a whole culture to follow. For we are witnessing not just the death of individuals but a menace to an entire culture. All the more reason to bear witness to the cultural movement.[68]

Third, Hollinghurst's novels recast the pattern of classic *Bildungsromane*. The heroes of *The Swimming-pool Library*, *The Folding Star*, *The Line of Beauty* and, to a lesser extent, *The Spell* undergo difficult processes of (personal and artistic) maturation which frequently fail, thus subverting the developmental structure of traditional *Bildungsromane*. Instead of rounding off the hero's individuation process, these novels describe trajectories after which the protagonists feel traumatised and uncertain. In *The Stranger's Child* and *The Sparsholt Affair*, the *Bildungsroman* is choral and chronological, making memory rather than trauma their driving force. Hollinghurst's early-fiction characters revisit —compulsorily or not— the past of same-sex desire through its textual traces. Out of this encounter, present-day characters undergo a transformation after which they redefine many concepts about themselves and their ancestors. This return to the past in search of formulas of homosexual representation is narrated in traumatic and nostalgic terms, especially in his first novels. Thus, nostalgia, trauma and fantasy are traits that characterise the anti-developmental structure of Hollinghurst's early gay *Bildungromane*. In his last two novels, it is not the past that returns to change the present. Instead, a bidirectional movement makes both past and present interact and mould each other. However, this does not preclude the traumatic

---

[66]   Hollinghurst: *Creative Uses*, 5.
[67]   Joseph Bristow: *Effeminate England. Homoerotic Writing after 1885*. Buckingham 1995, 168.
[68]   Edmund White: *The Burning Library. Writings on Art, Politics and Sexuality 1969-1993*. London 1994, 215.

nostalgia of previous novels to surface once and again. Parallel to trauma, Hollinghurst's novels have reified aestheticism and beauty. The male body is celebrated, though often forecasting a tragic *dénoument*. This tension between celebration of (male) beauty and the threat of coming traumata makes up Hollinghurst's liminal style.

The first chapter, '*The Swimming-pool Library*: The specular structure of (un)saying,' explores the dialogic poetics between the narrator, Will Beckwith, and the other protagonist, Charles Nantwich. The specular reflection of one on the other serves Hollinghurst to evoke the pre-gay London scenario and how it shaped the structure of the current gay scene until AIDS erupted. Clearly indebted to his thesis, the novel is an exercise of Narcissistic reflection that uses textual tropes to hide and disclose same-sex desire as both obsessed with beauty and doomed to extinction. The double-staged tempo of trauma is thus the structural basis of *The Swimming-pool Library*. The chapter analyses how the tragic queer is arranged on a first-level reflection, whereby the postmodernist text reflects the homosexual canon, and a second-level reflection, in which the postmodernist novel reflects itself. As a Narcissus-like character, Will's discourse draws on Echo. It comes only too late, a specular reflection of Charles's triggered by the trauma of AIDS. Although there are no explicit references to the disease in *The Swimming-pool Library*, Hollinghurst intended to write an epilogue with "William [the protagonist] 'writing' the book practically on his death-bed with AIDS, but [the writer] forgot that idea […]. It would have been too neat and turned the novel into a moral fable."[69] There are critics who consider his early fiction a displacement to the past meant to avoid having to deal with present issues. Gregory Woods regards *The Swimming-pool Library* as "a lusty celebration of pre-AIDS freedoms, already a historical novel by virtue of being set in the London in the 1970s, a decade so radically different from the 1980s in the common experience of urban gay men."[70] It is, the chapter argues, more than a celebratory detour that justifies the Narcissistic structure of the novel, though.

The second chapter, 'The specular tryptich: delusory Narcissus,' delves into *The Folding Star* as a morbid, melancholic extension of *The Swimming-pool Library*. Being both gay *Bildungsromane*, *The Folding Star* and *The Swimming-pool Library* work, according to John Bradley, as specular projections of each other.[71] Their protagonists are forced to confront (textual) traces of the past, frequently recalling traumatic episodes, after which they are supposed to learn something. However, this confrontation usually triggers a paralysis that threatens (rather than enhances) the protagonists' maturation process. The dual specularity of Hollinghurst's first novel now turns into a tryptich-like figure that replicates *ad nauseam*. This is done to address the melancholic scenario derived from the AIDS crisis that *The Folding Star* inevitably recalls. Narcissus is a leitmotif, as it is in *The Swimming-pool Library*. Yet, Edward Manners, the protagonist, is infatuated with a delusory Narcissus with whom he is haunted and to whom he hardly attempts to come back. The two-staged tempo of (AIDS) trauma determines Manners's discourse and his sense of an ending. *The Folding Star* earned

[69]   Burton: *Talking to*, 48.
[70]   Woods: History, 368-69.
[71]   John Bradley: "Disciples of St Narcissus. In Praise of Alan Hollinghurst." In *The Critical Review* 36, 1996, 3-18.

Hollinghurst the James Tait Black Memorial Prize and it was also shortlisted for the Booker Prize in 1994. However, it was too explicit a novel or it was perhaps too early for it to be awarded with the Prize itself.

'Orton meets Shakespeare in a Midsummer night's gay comedy' explores Hollinghurst's turn in *The Spell*. Narrated in the third person unlike his previous novels —both narrated in the first— *The Spell* offers a kaleidoscopic approach to (post)gay 'reality' from the perspective of four characters. Thus, the gay lifestyle and its representation is also the core of this novel, this time dispersed in four focalising strands that interweave with each other. According to David Alderson, *The Spell* is "less ambitious in scope in comparison to its predecessors [… and] barely inflected by [their] nostalgia."[72] Perhaps for this reason, some critics considered it a failure as they missed Hollinghurst's usual bookishness and nostalgic undertones. These differences apart, the novel follows a quadrangular pattern that somehow complements the dual and triptychal specularity of *The Swimming-pool Library* and *The Folding Star* respectively. This chapter's main purpose is determine to what extent the Shakespearean-Ortonian substratum in Hollinghurst's gay comedy of manners succeeds in screening the tragic queer and conveying the late-capitalist (post)gay scene.

The winner of the 2004 Man Booker Prize, *The Line of Beauty* has been extensively reviewed, mostly celebrating its excellence but, paradoxically, also criticised for its bookishness.[73] "The trauma of beauty: the Dionysian assault on the AIDS crisis" examines how Hollinghurst retraces himself. In other words, *The Line of Beauty* comes back to his first two novels, but with a turn, via Henry James. The novel is dense, full of intertextual references and it still focuses on a youth who undergoes a catastrophic process of learning and (self)-discovery. However, it is narrated in the third person, which grants the reader a distance from the traumata revisited. The setting of the novel takes the reader back to that of *The Swimming-pool Library* (in fact, there is even a reference to Lord Beckwith, one of the characters in the first novel), namely the London of the early nineteen eighties, of Thatcher and AIDS. However, the representation of gayness and the disease is in this case less indirect than in his earlier novels. The critical nineteen eighties are not perceived as vividly as before, but rather as a traumatic past that can be approached belatedly through satirical distance. However, not all critics think that satire succeeds. As Henry Hitchins has pointed out, rather than distancing from the Feddens' upper-class tory politics, *The Line of Beauty* cherishes it. There is, according to the critic, "too much of the echoing and affirmative chatter of patrician self-love."[74] Hence, this chapter wonders whether the novel, like its protagonist Nick Guest, is a conniving narcissistic Echo that recalls upper-class Feddens' voice(s) and sense of beauty. Or, on the contrary, it reveals the Dionysian underside of that beauty, showing the rawest side of AIDS as procrastinated trauma and eventual exclusion.

The Stranger's Child and *The Sparsholt Affair* work as an aftermath as well as a detour from the 'AIDS quartet'. In other words, as the chapter "Transgenerational blind corners of memory as myth of origins" argues, his last two novels do not constitute a rupture, but a redirectioning of Hollinghurst's fixed literary patterns. They do it in reference to a *status quo* where the effect of AIDS is no longer central, even though its aftermath has left unhealed scars and traumatic discourses are still prevalent and

---

[72] Alderson: *Territories*, 44.
[73] Henry Hitchins: "The Double Curve," *The Times Literary Supplement* (2004), 22.
[74] Ibid.

juxtaposed with celebratory ones. The myth of Echo and Narcissus keeps elucidating. However, Narcissus is not the main narrative agent, but the focal point of the narration. Unlike Will Beckwith, Edward Manners and Nick Guest and, to a lesser extent, the four protagonists of *The Spell*, the narcissistic protagonists of *The Stranger's Child* and *The Sparsholt Affair* are uttered rather than utterers themselves. It is others' voices that echo (hence their echoic nature) and are haunted by their narcissistic aura. Indeed, in current narcissistic culture, there is a shortage of aura, a sense of absence that both novels attempt to solve. The two texts draw on biography and memoir as genres that aim at filling the void left by aura. Nevertheless, the aura that protagonists Cecil Valance and David Sparsholt represent in First-World War and Second-World-War England respectively fades away as generations pass. The poetics of memoir and biography blur when memory falters or is politically biased. Moreover, their traumatic poetics of postponement are at variance with the first Hollinghurst. It is no longer a clash between generations that engenders a traumatic outburst that makes the new generation into a narcissistic aftermath echoing its predecessor. *The Stranger's Child* and *The Sparsholt Affair* convey a continuum of transgenerational allegiances and disengagements echoing each other. Hence, a scandal or a myth of origins can solidify in a work of art or series, but also be forgotten behind its traces. Be it as it may, Hollinghurst always addresses the substratum, no matter how oblivious, that makes up current (gay) discourses. Finally, although both novels are still committed to homosexual, gay and queer representations of same-sex desire, they open the scope to bisexuality. In a sense, this move towards bisexuality sanctions the juxtaposed artistic discourse of Hollinghurst's early fiction and breaks with prior self-centred narcissism in favour of ambiguity.

As mentioned above, influence is a key factor to delve into Hollingurst's texts. Most of them are engaged in a complex, specular intertexuality that confirms and transcends the very nature of influence. The writer himself regards the homosexual literary tradition as a useful intertextual network for his own literary aims. As he explains, in his novels, "there are a lot of quotations and literary references included, some of which will only be appreciated by me, I suspect. I am rather bookish in that way." [75] Hollinghurst always keeps an eye on the homosexual canon and he has thus been labelled as "the candidate of continuity" in opposition to David Mitchell, "the champion of change." Critics like Edmund White praised *The Swimming-pool Library* as perhaps the best novel on gay life ever, but also regarded his prose as too close to his Victorian and Edwardian predecessors in both form and content. [76] However, it should not be forgotten that, as Boyd Tonkin suggests, strict categorizations are often misleading, unfair and inaccurate. [77] Indeed, among the many canonical writers that Hollinghurst revises in his novels, White focuses on Oxbridge canonical E. M. Forster on purpose, leaving the subversive Ronald Firbank apart. Hollinghurst's camp juxtaposes both writers and traditions, since camp is the way whereby "homosexuals have pinned their integration into society on promoting the aesthetic sense" [78] and for them to convey the traumatic and celebratory. In fact, the interaction between contemporary hypertext and turn-of-the-century hypotexts is necessarily free from conflict. It is the way in which

---

[75] In Keehnen: "A Talk," 4.

[76] Edmund White: *The Faber Book of Gay Short Fiction*, London 1994, 246.

[77] Tonkin, Boyd: "A Week in Books." http://findarticles.com/p/articles/mi—qn4158/is/ain12 8172 43, 2004.

[78] Susan Sontag: "Notes on Camp," http://pages.zoom.co.uk/leveridge/sontag.html, 1964, 52.

Hollinghurst's fiction confronts the gay canon that will determine the characteristics of this intertextual dialogue and its identitarian discourse. In the limit between the narcissistic and the echoic, the Apollonian and the Dionysian, campy excess and the constraining (albeit promising) closet, repetition and coming back, corporeality and anti-relationality, and trauma and celebration arises the rare beauty and reality of Hollinghurst's novels. There is, this book contends, a shift from a sense of urgency to visibilise homosexuality and its discrimination in the 'AIDS quartet' to a more ambiguous tone and bisexuality in his last duology. In the former novels, there was a prevailing traumatic atmosphere which was achieved through self-centred obsessive narcissism; in the latter ones, trauma paved the way for memory to arise in the form of the echoic, echoes being transmitted inter and trans-generationally. In sum, it does not mean that narcissism is no longer present in Hollinghurst's final duology or that the echoic memories do not form a part of the tetralogy. There is simply a tendency from gay politics to post-gay politics that Hollinghurst recalls and contributes to.

1   *The Swimming-pool Library*: The specular structure of (un)saying

1.1   Critical reception and controversy

The Swimming-pool Library was published in 1988, at the peak of the AIDS crisis. Like the gay community, England was living its own national crisis as a consequence of the collapse of the Empire. The country was now a minor power in the world, a situation that Margaret Thatcher tried to mend with the Falklands war. At home, gays had to suffer the Prime Minister's homophobic politics: the government passed Section 28, a law that prevented the promotion of gayness with public money. But, what did Thatcher's cabinet mean by "promotion of homosexuality"? Nobody explained it; however, the subliminal message of the law was clearly homophobic. On the other hand, the gay community had to suffer an escalade of hatred and violence as a result of AIDS. Henceforth, power structures did not regard gays as criminals (like Wilde), but as infected bodies who could propagate the disease. In sum, *The Swimming-pool Library* was published in the context of a national crisis as well as one of identity and sexual politics.

As always with Hollinghurst's texts, there are critics who regard *The Swimming-pool Library* as a conservative, derivative and nostalgic text while others regard it as a subversive, postmodernist one. David Alderson puts forward a case for "Hollinghurst's apparent disenchantment with modernity [in *The Swimming-pool Library*]." [79] He explains this disenchantment as an answer to the fact that modern gay identity rejects English tradition. The novelist apparently regrets the current commodification and explicitness of gay sexuality, which has replaced former sublimation and innocence of gayness. Thus, as Alderson argues, the appeal of innocence exists "in the historical or individual past, prior to the emergence of an explicitly gay scene or the acquisition of an individual sexual identity and entry into the corresponding subculture, hence the generalised condition of nostalgia in the novel and the way that this structures desire" (36-37). [80] However, if Hollinghurst longs for sublimation, why does he opt for a sexually explicit discourse? In Alderson's view, the overt sexuality of *The Swimming-pool Library* is not "what the moralists might call 'gratuitous', since that very explicitness participates in but at the same time critically highlights the pornographic […] quality of contemporary desires. Hence, the ambivalence of many readers' responses to the novel, finding it deeply erotic yet simultaneously, if vaguely, troubling." [81] Unlike Alderson, Edmund White and Susanne Keen regard *The Swimming-pool Library* as conservative rather than ambivalent. For White, most English and French writers today suffer from a paralysing anxiety of influence with respect to their

---

[79] Alderson: *Territories*, 36.
[80] Ibid., 36-37.
[81] Ibid.

predecessors (Bloom, 1975). In his view, Hollinghurst is one of these authors who are unable to overcome the heavy burden of a long canonical tradition:

> Most English novelists are writing like their 19th century antecedents. Alan Hollinghurst writes like E. M. Forster, just to name one of the writers I admire. Obviously there are changes; for instance, there is a great deal more of interiority in contemporary fiction than in 19th century fiction, and a lot less incident, or plot. And there is far more sexuality now than then, and so on. But English novelists continue to be primarily concerned with analysing character in terms of social class.[82]

In White's view, *The Swimming-pool Library* simply adapts canonical texts to the political and aesthetic needs of the late twentieth century, adding no really significant thematic or structural innovations. Susanne Keen defends a similar thesis.[83] With "romance of the archive," Keen makes reference to a new genre arising out of the post-imperial crisis that has enjoyed a great success in England. In her opinion, romances of the archive represent the alternative to postmodernist literature: unlike the innovative character of postmodernist historiographic metafiction, these romances are conservative, realistic, truth-seeking and formally close to nineteenth-century literature. In chapter 7, "Envisioning the Past," Susanne Keen includes *The Swimming-pool Library* in a list of "conventionally realistic novels, linked by their shared interest in gender, sexuality, and identity."[84] Despite the variety of angles from which these topics are analysed, for Keen, these novels rely on:

> Traditional modes of characterization and plotting to tell realistic stories entailing episodes of archival research. The characters in these fictions exist in recognizable versions of contemporary Britain; their research quests draw them towards earlier periods of the British past where the people and problems they hope to understand dwell. [...] They successfully study historical documents, collections of photographs, and scientific reconstructions, discovering occluded truths and clarifying views of clouded pasts.[85]

In her view, the revisionist attitude of these novels aims "to correct misjudgements [...] according to the revised standards of the present, especially with respect to gender roles and sexual orientation."[86] In particular, the reparatory character of *The Swimming-pool Library* has ethical and political consequences, perceptible in the bafflement of the defeated, the identification of the villains and the restoration of the responsibility for making judgements. Moreover, it makes or encourages social and political changes by cultivating outrage.[87] I will return to Keen's analysis later on in order to decide whether Hollinghurst's novel fits into the category of romance of the archive.

Other critics, such as Christopher Lane, Luisa Juárez and John McLeod deal with Hollinghurst's novel from the point of view of post-colonialism. Lane analyses the different literary representations of the British Empire from a psychoanalytic

---

[82]   White: *Faber Book*, 246.
[83]   Susanne Keen: *Romances of the Archive in Contemporary British Fiction*, Toronto 2001.
[84]   Ibid., 181.
[85]   Ibid.
[86]   Ibid., 182.
[87]   Ibid., 182-183.

perspective.[88] He shows how the texts of canonical writers such as Forster or Firbank are ideologically implicated in British Imperial politics and concludes with a short epilogue on *The Swimming-pool Library*. In his view, this novel constitutes a paradigmatic contemporary response to the "vast confluence of racial and national difficulty, [and shows how] Britain has become mired in a renewed vision of colonial splendour and global influence."[89] In other words, the novel aims to solve the traumatic loss of the Empire that the old metropolis has proved unable to overcome. Likewise, Luisa Juárez 'denounces' what she considers a pro-Imperialistic attitude in Hollinghurst's novel. Out of the two narrative voices (Will Beckwith's and Charles Nantwich's) and the historical periods they represent (the eighties and the first half of the twentieth century), Juárez focuses on Nantwich's since "it connects with a British literary tradition that features a fascination for the exotic."[90] In portraying Charles as a kind, generous and patriotic officer in Sudan, Juárez contends, the novel not only validates the figure of the homosexual colonial. It also endorses British Imperialism as a whole. In this light, she argues, *The Swimming-pool Library* "distracts the problems existing in the representation of the colonial enterprise."[91] She also puts forward how the novel distorts history for the benefit of (homo)sexual wishfulfilment. The British government sent gays and other unwanted citizens to the colonies, an episode which, according to Juárez, is doubly problematic in *The Swimming-pool Library*:

> Firstly, the author presents a candid picture of the English government which was not sending them [homosexuals] to the colonies to remove them from the metropolis but because their better preparation for the work of imperialism was recognized. [...] Secondly, the colony offers a good opportunity for the homosexual who can both regain the masculinity denied him in Europe and a path to expression for his repressed and illegal sexuality.[92]

Juárez regrets that the author supports 'imperial nostalgia' —i.e. the use of nostalgia, sentimentalism and good manners to disguise and justify colonisation—[93] and the liberation of gays at the expense of the 'ethnic other'. In my view, one thing is Charles's discourse and another that of the novel, not to mention that of the author. The Lord sexualises/feminises the colonies and the colonised and thus he turns from oppressed homosexual (in England) to homosexual oppressor (in Africa). However, can the pro-colonial discourse of one character be extrapolated to the novel as a whole and, what is more, to Hollinghurst himself? Does the novel justify Charles's 'good colonialism' by

---

[88]   Christopher Lane: *The Ruling Passion. British Colonial Allegory and the Paradox of Homosexual Desire*, Durham and London 1995.

[89]   Lane: *Ruling*, 231.

[90]   Luisa Juárez: "Desire as Colonizer. A Reading of Homosexuality and Colonialism in Alan Hollinghurst's *The Swimming-pool Library*." In: Fernando Galván (ed.). *On Writing (and) Race in Contemporary Britain*. Universidad de Alcalá 1999, 67

[91]   Ibid., 68.

[92]   Ibid.

[93]   Linda Hutcheon: "Irony, Nostalgia, and the Postmodern." file:///C:/Users/Usuario/Down loads/pdfcoffee.com_irony-nostalgia-and-the-postmodern-by-linda-hutcheonpdf-4-pdf-free.pdf, 1998.

"putting excessive stress on the character of this individual"?[94] If so, that would involve identifying the ideology of the novel with that of the characters depicted in it, and also the ideology of the flesh-and-blood author with that of its cardboard *alter ego*. In my view, the novel intends to oppose Nantwich's early-twentieth-century aristocratic discourse to that of Beckwith, the first-level narrator, to address their similarities immediately afterwards. The problematic status of gayness as regards imperialism and cosmopolitanism is thus at the core of Hollinghurst's discourse. John McLeod points to what he calls "the ongoing vexed relations between gay marginality and political and institutional conformity." [95] Drawing on the debate on trauma narratives and postcolonialism that critics like Rothberg, Noak and Leys opened, Nantwich's twofold status is particularly problematic, being both marginal and conformist. Unlike victim and perpetrator, which are legal and political concepts, their interaction begs for a traumatic narrative. In this sense, *The Swimming-pool Library* is "a novel of complicities and repetitions that are hard to break."[96] Thus, the celebratory life its narcissistic protagonist leads echoes and is complicit with the suffering and injustice of others. The resulting sense of guilt makes trauma arise not only as a legal or political issue, but as a diagnostic effect that may affect victims and perpetrators. The specular structure of the novel represents the complex celebratory trauma of gays through a whole century.

In contrast to Keen or White, Richard Dellamora points out that the novel "takes the form of Linda Hutcheon's "postmodernist metafiction"[97] as long as the text mirrors and problematises itself:

> Undertaking a literary project more or less by accident, Beckwith begins in a delusory way to prepare to write the biography of Charles Nantwich. [...] The journals and other materials that Nantwich gives Beckwith provide a fragmentary secondary narrative that Hollinghurst interleaves through the framing story as Beckwith reads them. In this way, Beckwith functions as a hermeneutic figure of the process of 'reading' history. In the relation between the texts of these two 'I's, the problematics of being gay, white and privileged in Great Britain in the twentieth century become evident.[98]

That is, Dellamora puts forward the complex structure of the novel, its fragmented narration and its revision of the past and of homosexual identity. In his view, this type of identity is rendered unrepresentable as long as it is traumatic, as the narrations of both protagonists prove:

> The combination of [Will's] journal with Nantwich's records describes a set of textual limits [...]. But because neither of the narrating personas can find a vantage point external

[94] Juárez: "Desire," 71

[95] John McLeod: "Race, Empire and *The Swimming-pool Library*." In Mendelssohn, Michèle and Dennis Flannery (eds.). *Alan Hollinghurst: Writing under the Influence*. Manchester 2016, 61.

[96] Ibid.

[97] Linda Hutcheon: *The Poetics of Postmodernism. History, Theory, Fiction*. New York and London, 1988.

[98] Richard Dellamora: *Apocalyptic Overtures, Sexual Politics and the Sense of an Ending*. New Jersey 1994, 174.

to these limits, the [biographical] project can never be completed. Personal identity remains incomplete because it is always implicated in someone else's identity, and someone else's identity is always implicated in a variety of discursive practice.[99]

Closely related to this redefinition of identity, the novel also de/re-constructs gay history: when Will is commissioned to write Nantwich's biography, he becomes aware of its striking similarity with his own, a discovery that "changes the project from a historicist one to one about the relation between the two narrating personas."[100] Unlike Juárez, Dellamora puts forward Nantwich's ambivalence. In his view, this character is not only a sexual predator of blacks who participates and agrees with British Imperialism, he is a fragmented subject, "both privileged and victimized."[101] Although the commodification of working-class and black men by privileged homosexuals is morally dubious, these cross-class and cross-race practices provoked the persecution of thousands of upper/middle-class gays during the fifties. According to Dellamora, this traumatic episode would be the equivalent of AIDS, the trauma affecting the gay community in the eighties.[102] The critic justifies the absence of direct references to the disease as a symptom of trauma. This absence is terrifying for Bristow, Dellamora and Alderson, a symptom of Will's "dark insinuations."[103] Yet, this same absence is renewed when a new suntanned boy arrives at the close of the novel, "whose appearance most obviously offers a suggestion of the circularity of Will's life and a reminder that little has changed for him."[104] That is, the absence of AIDS serves for the disease to be present, but also to procrastinate Will's celebratory lifestyle. This delay in the traumatic unfolding of the disease, as the virus is latent, is circular, echoic and genealogical. Indeed, the difficulty in filling the memory gap surrounding the traumatic event explains the compulsive need to return to the past, or pasts. Unlike classic realistic literature, the traumatic realism of the novel discards any claim to objectivity, truth or closure. By contrast, it offers a problematic approach to gayness and its history.

Other critics such as Alan Sinfield and John Murphy agree with and complement Dellamora's analysis of Hollinghurst's novel. Alan Sinfield proposes a chronological revision of gay literary and cultural representation in England since 1945.[105] With this purpose, he focuses his attention on two novels —Wilson's *Hemlock and After* (1952) and Hollinghurst's *The Swimming-pool Library* (1988)— as representative of the evolution of gay discourses in England from post-War to post-Stonewall. Both deal with same-sex desire and the permanent menace of homophobia in Britain; the first was published at the height of the Cold War and the main subplot of the second is also set in that period. Though similar in some aspects, the novels differ in many others. In Sinfield's opinion, Wilson still believed in the possibility of merging gay and

---

[99]   Ibid., 178.
[100] Ibid., 179.
[101] Ibid., 178.
[102] Ibid., 179.
[103] In Johnson: *Alan Hollinghurst*, 59.
[104] Ibid.
[105] Alan Sinfield: "Culture, Consensus, Difference: Angus Wilson to Alan Hollinghurst." In Alastair Davis and Alan Sinfield (eds). *British Culture of the Postwar. An Introduction to Literature and Society.* London 2000, 83-102.

mainstream traditions. However, with the success of the gay liberation movement, gays established their own "distinctive tradition,"[106] as *The Swimming-pool Library* shows. Sinfield also puts forward how recent gay fiction frequently breaks the consensual boundary between high and low art: since gay subculture has been considered low art, gay affirmation implies the deconstruction of artistic hierarchies. Hollinghurst's novel participates of this blurring of boundaries which characterises gay fiction and postmodernist culture in general. Sinfield considers *The Swimming-pool Library* as a "troubled novel" as concerns gay identity, its discourses and especially its auto-indulgence. That is, it shows that gays (middle or upper-class and white by definition) are victims of social intolerance, but are also sexual predators who exploit underprivileged working-class and black men or youths.

Like Sinfield and Dellamora, Stephen Murphy regards Hollinghurst's novel as postmodernist. [107] Murphy approaches the novel from the perspective of historical discourses, literary traditions and the accessibility to the past in general. With this purpose, he makes use of trauma theory. In Murphy's view, trauma is the effect "not of encountering but of missing history."[108] As products of trauma, the narrations of *The Swimming-pool Library* establish a complex relation with the past that escapes traditional historiography. As opposed to Keen's "romances of the archive," Murphy contends that history is no more a truth that "we know, but something we are; [...] and history is no longer done in the name of intellectual curiosity but out of a sense of responsibility."[109] His view is in accordance with the current preference for memory over history, of which *The Swimming-pool Library* seemingly participates. As we will see, Hollinghurst's novel celebrates gays' oversexualised lifestyles; it is also a traumatised, testimonial text whose narrators explore the past nostalgically in search of a sense of identity but finally, as Murphy argues, "they provide us with a warning against the dangers of memory discourse and the abandonment of irony." [110] Like Dellamora and Sinfield, Murphy points out that history can only be accessed indirectly through texts and placing a special emphasis on irony. In Murphy's view, Hollinghurst's novel is a commemoration of Firbank's camp effeminacy and ironic style which Forster and others tried to detach themselves from. That is, *The Swimming-pool Library* recalls past traumata and their effects with irony. Hence, he argues: "Irony seems especially necessary now not only as a way to counter the excessive reverence in literary criticism for historical calamities [...] but also as a way, in fact, to honour the dead. It is precisely because Will Beckwith and Alan Hollinghurst refuse to respect history that they do it a service."[111] The 'disrespectful' process of rehabilitation of the closet and its literature of *The Swimming-pool Library* has political and ethical implications and consequences.

Joseph Bristow considers the novel as an archive of gay literary history, namely "the terminal point of a specific type of homophile writing that developed in England after

---

[106] Ibid., 95.
[107] Stephen Murphy: "Past Irony: Trauma and the Historical Turn in *Fragments* and *The Swimming-pool Library*." In *Ramifications of Trauma Theory, Literature and History.* Manchester 2004, 58-75.
[108] Ibid., 59.
[109] Ibid., 61.
[110] Ibid., 64.
[111] Ibid., 73.

1885."[112] Bristow focuses on the representation of masculinity and femininity since the late nineteenth century and, especially, on the increasing identification of effeminacy with homosexuality following Wilde's downfall. After a detailed chronological revision of the textual construction of identity, Bristow concludes that Will Beckwith is a compendium of previous representations of masculinity and effeminacy;[113] a character that bridges the gap "between once antithetical styles of masculinity,"[114] namely the scholar and the athlete. Both privileged —as a rich aristocrat, Will exploits working-class and black men— and marginal —he is gay and, therefore, victim of homophobic attacks— the hero of the novel is the result of a long tradition of gender discourses and especially of the crisis caused by the feminist and gay liberation movements.

Both John Bradley and Thomas Dukes read *The Swimming-pool Library* as a homosexual *Bildungsroman*. Bradley argues that Hollinghurst's first two novels "should be seen as coming from a tradition of *Bildungsroman*."[115] As he explains, the educational theme is more explicit in *The Folding Star*, but *The Swimming-pool Library* also revolves around the traumatic formation process of the young protagonist. Thus, Hollinghurst adopts and adapts the stereotypical and traumatic loss of adolescence. Many English authors, such as Forrest Reid, Henry James, Ronald Firbank or Hollinghurst himself cast heroes unwilling to grow up. In fact, as Bradley recalls, the dramatic onset of adulthood on a particular type of psyche can "solidify into the structure of a work of art, or a whole series of works of art in the hands of a good artist."[116] The arrested development of the hero characterises homosexual *Bildungsromane* in contrast to classic examples of the genre, where the protagonist fulfils his maturation process. In other words, Hollinghurst revises the pattern of the classic *Bildungsroman* to utter same-sex desire through a symmetric structure of parallels and contrasts where the onset of adulthood is recurrently recast. Thomas Dukes inscribes Hollinghurst's novel in the tradition of "*Bildungsromane* about uncloseting,"[117] or "coming-out stories;" *i.e.*: narratives where the repressed homosexual youth unfolds as a liberated gay adult. In my view, however, Will's story is not exactly a "coming-out story." The hero is already a liberated gay who, paradoxically, comes back to the closet as a visitor. In other words, the young Will Beckwith finds out his personal implication in homosexual history through the semi-closeted Charles Nantwich, his individuation process being a coming-back rather than a coming-out. The dialogue between both characters invites the reader to a first-hand discovery of the closet, the Empire and inter-class/race desire as lived by Charles and re-lived by Will.[118]

As concerns the colonial/racial discourse of *The Swimming-pool Library*, Dellamora differs from Juárez and Lane's one-dimensional standpoint. Hollinghurst's novel deals with African diaspora and with the "pattern of homoerotic patronage and loyalty

---

[112] Bristow: *Effeminate*, 171.
[113] Ibid., 172.
[114] Ibid., 176.
[115] Bradley: "Disciples," 8.
[116] Ibid., 4.
[117] Thomas Dukes: "'Mappings of Secrecy and Disclosure' *The Swimming-pool Library*, the Closet, and the Empire." *Journal of Homosexuality*, 31(39), 1996, 96.
[118] Ibid., 107.

between white master and black attendant;"[119] a pattern of interdependence and power manifest in the relationships between characters and in the artistic devices (i.e. Johnson's 'visual texts') throughout the novel. For instance, the Roman mosaic in Nantwich's house is an example of how Europe produced "the cultural capital calculated 'to define and justify' the roles of the colonizers."[120] That is, "late-nineteenth-century colonization of Africa depended heavily on invented traditions —for both Europeans and Africans."[121] However, the fact that the novel reflects these imperial discourses and practices does not imply that they are justified, even though its protagonists support them. On the contrary, as Brenda Cooper argues, *The Swimming-pool Library* does not connive in British colonialism, but rather, problematises it instead from the perspective of postcolonialism.[122] Cooper establishes a comparison between *The Swimming-pool Library* and *The Famished Road*, by the Nigerian Ben Okri, since "both oppose that colonial history and the racism that accompanied it."[123] Therefore, she points out the novel's —particularly Nantwich's— apparently contradictory commodification of black sensuality:

> [Hollinghurst's] novel abounds with objects, photographic images and fetishes that acknowledge the morally ambivalent history of gay oppression and imprisonment within this colonial dominance. Do the novel and its devices, however, partake of aspects of the colonial violence and domination that are simultaneously being interrogated and exposed? Is there not some tension between its celebration of gay sensuality, its utopia of a world populated apparently only by gay men, including beautiful black boys, and its critique of the oppression and dangers linked to that world?[124]

The answer to this would be that Hollinghurst's novel is too complex to allow for a simplistic, one-sided reading of interracial gay desire in colonial Africa and post-colonial London, and Cooper knows it. Both Charles and Will use their status to justify their sexual exploitation and worship of black males. Their ambivalent testimonies and behaviour keep the tension between gay wishfulfilment fantasies and their racist undertones. Sometimes, Cooper suggests, the author seems to approve of this tension through Will's love affair with black Arthur, "marred by some sinister undercurrents."[125] And she wonders whether the "magnetic pull of black bodies" is not a new metaphor for "the dark side," now making reference to the "absent presence of AIDS."[126] In other words, does *The Swimming-pool Library* endorse the traditional identification between blackness and Western fears and lust? Cooper's answer is that

---

[119] Dellamora: *Apocalyptic*, 175.

[120] Ibid., 189.

[121] Ibid.

[122] Brenda Cooper: "Snapshots of Postcolonial Masculinities: Hollinghurst's *The Swimming-pool Library* and Ben Okri's *The Famished Road*," *The Journal of Commonwealth Literature*, 34(1) 1999, 135-157; Brenda Cooper "A Boat, a Mask, Two Photographers and a Manticore: African Fiction in a Global Context." *Pretexts: Studies in Writing and Culture* 9(1) 2000, 63-76.

[123] Cooper: "Snapshots," 135.

[124] Ibib., 143.

[125] Ibid.

[126] Ibid., 144.

"Hollinghurst is fully aware of the problem, but only partially distances himself from it."[127] Still, although Charles may look like one of Conrad's heroes and share their discourses, it would be a mistake to extrapolate his views to Hollinghurst. The novel problematises interracial desire, as Mapplethorpe photographs do, for two reasons: because it forms part of gay erotica; and, on the other, because it brings about ethical conflicts since white gays have simultaneously adored and exploited black males. The novel does not solve conflicts, it rather problematises taken-for-granted concepts and truths. The roles of perpetrator and victim are often interchangeable, Will and Charles being one or another at different moments. Trauma narratives arise at the crossroads between different identity affiliations, particularly related to class, race and sexual orientation. Indeed, the novel breaks with the hierarchy of traumata as long as suffering is relative and movable. I do not mean there is not a logic of power that determines who is liable to inflict pain and who is to suffer from traumata. Will's grandfather, who prosecuted gays in the fifties, is undoubtedly a perpetrator with no trace of victimhood and/or trauma side-effects. But in most trauma cases, and *The Swimming-pool Library* is a good example, the event bursts in many directions with multi-levelled casualties. The specular arrangement of the novel constitutes an intertextual response to gays' politraumatic history, a purposeful uncomfortable reading.

1.2   The triangular speculum

The Swimming-pool Library is a very complex novel, both structurally and thematically. It is a piece of textual architecture which, as Hollinghurst himself confesses, follows a pre-established pattern: "*The Swimming-pool Library* I actually wrote in a desk diary. It was a leap year, so it had three hundred and sixty-six pages of manuscript. It had twelve chapters, each of which ended at the end of the month. So that book had a finite length before I even started writing."[128] The novel can be thus interpreted as a textual representation of a symbolic year: its pages coinciding with the days in a leap year and its chapters with the twelve months. Will's autobiographical narration and life story take exactly one year; a year which constitutes a turning-point in the hero's story and gays' history (especially voiced by Nantwich), and reveals parallelisms between one and the others. It can be argued that Will's year transcends itself since it mirrors other gay narrations, past, present and (presumably) to-be. Will's story stands for Charles Nantwich's which, in its turn, mirrors the stories told by homosexual writers such as Firbank or Forster. The experiences, memories and desires of the two narrators in the novel span a whole century of gay existence: Will meets Charles, who met Firbank, who met Wilde and his generation. Therefore, *The Swimming-pool Library* proposes a gay continuum that goes from —and connects— nineteenth-century Uranians to the victims of AIDS.

  The Swimming-pool Library is constructed on a multidirectional intertextuality and narcissistic   specularity: the   novel   simultaneously   recasts   the   canon,   reflects

---

[127] Ibid.
[128] In Canning: *Conversations*, 331.

Hollinghurst's other novels —especially *The Folding Star*—[129] and mirrors itself — Will's story mirrors Charles Natwich's. Like most postmodernist literature, *The Swimming-pool Library* does not hide its textuality and referentiality. In other words, the novel displays its artificiality. The stories the heroes narrate mirror each other as well as gay tradition in an all-enveloping intertextual network. Hence, the different stories in *The Swimming-pool Library* only mean as long as they make reference to each other. This is why gay history —from Wilde's trials, anti-gay raids in the fifties or skin homophobia in the eighties— is permanently deferred under and accessed through literary texts. This (self)mirroring is further enhanced by the juxtaposition of contraries, especially the concealment of the closet and the sexual display of post-liberation.

The specularity of the novel starts with Will Beckwith's double role as narrator and hero. As narrator, he claims to be a Narcissus, an excess of sameness (Hollinghurst, 1998a: 4).[130] The specular distance between Will as narrator and fragmented character explains the ironic comments that the former makes on the naiveté of the latter. Particularly ironic is Will's romance, which he says, covered sexuality under "'a protective glow" (5). As the novel advances, the glow fails and his destiny proves to be no longer charmed, but tragic. The wild early nineteen eighties come to an end. Indeed, even those days, his *belle époque*, already foreshadowed a tragic outcome (3). Will has two love affairs, parallel and opposed to each other, which divide the novel into two halves. In the first, Will is the carefree, naïve lover of Arthur, a black teenager involved in drug-dealing. In the second half, Will intends to cheat his fate through Phil, also a teenager, apparently unproblematic and naïve. However, with Phil's infidelity, Will finds out the unreliability of appearances and gets ready for other traumatic episodes back from the past. The rhythm and tone of the two stages in Will's individuation process balance each other, just as Nantwich's story complements the youth's, and also just as *The Swimming-pool Library* complements and is completed by the rest of Hollinghurst's novels and gay *Bildungsromane* such as Fielding's *Tom Jones*, L. P. Hartley's *The Go-between* or André Gide's *The Counterfeiters*.[131]

Will's dualism and fragmentation is in accordance with *The Swimming-pool Library* as a whole (both structurally and thematically). At a narrative level, the novel is fragmented into the intertwining voices of its two protagonists. Will Beckwith is the paradigmatic product of the gay liberation movement in the novel: he is overtly gay and he lives as such in the London of the early eighties. His counterpart, Charles Nantwich is also an aristocrat and a homosexual, but of the old generation. A pre-Stonewall specimen, Nantwich gives Will access to most manifestations of same-sex desire throughout the twentieth century.

Both men's encounter seems fortuitous. Will enters the public urinals of a London park where a group of old homosexuals search for sexual opportunities. As a liberated gay, Will feels poles apart these old queens. The scene reaches its climax when Charles Nantwich, one of these old voyeurs, faints, to the surprise of the rest. Will describes Charles's collapse in campy terms, merging the ludicrous with the serious, the irreverent with the pitiful, Will's elegant Oxbridge narration with a debased content and ultimately two generations of gays in a tragic-comic situation. Finally, Will gives Charles the kiss of life, a symbolic act whereby he enters homosexual history (8).

---

[129] Bradley: "Disciples," 4.
[130] Hereafter all references to *The Swimming-pool Library* (1998a) will be in the text.
[131] Bradley: "Disciples," 11.

As the novel advances, the emotional and political implication between the two character-narrators increases, and especially when Will "undertakes a literary project more or less by accident, [and] begins in a desultory way to prepare to write the biography of Charles Nantwich."[132] Reluctant at first, the youth is soon attracted, shocked and afraid of what he discovers. Charles's diaries reveal a life story which is suspiciously and uncomfortably similar to Will's. The old man is "an old Africa hand [who,] like Beckwith, was Winchester, Oxford, and gay and finds blacks particularly attractive."[133] The differences that Will claims from his predecessors are progressively reduced to eventually unfold as *alter egos*;[134] Narcissus and his reflection embracing to death and witnessed by the narrating Echo.

This duality of the novel is further complicated by Murphy. In his view, Will, Charles and the previous generation make up a three-staged structure of homosexuality: "Hollinghurst embeds their biographies in what has become a conventional tripartite narrative of gay history in the twentieth century."[135] Born in 1900, Nantwich embodies the century of homosexual history and, in particular, "the first third of the gay past;"[136] however, he emerges out of fin-de-siècle homosexuality, Wilde's traumatic trials in particular.[137] For Murphy, Will also plays a symbolic role in the evolution of same-sex desire: born in 1958 (the year of the Wolfenden Report, which suggested decriminalisation), he stands for the gay liberation and, more concretely, for the second third of gay history. In Murphy's opinion, while Charles connects with the turn of the century, Will's discourse foreshadows the era of AIDS, i.e. the third third of gay history. In fact, the disease is a suitable traumatic framework for Will to narrate his last summer in the retrospective and in Proustian imperfect past. It is not by chance that Will narrates this story in the summer of 1983, when the disease "came to widespread attention after the airing of a documentary on AIDS on the BBC".[138]

Dellamora reduces both heroes to mere hermeneutic figures to 'read' gay history.[139] Yet, he argues, "in the relation between the texts of these two 'I's, the problematics of being gay, white and privileged in Great Britain in the twentieth century become evident."[140] Dellamora's words point to the troublesome hermeneutic process *The Swimming-pool Library* constitutes. First of all, the characters are symbolic and functional. That is, they embody paradigmatic forms of representing same-sex desire throughout the last century, from the semi-closetedness of Nantwich (heir to turn-of-the-century camp writers such as Firbank and Wilde) to the overt, essentialist gayness of Will (heir to Forster). Secondly, whereas Will works as a mere epistemological tool to gain access to the past of gays, Lord Nantwich is the *agent provocateur* that orchestrates the youth's formation. In the penultimate chapter of the novel, when Will is reading

---

[132] Dellamora: *Apocalyptic*, 174.
[133] Bradley: "Disciples," 12.
[134] Ross Chambers: "Messing around Gayness and Loiterature in Alan Hollinghurst's *The Swimming-pool Library*." In Judith Still and Michael Worton (eds). *Textuality and Sexuality. Reading Theories and Practices*. Manchester 1993, 210.
[135] Murphy: "Past," 67.
[136] Ibid.
[137] Ibid.
[138] Ibid.
[139] Dellamora: *Apocalyptic*, 174.
[140] Ibid.

Nantwich's diaries, he discovers that his own grandfather carried out a crusade to eradicate male vice and thus gain socio-political prestige. To Will's —and the readers'— surprise, Nantwich was one of the victims of these raids as he himself confesses in his prison diary. When Nantwich finds out the identity of the young Beckwith in the eighties, he arranges his revenge. In learning about Will's identity, he had a "conviction of rightness. It was such a perfect idea" (Hollinghurst, 1998a: 281). Aesthetic and ethic, as well as poetic and political justice, mingle in Charles's discourse, which gives structural cohesion to *The Swimming-pool Library*. Nantwich's words corroborate the specular and traumatic structure of the novel: his suffering can only be neutralised, enhanced and re-surfaced with his tyrant's (or one of his relatives') suffering. As a consequence of this revelation, which indirectly implicates him in past homophobic practices (278), Will decides to give up writing Charles's biography (281). Therefore, the hermeneutic process seemingly fails since Will is not able to give definite form to Charles's biography. As an *enfant gâté*, the youth tries to escape political responsibility but, once he has explored the textual traces of the past, he is haunted by a traumatic *aporia*: he belongs to a marginal group, but he lives on the money that his grandfather made by persecuting gays. In other words, he represents the cultural schizophrenia and the traumatic narrative ascribed to gayness.

Related to intertextuality, trauma theory helps to understand the problematic access to the past (and the present) and the specular structure and the politics of (un)saying of *The Swimming-pool Library*. The novel partakes of the 'ethical turn' of humanities in the last decades. [141] In this context of renewed interest for political and ethical responsibility of late-postmodernism, trauma theory has greatly succeeded, not only in psychology, sociology or philosophy, but also in literary studies. Drawing on Freud, Onega points out that "the neurotics' 'compulsion to repeat' traumatic experiences over and over again constitutes an attempt to achieve a retrospective mastery over the shocking or unexpected event that has breached the defensive walls surrounding the psyche."[142] In other words, unable to cope with the traumatic episode, the victim recalls it belatedly and recurrently in the form of flashbacks, dreams or hallucinations. For Murphy, the survivor of the traumatic experience is moved by a double pulse: "the traumatised subject needs to testify to his experience and achieve some mastery over it in the form of narrative;" however, "to turn the catastrophe into just another story is to deny its power, because narrative's structure denies one of trauma's most salient features —its resistance to form."[143] This *aporia* lies in the heart of *The Swimming-pool Library*. Caruth's definition of trauma, "as a non-experience, causing conventional epistemologies to falter,"[144] is particularly useful in the context of postmodernism, when grand narratives collapse. Literature must adapt itself to voice trauma; with this aim, literary discourse must "depart from traditional sequential patterns and develop new forms […] and must revise received notions of time, memory and history" (Hartman

---

[141] Susana Onega: "Ethics, Trauma and the Contemporary British Novel." 20th Conference of the International Association of University Professors of English (IAUPE). Lund, 2007, 1.

[142] Ibid., 5.

[143] Murphy: "Past," 59-60.

[144] In Anne Whitehead: *Trauma Fiction*. Edinburgh 2004, 5.

and Caruth).[145] It is thus that trauma fiction aims to rehabilitate memory through alternative discourses.

Robert J. Corber and Stephen Murphy explain Beckwith's vicarious narration on trauma theory. Although produced after Stonewall (when gayness has become a public matter), Hollinghurst's novel still relies on —or rather plays with— the indirectedness of speech of more repressive times. Its narrators still speak and live through others' experiences in a specular intertextual fashion. Homosexual experience is mediated, accessed indirectly because it is frequently too traumatic to be represented literally; more so with the AIDS outburst in the background. Thus, the schizophrenic undertones in Caruth's words resound in the narrations of Nantwich and Will. Traumatised by his imprisonment, Charles can only bear witness to it in dreams and hallucinatory images. This is why he commissions Will to integrate the fragments of that episode in a coherent narrative. However, as could be expected, the youth fails. The trauma suffered by Charles is renewed when Will reads it and lives/witnesses similar traumatic episodes in the late-twentieth century. In fact, *The Swimming-pool Library* fictionalises Will's fall into trauma and, as mentioned above, his subsequent incapacity to write Charles's biography. As the novel advances, the rhythm of the narration accelerates with the avalanche of events that connect past and present, deflector and deflected, Narcissus and Echo. Will's best friend, James, is arrested for soliciting, which inevitably revives Charles's incarceration, itself a revival of gays' persecution in the nineteen fifties and Wilde's own downfall. Thus, the novel opens the debate on current homophobia. When Will's brother-in-law Gavin argues that gays do not suffer persecution any longer, a committed Will rejects the idea (265). The hero himself does not escape the direct effects of homophobia —he suffers a violent attack by a group of neo-Nazis— and personal deception —he bears witness to the infidelity of his "naïve" lover Phil. Assuming that traumatic events are never represented directly, but in a mediated, specular form, some critics consider that all the terrible episodes affecting Will and Charles somehow stand for AIDS. However, this is rather restrictive. Both narrators are haunted by insidious traumata, mostly derived from AIDS, which they displace and sublimate into past traumatic events.

The Swimming-pool Library uses Girardian triangles —which frequently adopt artistic forms such as music, architecture, painting or sculpture, and match Murphy's 'tripartite narrative'— to articulate homosexuality as an intertextual deflection of trauma. The preface to Sedgwick's *Between Men: English Literature and Male Homosocial Desire* (1985) addresses the seminal terms meant to explain Girardian triangles, or how males interact and establish structures of power: homosexuality, homosociality and homophobia. The first makes reference to the sexual attraction between people of the same gender; the second, to the tacit alliance between males to keep their social, political and economic —rather than sexual— privileges; and the third designates a mixture of fear and hatred against homosexuality. According to Sedgwick, the relationships between men usually follow a homosocial pattern and are structured in what René Girard calls 'erotic triangles'. That is, males establish bonds with each other through women who constitute the third element in the triangle. However, the true bond is still that between men while women are used as exchange value to keep the homosocial structure secure under an appearance of heterosexual normality. Sedgwick points to the dangerous proximity between central homosociality and marginal

---

[145] In Onega: "Ethics," 9.

homosexuality as follows: "The privilege granted to male-male relations stands in dangerous proximity to the very homosexuality that patriarchal fellowship is obliged to condemn." [146] If there is equilibrium between homosociality (disguised under heterosexual institutions such as marriage) and homosexuality, the system works. In fact, the ultimate aim of the system is that the boundary between homo- and hetero-identities and discourses is maintained. When any trace of explicit homosexuality comes to the surface, it is automatically suppressed by homophobic practices and discourses. In other words, homophobia is responsible for the balance between homosociality and homosexuality. The original Girardian triangle was later adapted to meet the interests of homosexual and gay authors by replacing the female with a third man so that the triangle is exclusively male. Sedgwick uses Wilde's *The Picture of Dorian Gray* and Herman Melville's *Billy Budd*, both published in 1891, as examples of all-male homoerotic triangles. Throughout the novel, characters meet in apparently fortuitous male trios, where females have been displaced. However, when analysed in detail, it comes out that these patterns are not mere coincidences, since they answer to a studied web of symmetries that makes the novel cohere both in form and content. The central triad of the novel is the one formed by Will, Charles and Lord Nantwich, whereas the rest (of triads) revolve around it. These characters make up a triangle whose vortices represent gays' classic roles. The triangle establishes intertextual references to previous texts —Wilde's *The Picture of Dorian Gray* or Melville's *Billy Budd*— with a similar pattern. In all these cases, an invulnerable, powerful figure (Lord Beckwith) stands at the top vortex and, from there, he desires and controls the characters at the lower vortices. The novel is quite cryptic about the relation between Lord Beckwith and Nantwich, except in that the latter was the victim of the former's homophobic crusade. However, Nantwich's diary hints at the possibility of an unutterable past affair with Will's grandfather, which would explain his unfair imprisonment. He remembers Lord Beckwith in the trial "to which he had come out of pure *vindictiveness*, and of his handsome suaveté in the gallery, his flush and thrill of pride" (Hollinghurst, 1998a: 260, my italics). The second character-vortex is an *agent provocateur* in the hands of the powerful first vortex: as happens with Claggart, in Melville's novel, or with Vladimir, in Wilde's. Through these *agents*, the upper-vortex characters, Captain Vere and Lord Henry, desire and control the third element in the triangle, Billy and Dorian. In other words, the powerful characters establish a vicarious relationship with the ultimate victims of the triangular pattern through the *agents provocateurs*. Thus, Billy, Dorian and Will Beckwith share tragic and/or dramatic ends.

Still, *The Swimming-pool Library* presents some differences with respect to its predecessors. The novel underlines the changeability of power roles in homoerotic triangles: a closeted Lord Beckwith takes revenge on the alleged object of his desire, Charles Nantwich, because he is unable to assume his sexuality. However, Beckwith cannot foresee the indirect effect of his repressive policy on his grandchild. Ironically and by chance Will turns the vicarious victim of Charles, in his turn Lord Beckwith's victim. Hence, the vortices of the triangle are interchangeable and the punisher proves to be punishable. Once Will finds out his grandfather's implication in the homophobic raids of the fifties, the roles of the different characters must be reformulated.

Close to the middle of the novel, in chapter six, Will, his friend James and Lord Beckwith make up a new triangle. The trio attends the performance of Benjamin

---

[146] In Joseph Bristow: *Sexuality*. London 1997, 205.

Britten's *Billy Budd*, an operatic version of Melville's eponymous novella. The scene is a new example of the complex interaction between the different vortices in a homosocial triangle. Still ignorant of his grandfather's implication in anti-gay raids, Will notices the problematic representation of gayness as a specular phenomenon: in the operatic performance, in the interaction between the creators of the opera, and in the box the hero occupies with James and his grandfather. Will feels thrilled once he understands its meaning (119-120). Further, Will is aware of the problematic interaction of the opera characters and the trio of spectators enacting an "intensely British problem: the opera that was, but wasn't gay" (120). That is, the Girardian triangles mirror each other, juxtaposed *en abyme* and breaking the boundaries between 'fiction' (the characters of *Billy Budd*) and 'reality' (the characters/spectators at the box). This symmetry gets more complex when old Pears —Britten's lover and the first singer of *Billy Budd*— enters the theatre when Lord Beckwith is remembering Forster's criticism on Britten's closeted music (121-122). This time, the novel confronts the triangle Britten-Pears-Forster and the one at the box, thus breaking the boundaries between past and present. For Will, Pears' life story is blurred itself with the story of Vere and Billy, just as his own does with Charles's diaries of adolescence (122). Gays' lives are thus arranged in triangles in a structure of infinite regress which enhances the traumatic difficulty of representing same-sex desire.

Will is the centre of other three triangles in which power and desire intertwine. In the first one, the hero mediates between his friend James and an attractive policeman, Colin. When James is cruising after Colin, the latter arrests him for soliciting. This episode makes intertextual references to Charles's arrest in the fifties and Wilde's in the eighteen nineties. As in to the story of *Billy Budd*, this story puts forward the vulnerability of the homoerotic triangle. Despite James's social status, his fortune as a gay is changeable. When Will and James ask Charles and the photographer Staines for help to blackmail Colin —paradoxically, one of Staines models for nudes— they find no satisfactory answer. This episode points to the internal homophobia characteristic of Girardian triangles. The *agent provocateur* (now Colin) is egged on by Charles and Staines against the victim, the upper-middle-class James. What is perverse about this is that heterosexual structures encourage internal homophobia.

Will is also the centre of two more triangles, one between his two lovers, Arthur and Phil, and another between Phil and Charles. The latter is also the main vortex of a series of triangles arranged *en abyme* with each other and with those turning around Will. Until he forms part of his main triangle —that constituted by Will himself, and Lord Beckwith— Nantwich gives first-hand information about the other triangular patterns in which he is involved. Like Will, Charles has two love affairs that make up the early phase of his individuation process. With his first lover, his elder Strong, he plays the role of a valet, following the hierarchical system of English public schools. Once he gets older ("sixteen" years old), Charles's role changes and he takes the control in all his relations thereafter. His next lover, Webster, is Strong's counterpart, a delicate and younger black boy. That is, with his two complementary lovers at school, Nantwich makes up a triangle where desire and power mix up as they do in the triangle constructed by Will, Arthur and Phil.

Charles reproduces this triangular structure along his life story, in the colonies, after the War and in the early eighties, as Will learns when reading his prison diary. As an officer in the Sudan, he takes two Nubian servants, Hassan and the youth Taha. The relation between master and servants soon becomes a complex one: Hassan jealously

competes with Taha for Charles's favour (206). The triangle acquires homoerotic
undertones when Taha is stung by a scorpion. Hassan displays pleasure for Taha's pain
and desire for his body (208-209), while Charles changes his role of master and
becomes the attentive carer of his servant. That is, roles and desire circulate and
fluctuate among the members of the trio in the desert. This type of triangle in which
power roles are momentarily blurred recurs later in Charles's life story. He even sets up
a weird patronage web of ex-prisoners and outcasts after he himself has been released
from prison. As happens with Taha and Hassan, Charles's current servant, Lewis, and
his former one, Graham, also fight for the Lord's favour. At one point, Will finds
Charles locked up and tied in a small room and, on bed, a "full-sized human effigy"
(91), forming part of a voodoo ritual whereby the servants try to gain his approval. In
sum, desire, jealousy and (post)colonial violence determine Charles's triangles.

    Nantwich's testimony of his traumatic imprisonment proves how a well-planned
triangle can be a trap against same-sex desire. Although Charles gives different,
dreamlike, and hallucinatory versions of his arrest —a common trait in victims of
traumatic episodes—, he recurrently evokes one in which he is set a trap by a couple of
policemen (251-252). An attractive man (the *agent provocateur*) seduces Charles while
cottaging and, with the help of a second officer (the executioner), arrests him. The
modus operandi is typically homophobic and brings to mind the cases of James, Wilde
or Risley in James Ivory's version of Forster's *Maurice*. That is, whenever the limits
between the homosocial and the homosexual are blurred, the heteronormative *status quo*
sets in motion strategies of homophobic repression.

    These triangular patterns arranged *en-abyme* throughout *The Swimming-pool
Library* make up a structure comparable to that of fractals. As Susana Onega —who
uses fractals to analyse A. S. Byatt's *Babel Tower* and Jeanette Winterson's *Gut
Symmetries*— explains:

> The fractal is a geometric figure that suggests infinite repetition. [...] The fractal's main
> capacity is to generate infinity of variations and forms out of a basic geometric structure,
> and so reveal the hidden order underlying seemingly chaotic forms [...] Fractals, then
> offer an infinitely flexible formula for the ordering of chaos.[147]

The revolutionary geometry of fractals relies on infinite repetition. They ramify in
countless variations and forms out of a basic structure, thus representing some sort of
order in chaos. This brings to mind one of aforementioned Hollinghurst's theses: in his
view, one aspect or theme can be treated from different angles and with slight
variations, making up in this way a whole series. Besides the triangular patterns
scattered throughout the novel, Will gives a metaphor for the logic of fractals when he
finally understands he is the recipient of a gay tradition condemned to echo itself in a
narcissistic iconography: "My dream dissolved one nostalgia in another" (Hollinghurst,
1998a: 250). In keeping with this, Charles's traumatic testimony adopts a multitude of
fragmented representations that branch out and echo others' testimonies, thus
establishing an apparent fractal order. The novel juxtaposes *en abyme* a whole series of
homo-social/erotic triangles that present slight changes with respect to each other. As
mere epistemological tools, characters adopt alternative power roles, confirming the

---

[147] Susana Onega: *Jeanette Winterson*. Manchester 2006, 10.

fragmentary and provisional nature of (gay) identity. This repetition with a difference in the triangles creates symmetric patterns that recur in the discourses of the two narrators and their intertexts. Gay generations, identities, *Bildungsromane* and triangles are juxtaposed *en abyme*, thus providing the illusion of order and infinite refraction.

1.3   Artefacts of triangulation

Alan Johnson speaks of visual texts as a potent metaphor of influence. Some of these visual texts coincide with Nantwich's 'treasured artefacts', which I consider signs of the specular and traumatic iconography of gay experience. A stele is the first artefact Will is shown. The piece of art has three contrasting heads of King Akhnaten incised (Hollinghurst, 1998a: 76), a bewitching rebel, an Amonhotep, who decided the Sun was the God to be worshipped (76). For several reasons, the stele works as a gay icon for Charles (77) and for the whole gay community by proxy. Firstly, he was a political and sexual revolutionary who rebelled against traditions. Secondly, he is represented as sexually ambiguous; as Will describes it, the king presents changing facial features, unrealistic and unnatural (77). Sexual androgyny increases as far as the king does not have the Pharaonic beard, a symptom of his adolescence. Finally, like most homoerotic projects or moments, the young pharaoh's apostasy lasted a generation (77). The stele transcends its artistic beauty and becomes an iconic symbol, or a concentrated *mise en abyme* of the whole novel. It represents a self-fragmented, sexually ambiguous, politically subversive, and ephemeral youth. As the stele suggests, most periods of gay freedom are brilliant but transient in contrast to long periods of silence, insidious trauma and persecution: the liberal eighteen eighties, which Nantwich longs for, ended drastically with Wilde's imprisonment; the happy nineteen twenties and thirties, both in the colonies and in Bloomsburian London, finished with the anti-gay raids during the nineteen fifties; and finally, the gay explosion of the nineteen sixties and seventies ended tragically with the AIDS crisis.

Charles's other 'artefacts' —namely the painting of an eighteenth-century black slave and the Roman mosaic of his cellar— are also metaphors of gay identity (fragmented, specular and power-controlled), and of the triangular pattern. Like the stele, the painting and the mosaic are figurative representations transcending themselves and announcing twentieth-century characters. Moreover, the three objects display homo-erotic-sexual undertones, thus confirming the millenarian presence of same-sex desire in London.

Nantwich keeps an oval portrait of Bill Richmond, a black man whom Will describes as a handsome "colonial servant" (78). Like the stele, the portrait represents a multiple identity. As Nantwich says, Richmond was "a man with several lives" (78). Richmond's different lives echo the stories of other exploited gay characters. Therefore, he represents how gays use power to dominate and exploit other gays. He was firstly imported as an exotic good for metropolitan homosexuals, such as Byron or the General himself. This is also the case of Taha, the Sudanese youth that Nantwich takes home as a servant after his experience as an Imperial officer in Africa. The master-slave relationship between the General and Bill Richmond echoes that between Nantwich and Bill Hawkins. In both cases, the powerful man places his underprivileged slave as a boxing instructor in his charitable organisation. That is, the different homoerotic affiliations of the black in the painting throughout his several lives reflect those of some characters in the novel. In spite of their different roles, the stories of Charles and Bill Richmond intersect at one point in particular. The latter and other slaves were pioneers of anti-ensalvement politics (78), just as Nantwich and pre-Stonewall homosexuals were the first to fight homophobic structures.

A last example of how Nantwich's symbolic pieces of art represent same-sex desire as narcissistic and part of a trans-generational continuum is the Roman bath in his cellar. The *tesserae* of a mosaic make up enigmatic figures: a bearded face, which Nantwich attributes to "the Thames God" (80) and two young swimmers. The scene is confusing and therefore open to different interpretations; happy for Charles but tragic for Will. The latter describes the enigmatic couple, the first youth "in full-face had his mouth open in pleasure, [...] speaking, [or in] pain" while the second stared at his partner (80-81). The fragment sends twentieth-century characters and readers a message that is difficult for them to decode. As Dellamora points out, "these forms suggest a likeness that speaks chorically the voices of an ancient knowledge, but the visual/aural representation escapes Will's ken."[148] Finally, the hero concludes that the figures are rather tragic, but he is unable to understand completely the dimension of the piece of art. It can be argued that the fragmentariness of the mosaic symbolises the infinite generations of swimmers expelled from paradise up to present-day London: after leaving Nantwich's cellar, Will narrates his meeting with Phil at the changing room of the Corry, an obvious transhistorical reference to the boys painted in the Roman baths. The fresco thus represents the continuity of homoerotic desire (and power relations) in England as a Roman colony or as a late-nineteenth-century Imperial metropolis. In Dollimore's view, the baths represent "what historians refer to as invented tradition";[149] that is, practices which are repeated and therefore become a tradition connecting the present and the past. The critic goes further. In his view, the mosaic is not an innocuous artistic device, but the material result of a cultural invasion. When Romans —like the English in the late nineteenth century— conquered a territory, they imposed cultural artefacts and traditions that legitimated the invasion. In this light, Dellamora argues that "the images [of the mosaic] signify not ecstasy but cultural dominance."[150] This takes us back to Bill Richmond as a symbol of Europe's (homo)erotic, political and cultural control over Africa.

This incursion of the present into the past is nostalgic, but also ironic. Otto Henderson, one of Charles's friends, painted a pornographic parody of (and on) the Roman mosaic. These explicit scenes provide a new reading of the original *tessarae*. Thus, art becomes a site of interaction between generations of gays, the post-Stonewall one trying to unbury and decipher the codes used by their ancestors. In this symbolic scenario, Nantwich commissions Will to write his biography, who feels initially reluctant, it being "a monstrous request" (Hollinghurst, 1998a: 81). Like the kiss of life with which Will saves Charles in the public urinary, this is an echoic moment that transcends itself and involves both protagonists. Through Nantwich's diaries, Will is haunted into the insidious traumata of homosexual history.

---

[148] Dellamora: *Apocalyptic*, 189.
[149] Jonathan Dollimore: *Sexual Dissidence, Agustine to Wilde, Freud to Foucault*. Oxford 1991, 189.
[150] Dellamora: *Apocalyptic*, 189.

The Swimming-pool Library proposes a rather postmodernist conception of historiography which has a lot to do with trauma poetics. Gays mirror and re-live their ancestors' stories, besides learning about them. As Murphy puts forward, the new concept of history is "a fundamental factor in the formation of individual and cultural identity. [It is] no longer something we know but something we are."[151] From this perspective, Will Beckwith delves into gay history to find out his personal implication in it. That is, he starts as a classic researcher/historian and ends up as part of a marginal tradition, a shift which has ethical and political consequences. The confrontation between the liberation movement and prior gay traumas constitutes the duplicitous and stimulating discourse of the novel.

Murphy summarises the complex interaction of fractalled triangles of *The Swimming-pool Library* arguing that "Hollinghurst embeds their (the heroes') biographies in what has become a conventional tripartite narrative of gay history in the twentieth century."[152] Nantwich, whose life spans and therefore represents the twentieth century, "stands for the first third of the gay past."[153] Murphy identifies Will —and the post-Stonewall generation as a whole— with the second stage of gay history.[154] To conclude, "the novel itself provides the link to the third stage of this history, the age of AIDS."[155] Nantwich works as the linking-point between the authentic first generation of homosexuals —that of Firbank, Forster or Wilde—, his contemporaries —the Bloomsbury group which emerged in the twenties— and Will's. Thus, Nantwich's imprisonment for 'gross indecency' in the fifties can be considered the central episode of the novel. It inevitably echoes Wilde's case and, as such, has a triple dimension, personal, political and symbolic. This episode transcends its immediate reference, and makes an impact on the lives of Nantwich, those surrounding him, Will, and even the contemporary reader, who is forced to revisit past traumas. In other words, the voices of the tripartite gay narrative get closer than expected as *The Swimming-pool Library* advances. Like layers, the different generations represented in the characters-narrators are placed specularly in the novel, with Will's voice reflected on Charles's and the latter's on those of the first homosexuals at the turn of the century. Therefore, *The Swimming-pool Library* re-defines the basic dualistic narcissism that characterises same-sex desire, proposing instead a more complex reduplication of triangles.

The question that remains to be answered is whether the poetics of (un)saying of *The Swimming-pool Library* are merely a narcissistic game on trauma or a working-through to come to terms with it or a celebratory text. As a whole, *The Swimming-pool Library* is a triangular fractal, whereby Will reflects on Nantwich, and both characters do on homoerotic trauma and celebration. Alan Sinfield has pointed out that *The Swimming-pool Library* celebrates Firbank, challenges Waugh and reinterprets Wilde and Forster.[156] In the next section, this statement will be set into question, with a view to seeing how and whether *The Swimming-pool Library* celebrates, challenges, commandeers and reinterprets texts of these (first generation) homosexual writers through a process of double reflection. I will firstly focus on how Nantwich's

---

[151] Murphy: "Past," 61.
[152] Ibid., 67.
[153] Ibid.
[154] Ibid.
[155] Ibid.
[156] Sinfield: "Culture," 95-96.

postmodernist biography results from the specular projection of recurrent topics and patterns characteristic of homosexual literature; namely those that Forster, Firbank or Wilde used to codify and sublimate same-sex desire. And secondly, I will show how the novel reflects itself as far as Will's *Bildungsroman* reflects that of Nantwich's, in a specular structure complemented by intertextual references to the gay canon. The novel works as a gallery of mirrors where the postmodernist text and its hypotexts reflect each other. Out of this reflection, the postmodernist text sublimates traumata, which overcomes through irony, and incidentally celebrates sexuality.

1.4   Some sort of a gay sensibility

A striking feature of *The Swimming-pool Library* is its wealth of references to gay (literary) stereotypes, which have made up gay sensibility, if such a thing exists. In order to assess their impact on the novel, I will firstly introduce some of the topics and genres (namely pastoral and elegiac literature, cross-class and interracial gay desire, camp and the tragic queer) through which the gay canon has represented (sometimes unfair) stereotypes and traumata and celebrated difference.

In Rictor Norton's view: "If any particular genre can be called a homosexual genre, the evidence would point most convincingly to the pastoral tradition."[157] Both E. M. Forster's *Maurice* and Evelyn Waugh's *Brideshead Revisited* respond to Norton's premise. In both cases, Oxbridge is an idealised scenario where youths can still love each other without the restrictions of adult heterosexuality. However, all (homosexual) utopias collapse sooner or later, and theirs' is no exception. Arcadia is always narrated as once enjoyed, imagined or dreamt of, but finally lost, as happens with Charles Ryder's Oxford[158] or Brideshead.[159] The pastoral scenario of Cambridge is replaced by the 'greenwood', a new and imaginary Arcadia where Maurice can fulfil his sexual desire with working-class youth Alec, and by heterosexual marriage in Waugh's text. In any case, the initial Arcadian tone progressively becomes elegiac and nostalgic to mourn loss.

The elegiac element in *Maurice* and *Brideshead Revisited* serves to lament the fall from innocence brought about by adulthood (123), rather than by the male beloved's death, as happened in the poetry of Theocritus, Virgil, Sir Phillip Sydney, or A. E. Housman. Homosexuals found it difficult to leave adolescence, a traumatic experience which they could only overcome and sublimate through recurrent references to the homoeroticism at school and university. Stephen Da Silva analyses how same-sex desire has been linked to immaturity or to preternaturally old age,[160] *i.e.* to the extra-ordinary. His analysis is based on Eve Kosofsky Sedgwick's association of the pair homo/heterosexual (and others, such as innocence/initiation, ignorance/knowledge, and old/new) as characterised by the opposition between underdeveloped children/gays and fully-developed male adults. Thus, in contrast to most criticism, Da Silva confers great

---

[157]   Rictor Norton: "The Homosexual Pastoral," http://www.infopt.demon.co.uk/pastor01.html.
[158]   Evelyn Waugh: *Brideshead Revisited.* London 1987, 23.
[159]   Ibid., 77.
[160]   Stephen da Silva: "Transvaluing Immaturity: Reverse Discourses of Male Homosexuality in E. M. Forster's Posthumously Published Fiction" *Criticism* 40(2) 1998, 242.

value on homoerotic literature. The critic challenges the widespread view that sublimation is more valuable than homoerotic explicitness in Forster. Indeed, "*Maurice* represents the realization of homosexual fulfilment as the recovery of a lost childhood object of desire."[161] The pastoral within the elegiac in these novels can be read as mere escapism, a way to evade the political problematic of homosexuality in Edwardian England. However, Da Silva finds some transgressive potential in these texts. He agrees that homosexuality is the symptom of an arrested development or immaturity. However, he considers immaturity a trope for homosexuality worth revising. It is a narcissistic event that, through procrastination, prevents trauma by keeping the child looking at himself in the mirror. References to Lacan's mirror stage and the conception of homosexuality as arrested and an excess of sameness are obvious as well as politically effective.

Once the homosexual has lost Arcadia and enters adulthood, albeit traumatically, he sublimates his illicit desire establishing erotic bonds with other 'others', mainly youths, workers, Arabs or black men. Homosexual literature has usually taken for granted that its heroes are middle or upper-class, white adults who establish power (as well as erotic) relations with less privileged men. Thus, *Maurice* adapts the pattern of classic *Bildungsromane* whereby the hero matures after two erotic relations with men of a higher or lower social class: from the High Sodomy Apollonian love with Clive to the "Dyonisiac spirit [...] in the tradition of Whitman and Carpenter,"[162] evoked in his sexual relation with Alec.

Eve Sedgwick gives a detailed analysis of the interaction between same-sex desire and class at the turn of the century. She puts forward how each class has approached and represented homosexuality from a different angle: "Between the extremes of upper-class male homosocial desire, grouped with dissipation, and working-class male homosocial desire, grouped perhaps with violence, the view of the gentleman, the public-school product, was different again. [It was grouped with] childishness."[163] Most literary representations of homosexuality have been narrated and addressed from the perspective of the upper-class (subject of desire) on the working-class (object of desire). As Sedgwick points out: "both aristocratic and middle-class English male homosexuality seem to have been organized to a striking degree around the objectification of proletarian men, as we read in accounts by or of Forster, Isherwood [etc]."[164] Thus, homosexuality was usually formulated by 'perverse' upper-class males who focused their desire on working-class men.

Most of Forster's works turn around a desirable combination and interchange between the aestheticism of aristocratic or bourgeois males and the athleticism of working-class ones.[165] Although the muscular working-class male undergoes a process of refinement, *Maurice*'s interest lies in the (re)-masculinisation of the effeminate

[161] Ibid., 7.
[162] Joseph Bristow: *Sexual Sameness. Textual Differences in Lesbian and Gay Writing*. London and New York 1992, 66.
[163] Eve Sedgwick: *Between Men. English Literature and Male Homosocial Desire*. New York, 1985, 176-177.
[164] Ibid., 174.
[165] Bristow: *Effeminate*, 57.

middle or upper-class gay. This inter-class hydraulics of virility is only apparently neutralised at the end of *Maurice*. Informed by the Oxonian appropriation of the "rehabilitation and elevation of same-sex passions in a democratic chivalry,"[166] the novel aims at erasing any trace of effeminacy and, consequently, of class consciousness in the relationship between Maurice and Scudder. That would explain why Forster places their love in the 'greenwood' where "they must live outside class, without relations of money; they must work and stick to each other till death."[167] Many critics criticised the novel for its escapism and utopianism, which made it politically ineffective. Besides, in their view, Forster's attempt to erase class from homoerotic love only serves to emphasise the relevance it has in shaping desire. That is, despite its forced happy ending,[168] the relationship between Maurice and Scudder is determined not only by inter-class attraction but also by the fear and exploitation characteristic of internal homophobia: In feeling exploited by Maurice, Scudder decides to blackmail him with incriminatory letters about their clandestine relationship.[169] In most homoerotic stories, little or nothing is known about or from the point of view of the working-class guy. Unnoticed for most of the novel, Scudder only acquires some relevance for Maurice to sublimate his unspeakable desire and solve the problem surrounding his loss of youth and innocence.

Forster fictionalised cross-class homoerotic relationships in many of his texts. The reticence with which he originally represented these relationships gave way to an increasing explicitness. In early novels, such as *The Longest Journey* and *Where Angels Fear to Tread*, upper-class homosexual characters feel driven to working-class men through women. This is the case of characters such as Edgar Carruthers in *The Longest Journey* and Phillip Herriton in *Where Angels Fear to Tread*. Both characters are the centre of homosocial triangles whereby they project vicariously their ineffable desire on lower-class males.

Maurice keeps this formula of homoerotic triangulation with a remarkable difference. As happens with other homoerotic texts at the turn of the century, women are definitely displaced from the triangle, and a third man is inserted instead. Maurice learns about his own sexuality through his Greek affair with Clive Durham, which he complements with his low sodomitic relationship with working-class Alec. In some of his later short stories —namely *The Life to Come and Other Stories*— homosocial triangulation is sometimes left apart and homosexuality is addressed directly. In *Arthur Snatchfold*, an upper-class old man, Conway, pays a young milkman, Arthur Snatchfold, for his sexual services. When somebody argues to have witnessed one of their sexual encounters, the shadow of blackmail and/or imprisonment looms in the horizon for Conway. However, when Arthur is arrested, he does not betray the old man,

---

[166] Bristow: *Sexual*, 67.
[167] Ibid., 208-209.
[168] The inspiring source for Maurice was a visit that Forster paid to his friend Carpenter and his lover George Merrill, the paradigm of "cross-class democratic harmony between upper middle-class intellectual and working man" (Fletcher, 1992: 68).
[169] E. M. Forster: *Maurice*. London 1998, 181-182, 188-189

who closes the story "taking a notebook from his pocket, [and writing] down the name of his lover [...] who was going to prison to save him."[170]

All in all, Forster condemned English laws and social hypocrisy against same-sex desire. In *The Swimming-pool Library*, Lord Beckwith contends that Forster wanted the libretto of Britten's opera *Billy Budd* to be "open and sexy" (Hollinghurst, 1998a: 121). However, the works where Forster vindicated an overt, essential homosexuality were only published posthumously. Besides, Forster himself established erotic —and frequently violent— bonds with working-class men similar to those in *The Swimming-pool Libray*: "I want to love a strong, young man of the lower classes and be loved by him and even hurt by him."[171]

Like other turn-of-the-century canonical writers echoed in *The Swimming-pool Library*, Ronald Firbank learnt how to deflect same-sex desire. The novelist displaced his homosexual message through different metonymic techniques. Firstly, he used celebratory camp. The settings and objects are always fantastic, bizarre and without a geographic referent,[172] while the characters (aristocrats and members of the church), situations (illogic or following the rituals of Catholicism) and conversations (mostly social gossip) are improbable and theatrical, thus escaping (heterosexual) standards. In fact, it is the improbability of fantasy and moral/behavioural eccentricity that allowed Firbank some freedom to approach same-sex desire. Moreover, according to Hollinghurst, the modernist writer disguised homosexuality behind femininity and lesbian characters: "The female viewpoint becomes more obviously a sly means of expressing his own [Firbank's] homosexuality."[173] Firbank made use of other metonymic displacements to disclose same-sex desire: in *The Princess Zoubaroff* (1920), religious imagery and art in general serve to sublimate homoerotic attraction for the male body. There are many other hints scattered throughout the narration that help the receptive reader to identify traces of same-sex desire: the Sapphic poem discovered in the excavations of the ruins of a Faubourg of Sodom in *The Flower beneath the Foot*; or the metaphor of floral pollination —taken from Proust's first volume of *Sodome et Gomorrhe*— to "convey the sexual freedom of [the Queen of Dateland's] 'Eastern' homeland."[174] However, it is especially by representing exotic men as objects of desire, that Firbank sublimated the otherwise ineffable sameness of homosexuality.

Like youths or working-class, exotic men have been frequently represented as objects of desire for and by homosexuals. In fact, the latter —white, adult and middle or upper-class by definition— have constructed their identity through a double process of attraction and exploitation of underprivileged men. Through this complex cathexis, writers such as Forster, Carpenter or Gide have expressed their desire, and a certain degree of identification, with the primitiveness associated with young men, foreigners

---

[170] E. M. Forster: *The Life to Come and other Stories*. New York 1987, 112.

[171] John Fletcher. 1992. "Forster's Self-Erasure: *Maurice* and the Scene of Masculine Love." In Joseph Bristow (ed). *Sexual Sameness: Textual Differences in Lesbian and Gay Writing*. London 1992, 73.

[172] In *The Flower beneath the Foot*, Kairoulla is a hybrid of an imaginary Vienna and somewhere in North Africa or the Middle East (Hollinghurst, 2000: xv). In *Prancing Nigger*, Cuna Cuna is also a hybrid territory mixing elements from Havana, Jamaica and Venezuela.

[173] Hollinghurst: *Introduction to Ronald Firbank*, xiii.

[174] Ibid., xvi.

and manual workers. Although this representation of same-sex desire as atavistic has been a recurrent trait in homosexual literature, this has been doubly so in interracial desire. From Beckford's orientalist *Vathek* (1782) through Ronald Firbank's *Prancing Nigger* (1924) to postmodernist literature, cross-race homoeroticism has been constant in the Western gay canon. In most cases, the exotic male has been —like the working-class at home— not only an object of desire and identification, but also one of exploitation whereby privileged homosexuals have affirmed and represented their identity. As mentioned above, Firbank's novellas are frequently set in exotic places; there, upper-class males hint at their attraction to Arabs or blacks, therefore accentuating "the absence of direct references to male homosexuality, leaving a surplus of nonreferential desire for the reader to interpret."[175] In other words, the exoticism of these texts has subversive possibilities against the restrictions of Western heterosexual culture. Thus, Firbank found the territory to escape English sexual restraints in the Caribbean or in a mythic East. The sexual potential of other races, like that of youths and the working-class, was uncontrollable for Victorian. This is why, if a homosexual established a bond with an exotic male, it was perceived as a perversion and, as such, was relatively free from Victorian strict morality. If Firbank showed his preference for exotic lands and peoples and apparently turned his back on England in *The Flower beneath the Foot*,[176] this tendency increased in his next novellas, particularly in *Prancing Nigger* (1924).

Prancing Nigger delights in depicting the innocence of the Mouths, a black family that leaves the countryside for Cuna-Cuna, Firbank's fantastic recreation of Havana. Hollinghurst recalls Firbank's own comments on the novella, an aesthetic *capriccio* about blacks' beauty and innocence: "As a bit of colour & atmosphere it is the best of all my others & some of the figures negroes and Spanish South American are as wonderful as their setting! [...] It is purposely a little 'primitive' rather like a Gauguin in painting —extremely gay."[177] That the novelist worshipped blacks as aesthetic marvels, but not as equals, can be inferred from Firbank's words in his novel. In their hometown, the family enjoys an atmosphere of sexual freedom: "torso-to-torso, the youngsters twirled, while even a pair of majestic matrons [...] went whirling away (together),"[178] and homosexuality is displayed in public: "Two young men passed with their fingers intermingled."[179] However, this sexual Arcadia breaks into pieces when the innocence of the Mouths crashes with the sophistication of Cuna-Cuna. Thus, according to Western prejudices, the black characters in *Prancing Nigger* are "'noble savages' whose endeavour to become 'civilized' (*i.e.*: white) precipitates their social and self-ruination."[180] This is why, unlike Hollinghurst, who considers Firbank's *Prancing Nigger* an Anglophilic text, critics such as Christopher Lane consider the novella a Eurocentric expression of imperial commodification of the exotic.

---

[175] Lane: *Ruling*, 192.
[176] Hollinghurst: *Introduction to Ronald Firbank*, xiv.
[177] In Hollinghurst: "I often Laugh when I'm Alone." *The Yale Review* 89(2), 2001, 12.
[178] Ronald Firbank. *The Complete Firbank*. London 1988, 604.
[179] Ibid., 594.
[180] Lane: *Ruling*, 183.

Other turn-of-the-century English writers also found the cryptic way to (un)speak homoerotic desire in the colonial native and his unexplored geography. As Sedgwick notes, "[Kipling's] *Kim*'s India is what Lawrence's warrior of Arabia had delusively promised to be: A kind of postgraduate or remedial Public School, a male place in which it is relatively safe for men to explore the crucial terrain of homosociality."[181] Despite some differences, Kipling, Lawrence and Firbank shared a common drive to identify with native males, which was undermined, however, by their participation in Europe's sexual colonisation of Africa. Thus, it is difficult to say whether Firbank's texts reject or rather reinforce the English social and moral codes in the colonies. What is worth noting, however, is that his novellas, like those of Forster, long for a scenario where the rules of a heteronormative adult world do not hold: be it a utopian 'greenwood' or a fantastic, exotic territory focalised through "naïve" eyes.

Like Firbank, Forster also used geographic or racial differences to boost same-sex desire; although, while the former did it in fantastic, ironic and campy terms, the latter did it from the perspective of Edwardian realism. Before gay and queer studies entered the canon, much writing by Forster (and other homosexual writers) was neglected, leaving many blanks unexplored, particularly interclass and interracial same-sex desire. I have pointed out how *Maurice* was undervalued due to its sexual explicitness while others, —especially those where any trace of gayness was not obvious or just suppressed— were highly estimated by criticism. *A Passage to India* is a paradigmatic example of the second group. Although the novel presents homoerotic undertones between the heroes, an English officer (Fielding) and an Indian (Aziz), overt homosexuality is always deferred and, finally, rejected. For a gay or queer critic, it would be obvious that the bond between both men transcends a mere friendship, and follows the pattern of Girardian triangles instead: that is, Fielding's fiancée is just an exchange good, a foil between himself and Aziz.[182] Christopher Lane underlines Forster's difficulty in representing interracial homosexuality. In his view: "Forster's narratives consistently frustrate these [interracial] encounters by wounding or destroying the protagonists who attempt to fulfil them."[183] The critic draws the emphasis on the closing lines of the novel, which "foreground a drama about the men's sexual intimacy and the abstract forces that keep them apart."[184] This is the case of *A Passage to India*, but can also be applied to Forster's posthumous *The Other Life and Other Short Stories* (1972).

As he had done in *A Passage to India*, Forster escaped European boundaries and placed same-sex desire in British colonies in some of his posthumous short stories. The complexity of homoeroticism shown in the first novel increases in stories such as "The Life to Come" or "The Other Boat." Both propose interracial affairs in which the exotic male —prince Vithobai and Coconut respectively— is associated with "primitive youthfulness"[185] and the coloniser —the missionary Paul Pinmay and Lionel— is associated with maturity and an apparent (sexual) self-control. That is, Forster used

---

[181] Sedgwick: *Between Men*, 198.
[182] Lane: *Ruling*, 148.
[183] Ibid., 147.
[184] Ibid., 155.
[185] Da Silva: "Transvaluing," 253.

developmental discourses whereby the coloniser tried to bring civilisation and maturity to the colonised, a hyper-sexualised brute. If in *A Passage to India*, forces of nature and an unbridgeable cultural gap abort an interclass homosexual affair, in these stories this is doubly so. The lack of restraint of the colonised transforms their desire into "something startling, disgusting, sinister [and] evil."[186] The gay coloniser desires and exploits the colonised, thus producing a deep sense of guilt in the former, which derives in a violent *dénouement*. In both stories, sex and death collide in sadomasochistic ends. Vithobai murders Paul in an act of colonial and sexual insubordination: the last lines of the story are eloquent; with Paul's death, Vithobai "rejoiced as in boyhood [...]. Mounting on the corpse, he climbed higher, raised his arms over his head, sunlit, naked, victorious, leaving all *disease and humiliation* behind him, and he swooped like a falcon from the parapet in pursuit of the terrified shade."[187] "The Other Boat," which tells the story of the English officer Lionel and the Indian secretary Coconut, shows similar aspects of cross-racial homoeroticism. In this case, the catastrophe also comes out of the European's sexual guilt, "which erupts when he strangles Coconut."[188] According to Lane, the narrator in these stories aligns with the white lover "proposing that the black man is responsible for his and his lover's social and psychic collapse."[189] He supports these words with Forster's personal experiences and opinion on cross-racial homoeroticism. As Lane recalls, in "Kanaya" (1922), Forster described his affair with an Indian boy in sadomasochistic terms, which again forecasts the poetics of desire in *The Swimming-pool Library*:

> It was now mixed with a desire to inflict pain. It didn't hurt him to speak of, but it was bad for me and new in me, my temperament not being that way. I've never had the desire which anyone else, before or after, and I wasn't trying to punish him — I knew his silly little soul was incurable. I just felt that he was a slave, without rights, and I a despot whom no one could call to account.[190]

Going on with the prototypical gay *Bildungsroman*, once the hero had mourned Arcadian loss and had experienced cross-class and interracial erotic affiliations, he had to confront a traumatic end. The tragic fate of same-sex lovers has been a common feature throughout Western literature and culture. The homo-textual iconography of (auto)destruction and death was already present in the myth of the Greek poet Orpheus.[191] However, the gay community inaugurated this apocalyptic narrative, 'the tragic queer', with Wilde's downfall. In fact, if there is a homosexual writer who epitomises the tragic queer in modern times that is, doubtlessly, Oscar Wilde. Both his life and literary production have helped to design contemporary gayness as fated, doomed to disaster. Like many earlier gay fictions, *The Picture of Dorian Gray* is peppered with omens announcing a tragic *dénouement*. However, although most examples of nineteenth-century gay fiction close with the violent murder of the hero,

---

[186] Lane: *Ruling*, 168.
[187] Forster: *The Life*, 82, my italics.
[188] Lane: *Ruling*, 172.
[189] Ibid., 173.
[190] Ibid., 174.
[191] Woods: *History*, 1.

Wilde's Dorian commits suicide. In fact, as Kopelson argues, suicide substituted murder as the trope for queer death at the turn of the century.[192] Anyway, what is at stake here is that homoerotic texts are culturally mediated by homophobic discourses: same-sex desire is fated even when put into words by gay writers. The hero of *The Picture of Dorian Gray* is a self-destroying dandy, the last member of his family —a clear example of *fins de race*— and the reincarnation of evil types:

> One had ancestors in literature, as well as in one's own race, nearer perhaps in type and temperament [...]. He felt that he had known them all, those strange terrible figures that had passed across the stage of the world and made sin so marvellous, and evil so full of subtlety. It seemed to him that in some mysterious way their lives had been his own."[193]

Like Des Esseintes, Gray is a decadent aesthete who symbolises the degeneration and sterility characteristic of aristocrats and gays.[194] It is precisely when Lord Henry gives Dorian a mysterious yellow book that the hero becomes a pervert, a corruptor, a collector of rare objects, a murderer, a blackmailer and finally a suicide, all of them common tropes for the sublimation of same-sex desire.

Like Melville's *Billy Budd* and other works analysed by Sedgwick in *Epistemology of the Closet*, *The Picture of Dorian* Gray turns around a fatal all-male Girardian triangle: Lord Henry introduces Dorian to amoral practices and controls his evolution — like Captain Vere does with Billy in Melville's novel— from the upper vortex of the triangle. Vladimir, the painter of Dorian's portrait, plays the role of *agent provocateur*, as Claggart does in *Billy Budd*. Through Vladimir, Lord Henry projects a complex homo-erotic/phobic relation with Dorian, which necessarily ends in the tragic murder of the painter. Similarly, in *Billy Budd*, Captain Vere discharges his erotic desire for Billy through Claggart. Finally, both Dorian and Billy die because beauty brings about tragedy in homoerotic texts.

However, it is *De Profundis*, the recriminatory letter that Wilde wrote in prison, which has definitely become the paradigm of the tragic queer. In the letter, addressed to his beloved Lord Alfred Douglas, Wilde assumes the auto-destructive drive of their 'fatal friendship', thus fashioning himself as "a man who had consented to his own ruin."[195] Throughout his confession, Wilde is oblique when dealing with homosexuality; he always speaks, justifies and displaces his unnutterable love for Lord Douglas through a homoerotic hagiography ranging from Hylas, Hyacinth or Narcissus, to Plato, Dante or Shakespeare.[196] That is, he sublimates his love affair with Douglas by having recourse to a well-established homoerotic tradition, a whole Oxonian anthology that he had learnt from Walter Pater. As the epistle advances, Wilde tries to overcome his traumatic relationship and subsequent incarceration, by embracing the moral he had previously despised, though subversively. Thus, he rejects —or at least redefines— camp and paradox, the basic traits of his literature and lifestyle, and searches for Christian values such as truth and expiation. Dollimore laments the measures of

---

[192] Kopelson: *Love's*, 27-37.
[193] Oscar Wilde: *The Works of Oscar Wilde*. London and Glasgow 1971, 166.
[194] Sontag: "Notes," 8.
[195] Bristow: *Effeminate*, 23.
[196] Wilde: *Works*, 889.

surveillance and punishment —not only the prison episode— which provoked the
writer's metamorphosis, rather than the writer's "renuntiation of his transgressive
aesthetic." [197] Traumatic realism is the genre to convey this metamorphic process.
Unable to bear witness to his own imprisonment, Wilde can only turn to a constraining
faith and tragic discourse to confront his homosexuality. That is, *De Profundis* is the
textual outcome of the coercive measures used by power against Wilde's reverse
discourses, of his own auto-destructive attraction to Douglas and, finally, of blackmail
and other homophobic practices used by the Marquess of Queensberry, Douglas' father.
Thus, the aesthete's final surrender is proof that he is assuming the construction of (his)
homosexuality as trauma, rather than of the rejection of his sexual identity.

Wilde entitled his letter to Douglas in the fashion of Popes' *Encyclicals*. [198] In
keeping with this tradition, *De Profundis* is presented as a confessional narration in
which Wilde introduces unprecedented concepts in his reverse discourses: he feels
repentance for his affair with Bosie; he searches for truth;[199] he condemns comedy and
paradox as part of his frivolous life;[200] he speaks like a puritan, using concepts such as
truth and honour or moralising about Bosie's shameful lifestyle without apparent irony.
Wilde's confessional conversion climaxes when he adopts an identitarian politics. In
transferring the paradoxical of his works to his own life, the hedonist writer searches for
his identity through pain: "suffering —curious as it may sound to you— is the means by
which we exist, because it is the only means by which we become conscious of existing;
and the remembrance of suffering in the past is necessary to us as the warrant, the
evidence, of our continued identity."[201] Dollimore labels Wilde's letter as the art of
expiation; a traumatic one, I would add, because in remembering suffering, past events
come back belatedly to configure pain anew and a continued identity. While many other
critics consider *De Profundis* as Wilde's more mature work, he regards it as "a tragic
defeat of the kind only ideological coercion, reinforced by overt brutality, can effect."[202]
Wilde's text is not an exception, since there is a fruitful carceral tradition in gay
literature. Indeed, Dollimore proposes this epistle as a paradigmatic example of the
contemporary concept of punishment. Foucault's *Discipline and Punishment* serves him
well to explain Wilde's forced conversion: "The expiation that once rained down upon
the body must be replaced by a punishment that acts in depth on the heart, the thought,
the will, the inclinations."[203] Dollimore then distinguishes between the soul of Christian
theology, "born in sin and subject to punishment" and the modern soul, "born rather out
of methods of punishment, supervision and constraint,"[204] and concludes that Wilde
would be the result of punishing discourses rather than an object of punishment. In other
words, power fabricated Wilde and his texts as symbols of its authority, as symptoms of
extrinsic cultural trauma.

197 Dollimore: *Sexual*, 95.
198 Wilde: *Works*, 1164.
199 Ibid., 1173.
200 Ibid., 1175.
201 Ibid., 884.
202 Dollimore: *Sexual*, 95.
203 Ibid., 97
204 Ibid.

Although Wilde surrenders to essentialist politics, as he moves to the endorsement of Christian values, he still keeps some of his former subversiveness. Like Saint Augustine in his *Confessions*, the Irish writer explains in *De Profundis* his evolution from pleasure to suffering and humility. In this sense, Wilde's letter may be read as a tragic *Bildungsroman*, in the tradition of gay literature. In fact, while Forster's and Firbank's characters regret the loss of innocence associated to childhood and youth, Wilde regrets the loss of his freedom after the trial. As the epistle advances, he feels progressively closer to Christ —the ultimate symbol of traumatic pain to counteract the original sin— rather than to Greek art and mythology.[205] However, his Christian conversion can also be interpreted as an expression of gay camp; *i.e.*: the predilection of gays for religious iconography, especially that involving pain. The dramatisation of the pain of Christ and Saint Sebastian has been recurrently associated with tragic gay aesthetics. At a conceptual level, Dollimore also enhances the heretic nature of Wilde's spiritual evolution, which, in his view, follows the example of Saint Augustine.[206] For the Christian theologian, sin is a privacy of good whereby man falls.[207] However, sin also offers the possibility of repentance to the transgressor who has the chance to return to God.[208] Dollimore's arguments lead to a heretic conclusion, which is also a paradox: man can only reach true virtue through sin.

De Profundis is also based on a Girardian triangle whereby the homosocial order punishes transgression. Bosie's father dominates and punishes from the upper vortex. Bosie plays the role of *agent provocateur*, taking Wilde to prison and, therefore, to social ostracism. Thus, the writer reveals that he is the object rather than the subject of his own downfall: "Indeed the idea of your being the object of a terrible quarrel between your father and a man of my position seemed to delight you [...]. His hatred of you was just as persistent as your hatred of him, and I was the stalking-horse for both of you, and a mode of attack as well as a mode of shelter."[209]

1.5   First-level reflection. The postmodernist text reflects the homosexual canon

As Christian Gutleben recalls, Linda Hutcheon points out that the myth of Narcissus is the guiding principle behind postmodern metafiction, because of the textual self-awareness of the genre. However, Gutleben prefers the myth of Echo, since in the last decades of the twentieth century, the novel "has fallen in love with his forebears," rather than with itself.[210] It seems to me that both myths conflate in Hollinghurst's fiction. Indeed, Narcissus was not really aware of himself and hence he died. Echo belatedly recalls his initial unawareness and his eventual demise. Yet, drawing on trauma, Echo makes the Narcissean myth recur once and again beyond death itself. Likewise, *The Swimming-pool Library* draws on repetition for survival. It displays a complex specular

---

[205] Wilde: *Works*, 1223.
[206] Dollimore: *Sexual*, 131-147.
[207] Ibid., 132.
[208] Ibid., 136.
[209] Wilde: *Works*, 895.
[210] Christian Gutleben: *Nostalgic Postmodernism. The Victorian Tradition and the Contemporary British Novel*. Amsterdam and New York 2001, 16.

structure whereby homo-textual traits are mirrored through gay generations and their texts. The effect is like the one produced by fractals: texts only mean insofar as they interact —reflect or deflect— with other texts.

Like retro-Victorian fiction, *The Swimming-pool Library* is an exercise in nostalgic backtracking; however, contrary to Gutleben's theory, nostalgia is not necessarily reactionary. It can be subversive and innovative. For the French critic, most English literature today suffers from a Bloomian anxiety of influence. Most contemporary novels, he defends, are simple pastiches of prior texts. At most, they introduce slight formal innovations, which cannot disguise the writers' inability to escape the influence of their predecessors. Gutleben also criticises that the structure of current fiction is normally fragmented and gender roles subverted in postmodernist fiction (46) because it is fashionable. However, *The Swimming-pool Library* looks back to homoerotic tradition consciously and with a purpose. The novel is structured around a double process of reflection: in the first one, homo-textual traits, genres and texts mentioned in the previous section are recast in Charles Nantwich's *Bildungsroman*, which is narrated in the first person. In a second reflection *en abyme*, as we will see, Nantwich's life story is also reflected in Will Beckwith's main narration, which means that the postmodernist text reflects itself. In narratological terms, Will narrates his life story at a diegetic level, in which the secondary character, Charles Nantwich, narrates his own story at an intradiegetic level. The textual dependence between characters and generations of homosexuals makes gay identity and textuality necessarily fragmented and specular. Moreover, this specular structure becomes both a symptom and a metaphor of gays' cultural and historical traumata.

The Swimming-pool Library proposes an iterative, cyclical structure that escapes the rules of classic realism. The different stories of same-sex desire are suspiciously close to each other. These similarities and coincidences make each story a symbolic item within a transhistorical continuum. The novel is narrated following a causal and teleological logic: traumatic events and the revelation of equally traumatic secrets leads to the final *dénouement*. However, most of these events and acts transcend their own meaning and acquire a symbolic dimension, so that the closure of the novel is just a mirage of other ends, past and present. For example, Nantwich's prison episode transcends itself and only acquires full meaning if read as a textual testimony of similar episodes, among them and principally Oscar Wilde's *De Profundis*. Will's traumas also echo those suffered by his gay ancestors and foreshadow new traumas to come. What is more, besides characters and texts, buildings and objects also help to understand the symbolic structure of the novel. The Corinthian Club, where Will swims, is an emblematic gay-meeting point; there, Greek homoerotic practices are reproduced centuries afterwards. As already mentioned, Nantwich's house is also a symbolic scenario: the building itself and the works of art that Nantwich hides make up a physical testimony of same-sex desire, its celebration and its traumata.

Both Will and Charles are forced to confront the onset of maturity through traumatic episodes. In fact, their narrations are the testimony of their failed attempt to leave youth. In this light, their life stories are gay *Bildungsromane* insofar as they do not find an adequate closure. Unlike Victorian literature, *The Swimming-pool Library* keeps open: firstly, Nantwich's project of having his biography written fails. Later, despite suffering traumatic revelations, the novel ends with Will cruising after a new boy, *i.e.*: the cycle starts anew.

With an all-male and all-homosexual cast, *The Swimming-pool Library* is a sub-versive text *a priori*. However, Hollinghurst's novel is not self-indulgent, as it simultaneously vindicates and problematises homosexuality and its practices throughout the last century, particularly internal homophobia and discrimination of less privileged gays. Hence, the post-gay-liberation generation is shown celebrating sexual freedom but also assuming their personal implication in homosexual history. Likewise, *The Swimming-pool Library* makes use of traditional genres such as the *Bildungsroman*, the public school novel and the pastoral elegy. But again, it does not approach these genres naïvely. They are problematised and adapted to a new ideological panorama that rejects black-or-white answers.

Turn-of-the-century homoerotic tropes such as Arcadia, Forster's cross-class and Firbank's cross-racial homoerotic love, and Wilde's imprisonment make up Charles Nantwich's *Bildungsroman*. His diaries put all these canonical gay topics or pieces together in just one and new postmodernist narrative comprising his fragmentary identity. Charles's story reflects each of these recurrent homosexual topics individually as well as the combination of all of them. His journals recall and arrange (like *tessarae* in a mosaic) the topics that have made up gay lives and fictions. As soon as Will starts reading Nantwich's documents, he notices and enumerates some of the old aristocrat's many lives: a schoolboy, Oxonian, imperial Comminssioner and the old man Will comes across (Hollinghurst, 1998a: 129). Nantwich's life story is not only fragmentary, but also ungraspable and transhistorically connected with generations of homosexuals. His life is, in Will's words, a "crazed mosaic" (162) of fragments which Nantwich wants to reveal and hide simultaneously. The old aristocrat commissions Will to write his biography but, paradoxically, his diary is queer, coded and, therefore, difficult to understand, "unreadable in more senses than one" (98-99). Nantwich means to be illegible and when Will deciphers him, he gets furious (242).

The mosaic of Nantwich's life and its connections with other gay lives and representations finds both material form and historical connections in his house. A seventeenth-century building, Nantwich's house is an isolated, enigmatic place haunted by "Edwardian ghost stories" (70) like the surrounding area, the millenarian London of Medieval streets close to the Thames, as described in Peter Ackroyd's *Hawksmoor*.[211] Will is received by Lewis, a severe ex-convict whom Charles employs as a servant. The austerity and bad temper of the servant forms part of the decadent scenario that announces Charles's private museum. Through a sort of initiation rite, he introduces Will to a semi-buried generation of gays; namely, those who had to sublimate their unutterable desire. Back to Charles's artistic pieces, they all address homoerotic undertones. The stele of King Akhnaten is an icon of androgyny, subversion, fragmentation and the ephemeral; Bill Richmond, the eighteenth-century colonial black servant represented in an oval portrait, stands for many other slaves and/or underprivileged men, both within and outside the novel; the enigmatic Roman bath at Charles's cellar represents the fragmentariness of postmodernist gayness and the millenarian association of homoerotic desire with political/erotic colonisation.

---

[211] Peter Ackroyd: *Hawksmoor*. London 1988.

Before learning to sublimate same-sex desire through artistic devices, Nantwich undergoes a maturation process that he narrates in his first-person diary. His first journals make reference to his years at Winchester and Oxford. Nantwich's narration is nostalgic of a homoerotic Arcadia, which has been lost forever. He remembers and dreams of a lost time from his present, post-fall adult standpoint, just as Charles Ryder does in *Brideshead Revisited*. Traumatised, Nantwich is haunted by that prelapsarian moment he implicitly celebrates. Never, he says, there will be "a time of such freedom [...] of pleasure" (Hollinghurst, 1998a: 113). Nantwich's Arcadia follows the stereotype: an all-male community, pre-homosexual at Winchester, homosexual at Oxford, and tragically broken when many of these youths become heterosexual men and forget their "*unspeakable* things" (113, my emphasis). However, Charles remains gay after university. He starts writing his diary as an Imperial officer in Sudan. There, Nantwich narrates with nostalgia his days at Winchester as part of a lost pastoral England. However, in spite of the Whitmanesque atmosphere of the bathing rooms, where all the boys mix democratically (109), Winchester is a harsh territory. At school, Nantwich overcomes his first initiation rite: one of the prefects, Stanbridge, tortures and finally rapes him with the connivance of their fellow students (110-111). After this violent episode, as Nantwich tells, "the teasing stopped" (111). Charles is thus accepted as a full member of the public school community. Later, he argues, the hero must get rid of homosexuality and displace his desire to his best friend's sister. Charles breaks this convention and keeps homosexual all his life. He also subverts the prescriptive two relationships, one "debasing, one exalting" (54), that the hero usually undergoes in his individuation process. Thus, at school, Nantwich soon sets up innocent bonds with Strong and Webster. Following the hierarchical structure of public schools (inspired by the Greek homoerotic model), the young Nantwich becomes firstly his senior Strong's valet. Since Strong is of a lower class than Charles, the latter increasingly feels "the fascination of authority" (111-112). Their erotic bond leaves its initial bliss and turns elegiac when Charles laments Strong's death while fighting in the Great War. Like the lyrical voice of many elegiac poems, Nantwich cries for the lost beloved, but especially for the transcience of Arcadia. Nantwich's other lover during his public school days is Webster, the first black in his life, and a definitive turning-point. Nantwich himself reflects on his evolution, first attracted by older guys and later by younger ones, which gave him power "over them" (113) and a problematic pleasure. Thus, moving from exalting a senior to debasing and mastering a junior, Charles reproduces the homoerotic model of ancient Greece, whereby age determines the roles of the lovers. As with Strong, Nantwich's affair with Webster forecasts his celebration of exotic males. The celebration of blackness is of an aesthetic nature, recalling that of Gauguin (113).

Nantwich's Oxford, which Will describes as "rather Bridesheady" (177), is a deterioration of Winchester and a terminal phase of Arcadia. Unlike canonical versions of Arcadia, Nantwich's is not perfect. In this sense, Nantwich's excursion to the country with his Oxonian friends is eloquent. Charles describes the scenario, the castle and the trees around, in quite depressing terms (124). Such a landscape announces the inevitable end of Arcadia from within. Even Nantwich's innocent desire for Strong and Webster turns into unsatisfactory sex (which, however, he still remembers with nostalgia) with middle-class Chancey. Furthermore, Nantwich's narration of his days at university is (homo)sexually explicit, thus breaking with the tone of classic public-school or

Oxbridge novels. His discourse combines the nostalgia of a lost time, an extraordinary sexual explicitness, and a touch of irony. While Chancey is looking for an Oxonian 'friendship', Charles is only interested in sex (127). Like Maurice in Forster's eponymous novel, or Charles Ryder in *Brideshead Revisited*, Nantwich suffers the arrival of post-Arcadian adulthood. While Ryder displaces his desire for Sebastian by marrying his sister Julia, and Maurice escapes to an imaginary 'greenwood' with the working-class Scudder, Charles Nantwich sublimates homosexual desire with working-class, black and Arab males.

After the pastoral, thus, another of the *tesserae* in Nantwich's fragmentary life (as represented in his Roman mosaic) is the simultaneous attraction and exploitation of his social inferiors. He places erotic pleasure in the differences of class, and therefore of power, when he is still an adolescent. As an upper-class member, he feels erotically inclined to middle-class Strong and Chancey, just like aristocratic Clive is attracted to Maurice. After his colonial experience, Nantwich reencounters his upper-class gay friends from Oxford, with whom he frequents cafes in search of working-class guys. Like Dorian in *The Picture of Dorian Gray*, Sebastian Flyte or Anthony Blanche in *Brideshead Revisited*, Nantwich assumes his non-democratic role of sexual predator (Hollinghurst, 1998a: 152). This vocational desire for underprivileged men takes him back to an idealisation of the 1880s peopled by soldiers and aristocrats in brothels (247). As happens in Forster's novels, Nantwich's cross-class affairs are based on a tension between sexual attraction and exploitation. However, while Forster tries to bridge class differences between characters through sentimentalism (*Arthur Snatchfold*), or a fantastic resolution (*Maurice*), the exploitative nature of Nantwich's cross-class homoeroticism is particularly conspicuous.

In prison, Charles meets working-class Bill Hawkins, also accused of sodomy, whom he soon takes as a loyal dependant. Once released, the Lord creates a feudal web through which he patronises a dependent homosocial community. His incarceration makes his status rather ambiguous: he becomes a favouritiser, a philanthropist, exploiter or 'exploited' by his slaves. Charles sets up a boxing Club for working-class boys and helps others in exchange for loyalty and erotic pleasure. The ambivalence of Charles's cross-class desire is especially obvious in the sadomasochistic relation with his two servants. Both of them are violent ex-prisoners *à la Genet*, who fight for their master's favour. In one of these episodes of love-hatred described by Will, they even practice voodoo in Nantwich's room (91). As Forster's characters, Nantwich makes use of working-class men to enjoy, suffer and define his own homosexuality. However, while in Forster's novels, cross-class same-sex desire is either fated to failure (*Where Angels Fear to Tread*), utopian (*Maurice*) or guilty (*Arthur Snatchfold*), Nantwich legitimises it as an aristocratic privilege. Thus, while upper-class Conway feels guilty about Arthur Snatchfold's imprisonment, Charles does not concede to moral rules but the celebration of sexuality. Pleasure is too short, though. Indeed, it is haunted as the original gay event (Wilde's imprisonment for too much pleasure) echoes traumatically with Charles's incarceration.

Nantwich's erotic inclination towards men of other races constitutes another fragment of his identity. As he himself tells Will, his life is a catalogue of desire for black men, which he labels as "blind adoration" (Hollinghurst, 1998a: 242). Nantwich shares this drive with Ronald Firbank, also a character in *The Swimming-pool Library*

(167). Like the modernist writer, Nantwich shows not only an aesthetic interest in Africa and black men, but also in their overt sexuality, unimaginable in England. Already at Winchester, Nantwich notices his lifelong inclination for dark-skinned men. Webster, the son of a rum-distiller from Tobago, is the first black Nantwich meets. The youth is described in aesthetic terms as long as the aristocrat is struck as if he was "a Gauguin" (113). However, Charles soon questions this prejudiced, turn-of-the-century appreciation of blackness. He finds out that Webster was an intellectual (113) and had a great skill for swimming. He considers his affair with Webster as an act of dissidence. Nantwich condemns the way in which English public-schoolers discriminate against Webster. Paradoxically however, his erotic and poetic interest in blacks increases during his experience in Africa as a colonial officer. How can one reconcile Charles's alleged Anglophobia with his participation in English Imperialism, or his aesthetic objectification of blacks? As an Edwardian aristocrat, he considers imperialism as part of a civilising project, and the colonies as the scenario for the fulfilment of his erotic fantasies. I am not trying to justify Charles's discourse and behaviour, but place them in their socio-cultural context. Already at Winchester, Nantwich's encounter with an Afro-American soldier summarises his/the whites' anxiety about black males. The soldier's oversexualised body and behaviour produces a schizophrenic combination of irrepressible desire and threat in the young Charles; a terrible desire to be dominated, even raped, by the 'uncivilised' man who is normally under control. As an adult worshipper and 'consumer' of blacks, he reveals this unfulfilled fantasy, when he misses the chance to have sex with an American soldier (115). Once in Sudan, Charles's idealisation of racial otherness fully unfolds. He worships the Nuba people's openness and apparent simplicity in Firbankian terms. Drawing on the narrator of Firbank's *Prancing Nigger*, Nantwich feels erotically aroused when he sees "a pair of adolescent boys sauntering along with their fingers intertwined" (108).

Charles's *Bildungsroman* also subverts the canon as concerns interracial desire. He justifies the English management of Sudan since, in his opinion, most officers were gay (241). Instead of maturing, like the heroes of imperial literature, Nantwich discovers in the colonies that he can remain a child for ever. Procrastination delays trauma unfolding until coming back. He considers Africa a huge public school where maturity can be postponed for the sake of idealism, the colonial project and same-sex desire (Lane, 1995). Being a colonial officer, Charles meets Taha, a young Sudanese whom he takes as a houseboy thrilled by his poetic body (206). Once more, blackness is rendered aesthetically, as a piece of art to Western eyes. Taha becomes a loyal servant whom Nantwich desires and disempowers, feels attracted to and exploits. This relationship echoes many others, both in gay history and fiction: when Charles comes back to England, he takes Taha with him, just as André Gide and other Western intellectuals did with their respective exotic youths at the turn of the century.[212] As happens with the Mouths in Firbank's *Prancing Nigger*, Taha is a noble black in Africa but an odd specimen in the 'civilised' metropolis. Both Firbank and Nantwich mix Anglophobic and Anglophilic drives: they desire otherness, but they do it from the privileged standpoint of Europe and 'civilisation'. As time passes, Nantwich's worship of black men('s bodies) deteriorates, and he becomes a grotesque parody of what he used to be.

---

[212] Dollimore: *Sexual*, 336-339.

As an old Lord, he uses Abdul, Taha's son, as one of the actors in the amateur porn film he produces with his friends. The echoes of Firbank are obvious, especially from *The Princess Zoubaroff* (1920) and its homoerotic religious imagery with Baron Von Gloeden making orgiastic/artistic use of young men. Charles and his friend, the photographer Ronald Staines, also exploit underprivileged (black) men for the sake of art, either in porn films or in photographic exhibitions. The controversy of Mapplethorpe's black male nudes in the eighties resounds throughout the session. The limits between ethics and aesthetics, censorship and freedom, sexuality and emasculation are more blurred than ever. Will condemns the session from his post-liberation standpoint. However, the novel's specular testimony suggests, he is not so different. Generations of privileged gays owe too much to each other and thus, Charles cannot be understood without Firbank or Will without Charles.

Ronald Firbank is ever-present throughout the novel: firstly, and directly, in Nantwich's life story and later, indirectly, in Will's. The author of novels about bizarre characters (Hollinghurst, 1998a 153), Firbank is the paradigm of camp and a referent to understand Charles's (and homosexual) identity. In his incomprehensible exotic camp (153) Charles recalls his first encounter with Firbank, a fascinating man he met in rather theatrical terms (154). The scene is a good example of camp ambiguity: performative and comic but serious; childish but emotionally violent; titillating but ephemeral. Henceforth, Firbank's camp becomes part of Nantwich. Indeed, Will describes Nantwich as a "Firbankian figure" (242) because he behaves like an over-indulged child. In fact, the character of Charles can be read as a tribute to Firbank's camp. His behaviour is frequently extravagant and mysterious as well as his language. Drawing on camp, he unexpectedly uses foreign terms to highlight the artificiality of the medium.[213] Usually camp talk makes use of French as a cultural stereotype of style and sophistication,[214] and *The Swimming-pool Library* is not an exception. Keith Harvey reproduces excerpts from chapter 4 of the novel, when Charles shows Will his home using French terms (Hollinghurst, 1998a: 75, 80). These excerpts are used by Harvey as evidence that camp is citational, makes reference to the mechanisms of the medium (*i.e.*: language) and, in consequence, "plays around with and blurs the distinctions in the binarisms spoken/written, voice/print [...] authentic/represented, natural/unnatural."[215] In other words, camp works as a reverse discourse whereby gays can deconstruct conventions. It both celebrates gay difference and makes a tragedy out of it. Charles is both an ultramasculine prototype in an all-male world and a decadent queen. He (and Will) is a worshipper of blacks and working-class men but also their sexual predator. He is socially privileged but also an outcast punished by the system. Nantwich is the paradigm of Firbank's melodramatic camp, a mystery that Will fails to decode successfully but one that conveys the traumatic/celebratory discourse of Hollinghurst's.

After Arcadian Winchester and cross-class and interracial erotic affiliations, Charles's fragmentary life story meets the paradigm of gay literature, namely the tragic queer. Trauma is latent but haunting for most of the novel. Yet, it is the last entry of his

---

[213] Keith Harvey: 2002. "Camp Talk and Citationality: A Queer Tale on "Authentic" and 'Represented' Utterance." *Journal of Pragmatics* 34, 2002, 1153.

[214] Ibid.

[215] Harvey: "Camp," 1154.

journal, which bears witness to his imprisonment, that triggers the trauma back. The episode is inscribed within the gay carceral tradition and is an obvious reference to the paradigm of the genre, Wilde's *De Profundis*. Like Wilde, Charles is convicted of gross indecency (*i.e.*: homosexuality) and condemned to hard labour. Both suffer and represent the psychic trauma of a terrible downfall, a "change of station" (Hollinghurst, 1998a: 249) from a privileged position, which has proved to be a fascinating metaphor for the tragic fate usually attributed to gays.[216] While Wilde sublimates his affair with Bosie as a mere friendship, or through Greek myths, Charles defers his traumatic experience; that is, he is only able to narrate the episode after being released from prison (Hollinghurst, 1998a: 248). Victims of unfair conspiracies, Wilde and Nantwich take refuge in sentimentalism, self-pity and philanthropy. Both feel auto-destructively driven to tragic ends by attractive youths and homophobic agents. However, despite the many similarities between these stories at a psychic level, Nantwich's letter differs from that of Wilde in a few aspects. Most of these differences derive from the historical contexts in which they are narrated, the nineteen fifties and the eighteen nineties respectively. Charles narrates his own detention after the fashion of the spy novel or classic Hollywood *film noir*: the whole scene takes place in a dark atmosphere of shadows, footsteps and threatening corners where, as he confusingly remembers, two policemen —a youth with a hat obscuring his eyes and another one in a dark overcoat— set a sexual trap to arrest him (251-252). This Cold War atmosphere of homophobic blackmailing recasts the persecution that Wilde suffered during the decadent *fin de siècle*. Moreover, the consequences of both imprisonments also differ; chiefly because the socio-political circumstances were also different. Wilde learns from his incarceration how to overcome his tragedy through "the meaning of sorrow, and its beauty."[217] In appropriating, revising and adhering to Christian values from Dollimore's 'transgressive reinscription', he converts punishment into expiatory bliss. By contrast, Nantwich's transformation is political rather than personal: after his tragic incarceration, he understands himself as part of the gay community. Wilde keeps subversive, but only from a dialectic point of view; Nantwich, however, adopts the political resolution of helping his peers (Hollinghurst, 1998a: 260). Although both men adopt a patronising attitude to other prisoners, it is Nantwich who foresees the potential of sexual punishment and martyrdom for sexual liberation. He meets a community of sexual dissidents in prison where, paradoxically, they reverse what could be expected as long as they can set up bonds apart from "the outside world" (255). His philanthropy and consciousness of belongness announce the gay liberation movement of the nineteen sixties.

Nantwich's imprisonment diary is a masterful fictionalisation of trauma theory. It represents Nantwich's inarticulated discourse in the aftermath of his downfall: the PTSD that affects, in Caruth's view, the victim of traumatic episodes haunts Charles and prevents proper narration. Thus, his mental and affective lacunae, particularly his nostalgic references to childhood, can only be referred in a direct speech that breaks with classic logical narration and captures instead Nantwich's sorrowful hallucinations and dreams. Moreover, his traumatic diary is poly-referential. Simultaneously a fictional

---

[216]   Hugh Stevens: *Henry James and Sexuality*. Cambridge 1998, 146.
[217]   Wilde: *Works*, 957.

representation of the historical persecution of gays in England during the nineteen fifties, of Wilde's *De Profundis*, and once read by Will, an omen of future disasters for the gay community. For Nantwich to render testimony to his arrest belatedly, he hides behind *film noir* conventions. With this aesthetic framework, the novel rescues a shameful episode of recent homophobia in England. During the nineteen fifties, gays suffered raids which sent many of them to prison. The most outstanding case was Lord Montagu's, which, in Nantwich's view, recalls social and policial double dealing (253). Montagu's trials were planned by three prominent figures: "The Home Secretary Sir David Maxwell Fyfe, the Director of Public Prosecutions Sir Theobald Mathew; and the Commissioner of the Metropolitan Police, Sir John Nott-Bower."[218] Similarly, in *The Swimming-pool Library*, Lord Beckwith turns out the crusader that took Charles to prison. As Charles observes, he is the leader of "this 'purge' as he calls it, this crusade to eradicate male vice" (Hollinghurst, 1998a: 260). The echoes between the historical figure and the character go even further: Sir Maxwell Fyfe was nominated Viscount Kilmuir in 1954 and Earl of Kilmuir in 1962, while Will's grandfather, as Nantwich sees in *The Times*, leaves the DPP's office and takes a peerage too (260).

Nantwich's disclosure of this traumatic episode corroborates transgenerational gay trauma as well as the necessity and impossibility of rendering it but in an intertextual narcissistic trauma realism. The novel keeps trapped in a Girardian triangle that confirms Sedgwick's vicious circle between homosexuality, homosociality and homophobia: Lord Beckwith stands on the top vortex, while Lord Nantwich and Will Beckwith rotate in the other vortices. The relation between the two old Lords remains an enigma through the novel, though some information is hinted at. When Nantwich recalls his school days, he regrets how things have changed. The boys in that homoerotic past being the same who punish him so severely (113). Lord Beckwith belongs to the group that, having overcome the homosexual phase, become part of the homosocial establishment and homophobic repressors of recidivist homosexuals like Nantwich. Charles's incarceration seems the result of a previous personal (perhaps sexual), rather than political, affair with Lord Beckwith. Otherwise, why should the latter feel resentful? As in many other triangles, the dividing line between homosexuality and homophobia is easily trespassed. Charles works as the *agent provocateur* of the triangle: as soon as he reveals Lord Beckwith's political activity, he converts Will into part of the (hi)story. Thus, the youth, who has paradoxically enjoyed a well-being out of his grandfather's homophobic practices, becomes Charles' weapon to respond to Beckwith's former aggression. The triangle is an aesthetic and political artefact that makes the novel a coherent unit that responds to the (im)possible representation of trauma; besides, it puts forward a complex set of relations of power and powerlessness that informs how homosexuality has been formulated throughout the twentieth century.

---

[218] Patrick Higgins: *Heterosexual Dictatorship. Male Homosexuality in Post-War Britain*. London 1996, 249.

1.6   Second level reflection. The postmodernist novel reflects itself

The Swimming-pool Library puts forward a second reflection. If in the first one, Nantwich's story works as a specular projection of canonical gay texts, in the second one, Will's auto-biographic narration reflects Nantwich's failed biography. In other words, the postmodernist text reflects itself.

Unlike his predecessors, Will is theoretically free to live and utter his gayness. However, as he learns, his life story is not only a sexual option. It is the product of the effect on him of the gay canon and its codes of unnutterability. Hence, although sexual politics in (Will's) postmodernist era are more permissive, he cannot escape history or the formulas that the homosexual literary canon used in order to avoid censorship. Thus, although Will's story is meant to be the definitive gay text, the postmodernist answer to Nantwich's unwritten biography, it finally fails. Will Beckwith is the narcissistic, albeit haunted, product of the post-liberation era: openly and proudly gay (as his sexually explicit narration proves), he is not ready, however, to give a definite form to Nantwich's journals. If Charles is a victim of institutional homophobia, Will is equally unable, though for other reasons, to reject Nantwich's commission: the better he knows Charles, the more aware he is of his commitment to the past and of its traumatic return in the future. It is for these reasons that prior sublimating strategies prove to be useful again at the end of the twentieth century.

Will's *Bildungsroman* echoes Nantwich's (which itself echoes many others), in a fractal structure. Will's identity is ambiguous and fragmented, like that of his predecessor. As a Gemini, he is split into two halves or facets, one hedonistic and the other puritanical (Hollinghurst, 1998a: 4); he is liberal, but he foreshadows times of repression. Thus, Will's narration starts with a nostalgic retrospection of Arcadia (3). From the very beginning, Will adopts traumatic undertones to narrate his naïve youth, when he could not make out the fate awaiting him. It is as if Narcissus spoke the moment he embraces himself in the water after Echo's reverberations. As Narcissus, finally conscious of his reflection, Will finds himself paralysed when he learns of his grandfather's homophobic campaign. The transgenerational trauma, silenced for long, finally bursts (278). Nantwich's incarceration is a turning point, the traumatic trigger, that Will cannot avoid. Indeed, the trauma that haunts him is that his life story is a reflection of previous gay stories he cannot bear witness to. That is why he feels compelled not to write down Charles's biography: "All I could write now would be a book about why I couldn't write the book" (281). That is trauma's aporia, the 'truth' (be it internal homophobia, AIDS or the visibility of same-sex desire) that must but cannot be narrated, the reflection that is (but cannot be) seen.

Will Beckwith and Charles Nantwich intertwine their narrations, thus breaking with classic univocity and rendering instead a two-staged trauma narrative. Both differ greatly at first glance: young and openly gay the former, old and semi-closeted the latter. However, as soon as Will starts reading Nantwich's diaries, the parallelisms are conspicuous. Ross Chambers regards them as 'alter egos' —I would say events in a traumato-celebratory continuum— since "the last [Nantwich's] diary entry links with the date of the younger man's birth."[219] Will's life updates Charles's diaries to a new

---

[219] Chambers: "Messing," 210.

socio-political panorama. Like his predecessor, Will studies at Winchester and Oxford, feels attracted to working-class and black men and foreshadows tragedy.

When Will reads Charles's nostalgic narration of his school days, he cannot help thinking of his own as an aftermath of the former's account (Hollinghurst, 1998a: 129). Will shares the sentimentalism of Nantwich, Maurice or Charles Ryder in remembering an English Arcadia which never existed (122). However, Will's lost *locus amoenus* is the Winchester swimming-pool, which he describes as the projection of an unfulfilled wish and genuine naïveté: "I still dream [...] of the Swimming-Pool library [...] that empty place [...] where at heart I want to be" (141). This is a primordial scene which revises and foreshadows other aquatic spaces throughout the novel: from the Roman mosaic at Charles's house to the swimming-pool of the Corry. Will recalls the traumatic loss of naïve childhood and the subsequent entry into adulthood that most public school novels regret. Like Narcissus's river, the swimming-pool reflects oneself as a pre-symbolic entity, a nothingness akin to loss and a way to overcome the trauma of the fall into the restrictions of the symbolic. Although Will's narration of his school days is rather escapist, it also presents ironic undertones. His nostalgia and sentimentalism can be read as a psychic response to the AIDS crisis. But, in view of his promiscuity, Will's discourse is ludicrous to say the least. Like Firbank's texts, *The Swimming-Pool library* looks back in sorrow for a lost time, but, as Stephen Murphy has put forward, it does so ironically. Like Charles before him, Will is just playing with and recasting classic public-school novels in an ironic and subversive fashion.[220] As narrator, he recalls his school days ironically. A narcissistic student only gifted for sex, Will is appointed as responsible of the swimming-pool (140).

Will's days at Winchester and Oxford are bucolic, first as a student and later as a *flâneur*, a parasite and, finally, a promiscuous lover; no trace of Charles's traumatic undertones in his school days. However, the course of his life changes when he meets his best friend, James. An archetypal Forsterian middle-class intellectual, as he himself protests (220), James is a hermeneutic figure in Will's *Bildungsroman*. He introduces Will to Firbank's literary production and encourages him to write Charles's biography. Thus, when Will starts reading Nantwich's and James's diaries, he feels compelled to analyse himself through the other. However, instead of feeling dissociated, as trauma victims do, being dispersed in his 'alter egos' feeds his vanity and reveals his naïveté (217). Will firstly fails to notice his trace is implicit in every gay text, which necessarily begs for re-evaluating his bucolic *Bildungsroman*.

Despite logical differences, the life stories of the old and new generation of gays are specular. Like Nantwich, Firbank and many other gay writers and characters, the young Beckwith feels inclined to foreigners and underprivileged men. James censors, not without some envy, Will's exploitation of this type of men (218). This is ironic of James's though, since he is subscribed to a pornographic magazine published by the Third World Press (215). In brief, Will and James keep (ab)using black and working-

---

[220] The nostalgic tone of classic school novels turns more tragic and direct in the sixties. Stephen Adams (*The Homosexual as a Hero*, New York: Barnes and Noble 1980) addresses Simon Raven's *Fielding Gray* (1967) or Michael Campbell's *Lord Dismiss Us* (1967) as examples of this transformation of the genre, which persists at the end of the century, particularly in *The Swimming-pool Library*.

class males. However, the new political circumstances −especially the success of the campaigns for equal rights− make the new generation's desire for the exotic much more problematic than it was for the old one. As the gay liberation generation in the novel, Will and James cannot accept that their sexuality is shaped on their attraction and, above all, their exploitation of the underprivileged. Yet, Will is not the liberated version of Nantwich that he pretends to be, but a hypocritical post-imperial reflection of the old man's experiences and desire.

When Charles and some friends invite some working-class boys, a black man and an Italian, to participate in a porn film, he does so unproblematically (245). Will can only feel "Charles was [...] a fixer and favouritiser" (245). But he is the victim of his double morality. He is not afraid of the old one, but of his own exploitative desire, of his own process of dissociation whereby he bears witness to his own desire and its potentially traumatic consequences. In othering the other, Will is building up himself as the Same from whom he tries to keep apart. Thus, although the young aristocrat is sexually aroused by the *myse en scène* and the actors, he censors his/their desire in moralistic terms (187). Will escapes from his awakening, rather than from the sexual scenario itself. After the film episode, he intends to maintain his feeble truth despite trauma symptoms all around. Thus, he decides to leave Charles's world and welcome instead the presumably naïve "company of Phil" (189). However, he objectifies and fetishes working-class Phil in a sadomasochistic affair that reproduces Will's sadistic use of the youth in their regular life (163). The young Beckwith is not less a fixer and favouritiser than Charles. The only difference is that, while Nantwich assumes his cross-class and interracial desire, Will tries to deny his own. It is significant that Will meets Phil just after admiring the mosaic in Charles's basement. That is, the message of sexual control and colonisation of the mosaic is presumably applicable to Will's affair by juxtaposition. Besides, as happens recurrently throughout *The Swimming-pool Library*, things are not what they seem at first sight. Phil is not the naïve he seems, since he keeps a parallel relationship with Bill Shillibeer. When Will comes across "Phil and Bill kneeling face to face on the bed" (276), it constitutes a new trigger to awaken the latent trauma.

The scene is a new example of the specularity —triangulated by a third element— of the novel. Both men mirror each other in a scene that echoes the sense of balance of Greek art. Besides, their names, together with Will's, are phonetically similar, a metaphor for the blurring of gay identities Will addresses (278). The three men form a new triangle whose vortices are so similar that they are interchangeable. The symbolism is clear: gay lives and texts mirror each other so that roles or positions can change at any time. As John Bradley has pointed out, there is a reference to Hartley's *The Go-Between* on the centre page of *The Swimming-pool Library*. This strategic position is very significant. Phil is reading Hartley's novel when he highlights its climactic scene and its impact on the hero's individuation process: "The idea is that seeing Ted and Marian shagging in the barn freaks him [the hero] out so that he can never form a serious relationship with anybody when he grows up."[221] The parallelism between this scene and the one in which Will discovers Phil's infidelity is obvious but, in Bradley's view, they differ in the effect on the heroes (6). Thus, while the hero of *The Go-Between*

---

[221] Bradley: "Disciples," 6.

suffers "an arrested development," Will reaches "self-realisation and maturation" (6). An avalanche of traumatic episodes, all of them different versions of the same, compels Will to revise his premises. However, it is unlikely that the hero succeeds in completing his maturation process, as far as he keeps his life style to the end of the novel. *The Swimming-pool Library* does re-work the primordial Freudian scene of Hartley's *The Go-between*, when the young hero witnesses a surrogate of his parents' coupling into one of homosexual infidelity.

Will also draws on Charles's erotic attraction to black men. Already on the first page of the novel, Beckwith confesses his attraction for West Indians. However, the political circumstances of both characters differ and so does their inclination to exotic men: Charles is an Imperial officer and aristocrat and, therefore, feels legitimised to control these men politically and sexually. Moreover, he still sublimates his desire for them addressing their beauty. By contrast, Will's cross-race affairs are overtly sexual and allegedly non-discriminatory. Nantwich's devotion for blacks −from Wesbster to Taha and even, to some extent, Abdul− has an artistic, quasi-religious character, which he associates with camp and imperial aesthetics. It is precisely the poetic approach of Europeans to the natives that made the imperial adventure apparently devoid of the dramatic effects of colonialism. The fact that, as usual, the social inferior is silenced makes the reader only familiar with his beauty, as described by the coloniser. Will's interracial affairs recreate *mutatis mutandis* Nantwich's colonial ones. Instead of the sexual expeditions to Africa that Nantwich and his friends carried out in the nineteen twenties, Will has black men available at home. The African savannah has been replaced by the poor neighbourhoods on the outskirts of London for cross-race sexual exchange. Charles describes blacks and their lands in idyllic terms that recall Firbank's camp aesthetic (Hollinghurst, 1998a: 108). What for Nantwich is an unfulfilled sexual fantasy becomes a reality for Will. That is, whereas Nantwich 'adores' (yet colonises) black men in exotic scenarios, Will exploits them in post-imperial London. Arthur is a Caribbean teenager, whom Will uses as a sex object. Hence, the former is described in racist and classist terms, a poor guy from a tower block in the outskirts (20). Conscious of the role of class and race, Will regards his love affair as an example of Lower Sodomy with an inferior, more primitive male. In other words, the hero maintains nineteenth-century prejudices on race and sexuality despite his apparent post-liberation discourse.

When James reminds Will that he shares Nantwich's inclination for blacks, the youth rejects the comparison, arguing his desire is well intended (178). As happens when Will leaves Charles's porn film, his answer to James brings to the fore the irreconcilability of his double status as liberated gay and sexual predator. The contradictions between his desire and the politically correct, between his post-imperial use of blacks (now at home) and the postcolonial politics that he claims, explain Will's outbursts of sadomasochism and sentimentalism with Arthur. Will himself detects the symptoms, sentimental and brutal at the same time (5). The extreme violence against Arthur brings to mind some of Forster's short stories in *The Life to Come* collection, especially "The Other Boat." After their short affair, Arthur disappears leaving no trace. Only some time later does Will decide to visit the outskirts of London in search of Arthur in what turns out to be a post-imperial parody of Nantwich's sexual expeditions to the colonies. Arthur's neighbourhood in London is not less unfamiliar to Will than

Africa was to Charles (168-169). The marginal neighbourhood is not only a foreign territory, it also produces in Will a feeling of hostility owing to the racist graffiti and bands of skinheads around. That is, Will's 'journey' is more dangerous than Nantwich's sixty years before.

Will's exploitation of blacks gets more complex and problematic when he comes across Abdul, the son of Charles's Sudanese servant. Recalling Charles's unfulfilled fantasy with an American black soldier (115), Will feels attracted to Abdul. It is at the amateur film of Charles and his pals that Will is shocked by his sexualised body. In a fur coat, Will spots Abdul's scarred skin and fantasises with playing "some exquisite game animal" (188). Drawing on sterotypes, Will's description associates primitiveness and bestiality with blackness. This explains the sadomasochistic visual pleasure that Will experiments. Being afraid of his own desire to be desired —something which finally happens— he regards Abdul as both pleasurable and abject after Edelman's *Homographesis* (1994). At the end of chapter eleven, Will meets Abdul once more. This time, however, the youth is no longer as self-confident as he used to be, and it is the black man who 'emasculates' him: Will enjoys and suffers the brutal sex and pain inflicted by Abdul, thus turning upside down roles and positions (262) and making good the novel juxtaposition of sexual celebration and trauma. Abdul's sexual violence is the culmination of Will's trajectory, one of celebration, traumata and social violence, as he himself announces (3).

When Will goes to the outskirts of London in search of Arthur, he lives a new traumatic episode which problematises the discourses of class, race and sexual orientation. As Robert Corber points out, Beckwith is once more victim of his own sentimentalism. When he notices the racist graffitis of the neo-Nazi National Front on the stairwell of Arthur's building, he imagines his lover's family "forced to contain their anger, contempt and hurt in such a world."[222] Will bears sentimental witness to the trauma of racism against Arthur, ignoring the danger his own gayness brings about. In fact, his sentimentalism breaks down when he is assaulted by a group of skinheads and understands he is as vulnerable as Arthur and his family. At first, Will feels attracted to them, as he recalls his own affair with a neo-Nazi (Hollinghurst, 1998a: 171-172).

As in Genet's texts (Sinfield, 1998) or Tom of Finland's pictures, Will finds in the brutal masculinity of these men the erotic thrill that Nantwich and the characters of Firbank and Forster feel about blacks and working-class men. Beckwith even dismembers the skins' uniformed bodies into parts that he fetishises, as he does with Arthur and Phil. While he is infatuated by the gang, Will is unable to foresee the imminent danger. As a privileged aristocrat, he thinks himself immune to any violence. However, as Corber points out, it is precisely because "privilege is so legible —in his well-tailored clothing, his educated manner of speaking, the Ronald Firbank novel he is carrying— [that] the skinheads recognize him immediately as a 'fuckin' nigger-fucker' (173)."[223] Upper-class Will is associated with sexual perversity, other races (Arthur) being the former's object of desire, and the frustrated working-class (the skins) are associated with homophobic violence. With this class-conscious concept of desire, Will

---

[222] Robert J. Corber: "Sentimentalizing Gay History; Mark Merlis, Alan Hollinghurst and the Cold War Persecution of Homosexuals." *Arizona Quarterly* 55(4) 1999, 131.

[223] Corber: "Sentimentalizing," 131.

dissociates from himself, splitting into character and narrator of his homophobic aggression in a classically paranoid fashion. Thus, he bears witness to his copy of Firbank's book and the boot on his face (Hollinghurst, 1998a: 174). Will's narration is the realistic representation of a social problem with a symbolic meaning in *The Swimming-pool Library*. He suffers a physical aggression but also a psychic and a symbolic one. He has his nose, self-confidence and narcissism broken. Back to the origin of trauma, physical harm is soon incorporated in a melancholic state. Moreover, its very specularity makes it mandatory, yet impossible, to bear witness to. Drawing on Dorian Gray, Will feels a narcissistic pleasure when looking at himself in the mirror, which finishes when he is attacked (176). Will's traumatic aggression can be extended to the whole gay community since *The Flower Beneath the Foot* —the paradigm of homoeroticism in the novel— is also the target of the skinheads' fury. In fact, both the hero and the book represent literally and symbolically the social hatred and violence against gays and their personalised and cultural trauma (174).

Will is exposed to other traumatic discoveries and episodes: his family's shameful past, blackmail stories implicating Charles and Bill, Phil's infidelity or James' arrest for soliciting. The young Beckwith is not arrested and imprisoned like Wilde or Nantwich. However, AIDS becomes his rhetoric and cultural prison, one that permeates his whole life with insidious trauma no matter how privileged he may be. According to most critics[224] what lies behind the catastrophes in the novel is the disease. For Dellamora, "the absence of explicit reference to AIDS is part of the history that Hollinghurst represents."[225] In other words, the novel is indebted to the tradition of the closet. While this tradition used strategies to silence and/or sublimate homosexuality, *The Swimming-pool Library* does it with the disease. In juxtaposing this language of indirection with current sexual and textual explicitness, *The Swimming-pool Library* has a double motivation: aesthetic —recalling forgotten voices of gay literature— and a psychic and political one —being set in the pre-AIDS era, the novel renders the disease absent. Set in the transition between the happy seventies and the catastrophic eighties, *The Swimming-pool Library* displaces AIDS to other traumatic events such as Wilde's downfall, the loss of the Empire, or the homophobic purges during the Cold War. Yet, in being sublimated, AIDS is addressed. That is, the poetics of indirection serve Hollinghurst's text to utter two-staged traumata, the present absence being haunted by the past presence.

In spite of the omens of future disasters (AIDS in particular) Will comes across, he is unable to decipher them. He does not suspect about his grandfather when a senior police officer enquires if, he "was related to the former Director of Public Prosecutions" (Hollinghurst, 1998a: 216). His stupidity and self-confidence do not allow him to suspect Phil is having an affair with Bill either. In front of a poster with broken-nosed pharaohs in the British Museum, the hero notices how he and Phil are being observed by Bill. He fails to see what is really happening once more (195). However, it is the oracular and subliminal references to AIDS that definitively reflect former gay traumata throughout the twentieth century. Again, Will is just the last in a list of victims of

---

[224] Keen: *Romances*, 187-188; Woods: *History*, 368-369; Burton: *Talking*, 48; Chambers: "Messing," 217; Dellamora: *Apocalyptic*, 173, 191; Bristow: *Effeminate*, 173.

[225] Bristow: *Effeminate*, 173.

(internal) homophobia, ranging from Wilde or Firbank to Nantwich. At the beginning of
the AIDS crisis, the American and British governments ignored the problem. That is
why the slogan 'Silence=Death' became widespread among the victims of the disease,
many of them gays. *The Swimming-pool Library* is textual evidence of a historical
traumatic *aporia*: sexual dissidents cannot bear witness to their own tragedy, but must
address it (albeit indirectly/intertextually) to survive.

Through Charles's diaries and Firbank's novellas, Will learns that gay identity is
inescapably textual. Thus, although he is a post-Stonewall gay, he finally understands
his identity is inevitably linked to the homosexual canon and history. That is why Will's
answer to the plague can only be textual, namely the writing-narration of *The
Swimming-pool Library*. The novel is a symptom of the trauma and part of the trauma
itself, irony being its only redeeming feature. When Will decides to write Charles's
biography, he ignores the pedagogic and political implications of the project. The novel
itself is an *aporia*, paradoxically proving the impossibility of writing (280).

In an interview by Richard Canning, Hollinghurst confesses he thought of "having
the whole thing written by Will when he was very ill."[226] He finally gave up the idea,
for "it was too much of a cliché. It would have been too neat and turned the novel into a
moral fable." [227] Moral or aesthetic reasons apart, *The Swimming-pool Library* is
narrated in traumatic terms. Following a pattern whereby gays' culture is haunted
cyclically, some events trigger the return of trauma in between celebratory phases. As
Dellamora points out, "the sense of imminent apocalypse floats across other ways of
organizing time in the novel. […] One effect of approaching catastrophe is to convert
much of Will's memoir into a retrospective apocalypse of gay bliss. This effect is
analogous with the widespread tendency in contemporary gay existence to project back
onto the period between Stonewall and AIDS a myth of sexual and social plenitude."[228]
Like Nantwich's imprisonment, the disease works as a symptom of cultural trauma.
Likewise, Will's narration is peppered with apocalyptic signs simultaneously
foreshadowing and sublimating AIDS. Thus, he recalls his last summer of sex and self-
esteem before the unspeakable (which can occur and, what is worse, it is "perhaps
deserved" (Hollinghurst, 1998a: 4)) came up abruptly, as traumatic reverberations do.
Will's 'something' constitutes the very essence of gay traumata as intertextual
phenomena. It makes reference to Lord Beckwith's homophobic raids, but also to AIDS
as, for many leaders, a God-sent punishment and the rest of events that abolish gay lives
and culture. No celebration left, cornered by traumata, Will's discourse turns elusive.
Indeed, as Žižek argues, for trauma discourse to be credible it must be unrealistic.[229]
Too much realism makes trauma realism unreliable. Hence, like Nantwich's
hallucinations, Will's dreams prove to be valid metaphors of cognitive impairment and
psychic dissociation: "I had several dreams of siege [and] woke up in the certain
knowledge that I was about to die" (Hollinghurst, 1998a: 33). Being a liberated gay,
Will is still a prisoner in a metaphoric closet with Arthur. The dream confusingly
foreshadows disasters to come, individual and cultural traumata abolishing gay culture.

---

[226] Canning: *Conversations*, 337.
[227] In Burton: *Talking*, 48.
[228] Dellamora: *Apocalyptic*, 174.
[229] Slavoj Žižek: *Interrogating the real*. New York 2005, 29.

A whole generation of gays was to suffer an unprecedented violence: that produced by the disease, as well as by social and political disregard.

Other than hallucinations and dreams, the narrator speaks in metaphors that address and elude AIDS. Will's visit to Brutus Cinema is a case in point. Before entering the porn room, he has a look at the attendant's television screen, where a different channel is on. A documentary is on a termite colony being attacked by an ant-eater (48). The traumatic undertones of the scene makes Will feel disappointed at the banality of the gay porn he watches next. He feels both impressed and attracted by the idea of extermination conveyed by the ant-eater eradicating the community of termites. Although unable to bear witness to the trauma of AIDS directly, his troped discourse is equally (or even more) effective. As mentioned above, the presence of absence is particularly threatening. The aesthetic terror produced by the abject monster recalls AIDS homophobia more effectively than actual details and figures about the disease: AIDS becomes a spectacle for its own victims.

'Trouble for Men', a talc and aftershave lotion, is also the recurrent trope for the disease and its rapid spread. As Will argues, the talc had become popular among gays rapidly, being "*decadent* and *irresistible*" (27, my emphasis). The deadly talc has the same oracular and symbolic force as the program at the Brutus. The scene of termites being devoured is revived when Will gazes at men in the gym "clouding the air with Trouble for Men [...] as [...] menaced by brutal predators" (223). As the novel advances, the metaphors of AIDS are more frequent and obvious, even assuming a medical imagery. Will inexplicably turns his sexual brutality with Phil into careful attention, as if announcing the gay solidarity after the AIDS outburst. He feels as if "afflicted by some cruel, slowing illness" (179) about to change everything. Drawing on the nineteen-fifties-inspired homophobic assaults recalled by Jeffery-Poulter (1991), Weeks (1990), and Higgins (1996), *The Swimming-pool Library* refers to an imminent eruption of "pockmarks" (279). The latter make reference to the marks, physical and psychic, left by AIDS. A few lines later, Will decides to do something for the gay community (280) to repair Nantwich's memory. Will's messianic project is determined by a traumatic past and threatened by a future marked by the disease as he feels "some test was looming" (280).

Wilde's downfall inaugurated homosexual identity, Nantwich's incarceration foreshadowed the gay movement and Will's generation constitutes the transition from celebratory liberation to the threat of extinction. This liminal status is persistent for most of Hollinghurst's fiction. As a prisoner, Charles gives voice to transgenerational gay traumata (250). That is, the fractal, specular character of the novel prevents the closure of classic realism. Instead, *The Swimming-pool Library* holds a chain whose last element is Will Beckwith. He is compelled to look back, though not in anger, but to see himself reflected. This is however not only an event of narcissism, but one that bears witness and echoes that narcissism.

2 The specular tryptich: Delusory Narcissus in *The Folding Star*

Although *The Folding Star* was shortlisted for the Mann Booker Prize in 1994 and included in Carmen Callil and Colm Tóibín's anthology *The Modern Library. The 200 Best Novels in English since 1950*,[230] it did not reach the impact of *The Swimming-pool Library*. There is not much criticism on Hollinghurst's second novel, except for reviews and comparative analyses with his more successful first one. Thus, I will firstly make reference to the critical reception, focusing especially on to what extent *The Folding Star* follows the path started by its predecessor. Is it vindicative and celebratory or nostalgic and traumatic? Or does it inhabit a liminal territory like *The Swimming-pool Library*? Hollinghurst has contended that his four first novels form part of a cohesive group. Indeed, all of them deal with gay experience and its representation (mostly in England) throughout the twentieth century. However, they differ in many other respects and, therefore, cannot be labelled as a tetralogy *stricto sensu*, but for the sake of working out Hollinghurst's production. Despite their thematic and structural similarities, there is also an evolution that is more conspicuous in his last two novels. However, *The Swimming-pool Library* and *The Folding Star* are especially linked to each other both in form, content and scope, thus forming a self-contained unit.

Like *The Swimming-pool Library*, *The Folding Star* is narrated retrospectively by an intradiagetic gay hero who initiates a *Bildungsroman* guided by an elder homosexual. Edward Manners is a 33-year-old teacher of English undergoing his individuation process in a voluntary exile in a Flemish city. There, he becomes infatuated with one of his two pupils, the problematic teenager Luc Altidore, recently expelled from school for a mysterious offence. Like Will Beckwith, Manners is a postmodernist *flâneur*, a voyeur and a fetishist who focuses his attention on those below him. Though obsessed with the young Altidore, Edward leads a promiscuous life, recklessly exploiting 'exotic' men. Another key character in the hero's *Bildungsroman* is Paul Echevin, the father of his second pupil, Marcel. Echevin is the director of the Orst Museum. Indeed, he claims to have devoted all his life to the late Flemish painter, fictional Edgar Orst. Like most Hollinghurst's elders, Echevin is a closeted gay man. Fascinated by Manners, he offers him a job as translator and reader of Orst's catalogue he seems unable to end. In the course of his collaboration with Echevin, the hero learns about Orst's own obsession with a famous actress who disappeared mysteriously, as Luc eventually does. Old newspaper articles, Orst's paintings and Paul Echevin's account give Edward privileged access to a story of decadence and trauma —particularly Orst's personal downfall and the Nazi occupation of Belgium— which uncannily mirror his own traumata. Coinciding with the middle of the novel, Edward must return home to attend the funeral

---

[230] Carmen Callil and Colm Tóibín. *The Modern Library. The 200 Best Novels in English since 1950*. London 1999, 86.

of his first lover, Dawn. Like an island in the middle of his Flemish experience, this return to England is not just geographic. The hero longs for a space and a time lost forever and hence his narration of this episode becomes emphatically nostalgic. He mourns Dawn's death which constitutes the turning-point of the novel, the symptom of the end of an era in an extended elegy and the trigger of prior traumata and others to come.

Most critics lament the bookishness and sexual explicitness of *The Folding Star* and seem reluctant to appreciate its literary worth. Several literary supplements of prestigious newspapers have published illuminating interviews with Alan Hollinghurst, though. *The New York Review of Books* dubbed the novel "a miniature *Remembrance of Things Past*. Or an expanded *Death in Venice* … or a homosexual *Lolita*" (in Hollinghurst, 1998b: ii).[231] Although Proust, Mann and Navokov's novels are the more obvious intertextual references of *The Folding Star*, they are by no means the only ones. Like *The Swimming-pool Library*, Hollinghurst's second novel relies on the canon —mostly, though not exclusively, homoerotic— for new formulas of representation of same-sex desire. As Hollinghurst himself has noticed, *The Folding Star* is a self-conscious text "in terms of literary analogues and prototypes, in the deliberate play with *Lolita* and Thomas Mann's *Death in Venice*."[232] The author rejects being pigeonholed as a gay writer, claiming the influences and intertextual references in his novels, whether conscious or unconscious, not to be necessarily gay. One of the key intertexts of *The Folding Star*, Georges Rodenbach's symbolist *Bruges la Morte*, is a case in point. It is the story of the obsession the hero feels for two women, or rather for the idea(lisation) of femininity.

Hollinghurst's indebtedness to the gay canon is however undeniable. As David Alderson has pointed out, "there are connections between Hollinghurst's [*The Folding Star*] and that earlier twentieth-century English tradition of gay writing which is arguably more of an influence on this novel that either of the most frequently invoked prototypes, *Lolita* and *Death in Venice*." [233] For Alderson, Forster is the main representative of this tradition which goes back to Forrest Reid and A. E. Housman. Alderson recalls Hollinghurst's main contention in the Thesis that the three writers focus on the disruption of homosexual innocent/adolescent eroticism by "harsher adult forces untransmuted by fantasy."[234] These canonical gay writers invariably identified gay loss of innocence with a long vanished England. This feeling of an irrecoverable past takes us back to the elegiac, pastoral tradition addressed in reference to *The Swimming-pool Library*. Hollinghurst has acknowledged his interest in Milton, especially *Comus* and the very end of *Paradise Lost*, which he used "for the imagery of the woods and lawns, and is reused in the common in *The Folding Star*."[235] However, in John Bradley's view, *The Folding Star* transcends English Renaissance pastoral to inscribe itself in a millenarian tradition, since, "by bringing in the 'folding star' found in Milton's *Comus* and Collins 'Ode to Evening', Hollinghurst's novel evokes the tradition

---

[231] Hereafter all references to *The Folding Star* (1998b) will be in the text.
[232] In Canning, *Conversations*, 346.
[233] Alderson: *Territories*, 40.
[234] Ibid.
[235] In Canning, *Conversations*, 359.

of pastoral verse going back through the Restoration and the Renaissance to, by logical extension, Virgil's second eclogue."[236]

Critics such as Peter Kemp (*The Times Literary Supplement*) or Nicholson Baker (*London Review of Books*) have pointed out the ambiguous character of *The Folding Star*, and its tendency (also in *The Swimming-pool Library*), to juxtapose Victorian sublimation with the (sexual) explicitness of twentieth-century literature. Kemp puts into words this apparent contradiction as follows:

> It [*The Folding Star*] swings between the rarefied aesthetic satisfactions and thrills of a more fundamental kind [...]. Ranging from romantic obsession to anonymous sex in the undergrowth, from amused observation of a dinner-party to submersion in the symbolic shadows of nineteenth-century Decadent painting, making detours down literary and musical by-ways of the twentieth century, inspecting Gothic architecture and gay bars, two-way mirrors and differences between the placings of the eyes in Flemish and Italian Renaissance pictures.[237]

Sexual explicitness and the postmodernist melange of high and low culture and of past and present that Kemp greatly values are questioned by Craig Seligman and Nicholson Baker. Seligman finds particularly problematic the plot of the novel. In his view, it is a "Jamesian jigsaw puzzle in which pieces —confessions in this case— slowly accrete until, by the end, the reader has the big picture." [238] Thus, Hollinghurst's over-intentionality results in a postmodernist metafictional text: "He lets the machinery show through so nakedly, that there were moments when I [Seligman] wondered if he wasn't being archly postmodern [...]. But the effect of all this meticulous craftsmanship is mainly prissy."[239] Nicholson Baker finds fault with the (homo)sexual explicitness and repetitiveness of *The Folding Star*, and the fact that "an awed or intrigued reference to the male 'genital ensemble' occurs every fifteen pages or so."[240] Most condemnable for this reviewer is the fact that Edward views the straight world with fastidious distaste. As Baker notes, through this behaviour, the hero establishes a dangerous chasm between "the gay cosmology and the prevailing straightgeist."[241] Baker's words bring to mind some of the analyses of *The Swimming-pool Library*, identifying the voices of the narrator and of Hollinghurst's. This is particularly surprising in Baker's case, for he fails to notice Edward's ironic undertones: he performs the very same 'indignities' he criticises in others with his Arab lover, Cherif, and with his teenager pupil, Luc. Indeed, like *The Swimming-pool Library*, the irony of *The Folding Star* lies in how post-Stonewall gays frequently repeat the attitudes they censure in their predecessors. Hence, *The Folding Star* draws on an echoic narcissism to outline the similarities between gay generations, their celebratory and traumatic discourses.

---

[236] Bradley, "Disciples," 10.

[237] Peter Kemp: "Aesthetic Obsessions," in *The Times Literary Supplement*, No. 4756, May 27, 1994.

[238] Craig Seligman: "Sex and the Single Man." *The New Yorker*, October 24, 1994, 95.

[239] Ibid.

[240] Nicholson Baker: "Lost Youth", *The London Review of Books*, 1994, https://www.lrb.co.uk/the-paper/v16/n11/nicholson-baker/lost-youth.

[241] Ibid.

James Wilson's review for The Michigan Daily is even harsher than either Seligman's or Baker's. According to this review, Hollinghurst's talent is hidden behind "an over ambitious, poorly constructed, clumsily delivered bulk."[242] Hollinghurst's attempt to normalise the gay life-style is questioned, because "he only succeeds in scandalizing it."[243] Like Seligman's, this review draws attention to the improbability of the plot and of his hero. Manners is an interesting character *a priori*: he is complex and contradictory, as is expected in postmodernism. But, in the reviewer's opinion, the character becomes a parody of himself when he turns out to be a fetishist obsessed with his pupil, seventeen-year-old Luc.[244] Unnecessary, ludicrous and unbelievable, "all this is presented as a sign of Manners' love. But the fact is this obsession is for a boy Manners hardly knows. He wishes to tell Luc he loves him before they had even exchanged a few words." [245] However, this is precisely what happens with the protagonist of Thomas Mann's *Death in Venice*. Gustav von Aschenbach is also obsessed with a teenager he does not know and with whom he virtually does not exchange a word. In both novels it is the voyeur's obsession that matters. There are, however, obvious differences: Mann's novel rejects any overt reference to sexual activity, after the norms of Platonic High Sodomy. By contrast, *The Folding Star* focuses on the hero's sexual acts and fantasies, which are frequently sadomasochistic. Avowedly, the heroes of Hollinghurst's first two novels fit into a well-known gay type, namely the middle-upper-class homosexual who exploits youths, foreigners and workers. This can be evidence that the novels reproduce a stereotypical representation of gayness. However, *The Folding Star* can be read ironically, as a problematisation of post-Stonewall same-sex desire and identity and a denunciation of the constructedness of set gay types. As Hollinghurst himself has suggested, albeit indirectly, the novel shows and sets into question the representation of homosexual practices and identity in a homophobic context.[246] Another fact to consider is that Will and Edward are not the only representatives of the gay community. The other characters belong in a wide range of homosexualities. Wilson regrets that *The Folding Star* is a failure as a whole, especially in view of the literary quality of its second section, "Underwoods." This section, Edward's elegiac narration of his return to England to attend his friend Dawn's funeral, is unfortunately "extraneous to the central plot."[247] Hence, the novel is not just a fragmentary postmodernist text, but a chaotic and failed attempt at vindicating gay identity and history. Conversely, David Alderson argues instead that "the central section to *The Folding Star* is not abstractable from the rest of the novel, and casts its shadow over the events which both precede and succeed it."[248] Indeed, Hollinghurst's second novel as a whole conveys gay celebration thwarted by traumata in a nostalgic tone and specular structure, as *The Swimming-pool Library* does. Eve Sedgwick's 'sense of

---

[242] James Wilson: "*The Folding Star* Review." *The Michigan Daily*. https://digital.bentley.umich. edu/midaily/ mdp.39015071754951/258, 1996, n.p.

[243] Ibid.

[244] Ibid.

[245] Ibid.

[246] Ibid.

[247] Ibid.

[248] Alderson: *Territories*, 40.

touch', as "out of any dualistic understanding of agency and passivity" [249] helps understand celebration in Hollinghurst. In other words, pleasure in Hollinghurst breaks with the tendency to "comprehension, to prioritize the imaginative over the corporeal, to follow the twist of the plot rather than the turn of the page." [250] There are many tropes Hollinghurst's fiction addresses to delimit its liminality and convey pleasure on the book as organic, inorganic and eventually on "the male form," [251] namely "lines, folds and libraries." [252] In the end, as in *The Swimming-pool Library*, gay characters are dispossessed of their sense of beauty when triggers activate latent traumata.

2.1   *The Folding Star*, a thwarted sequel of *The Swimming-pool Library*?

Strictly speaking and in answer to the subtitle above, *The Folding Star* is not a sequel to Hollinghurst's first novel, but it shares key structural and thematic elements with it:

> *The Folding Star* is a continuation and development of the themes and ideological perspective already established in the previous novel, except that the nostalgic qualities of that novel —those expressions of the desire to repossess some former moment of pure, unselfconscious sexual being— are, if anything, intensified and bound up even more explicitly with the awareness of mortality enforced by AIDS. This is especially the case with the central section of the novel. [253]

Though not directly, AIDS is more conspicuous in his second novel than in the first. *The Swimming-pool Library* is a transitory text, mostly set before AIDS but narrated during the crisis, whereas *The Folding Star* is a fully-AIDS text. In the former, the disease is hinted at through numerous omens; in the latter, through an introspective melancholic narration. *The Folding Star* reconciles melancholia with the ironic undertones. Indeed, as Nick Rennison argues, the novel is "infused with Hollinghurst's characteristic brand of sensuality and melancholy irony." [254] Before Rennison, Linda Hutcheon addressed how apparently contradictory concepts like irony and nostalgia match together as long as postmodernism demands a new, less naïve, perspective on nostalgia (2002). The past is irremediably lost, but it is recalled with ironic distance. Hence, it seems to me, *The Folding Star* recasts Thomas Mann's *Death in Venice*, adding to it the irony that postmodernism requires to make nostalgia palatable. The general tone of Hollinghurst's novel is pessimistic and introspective, but also comic. Edward Manners is a frustrated young man who looks back nostalgically on his childhood and early youth, especially when his friend Dawn dies. However, this trip back in time is funny to the degree it can be, a mixture of ludicrousness and camp.

---

[249] Eve Sedgwick: *Touching Feeling: Affect, Pedagogy, Performativity*. Durham 2003, 14.
[250] Angus Brown: "The Touch of Reading in Hollinghurst's Prose." In Mendelssohn, Michèle and Dennis Flannery (eds.). *Alan Hollinghurst: Writing under the Influence*. Manchester 2016, 26.
[251] Ibid., 27.
[252] Ibid., 26.
[253] Alderson: *Territories*, 39.
[254] Nick Rennison: *Contemporary British Novelists*. London and New York 2005, 85.

John Bradley also defends that Hollinghurst's two first novels are closely connected with each other:

> They are variations on the theme of the onset of adulthood on a particular type of psyche. Both dramatize the theme of the crippling psychological effects of an unsuccessful initiation into adulthood after a prolonged, narcissistic homosexual adolescence, and the way the protagonists come to terms with this sense of loomed melancholia.[255]

Like Will's, Edward's narcissism is pathological, a symptom of an arrested development that their respective narrations and novels echo as if specular prisons where trauma and its reverberation concur. This excess of sameness, which equates erastes and eromenos[256] or "master and pupil, subject and object,"[257] explains Edward's sexual cathexis with Luc. Although his infatuation with the youth draws on "the narratives of pedagogical eros penned by James and others,"[258] he, like Narcissus, conflates master and pupil.[259] That Will and Edward are constantly looking at themselves, and others, in mirrors serves as a metaphor for the specular pattern of these novels. According to Bradley, each novel and the interaction between them relies on different parallels and contrasts. He argues that "despite a series of reversals and a difference of location, it is obvious that the narrators of these two novels are essentially the same type of person, and that they are made to play similar scenarios."[260] They are the same and complementary as long as they are opposed to each other, like an image and its reflection in a mirror. Thus, *The Swimming-pool Library* longs for the seventies from the eighties, whereas *The Folding Star* mourns the eighties from the nineties. Bradley's list of parallel oppositions is long:

> Beckwith is absurdly, almost offensively wealthy; Manners is embarrassed by his lack of money. [...] Beckwith is overwhelmed by what he perceives as his potential for success and fulfilment; Manners is continually swamped in a "sense of failure and imbecility." [...] Beckwith exists in a sort of all-male homosexual world [...]. *The Folding Star* is more diverse in its presentation of heterosexual men and even women [...]. *The Folding Star* is a quiet, melancholy, domestic novel, and its impressive architectural commentary is chiefly concerned with the interiors of the houses. By way of contrast, *The Swimming-pool Library* [...] tellingly concentrates [...] on the structures and façades of buildings.[261]

Briefly stated, although there are parallel oppositions between both texts, *The Folding Star* constitutes a move forward: it does not feature an exclusively gay cast and canon and it is an intimate recall of AIDS.

As in *The Swimming-pool Library*, art plays an important role; principally, it helps to sublimate (otherwise) overt homosexuality in the problematic atmosphere of post-

---

[255] Bradley: "Disciples," 4.
[256] John Elsner: "Naturalism and the erotics of the gaze: imitations of Narcissus." In Natalie Boymer Kampen (ed.). *Sexuality in Ancient Art*. Cambridge 1996, 249.
[257] Johnson: "Alan Hollinghurst," 74.
[258] Ibid.
[259] Ibid.
[260] Bradley: "Disciples," 5.
[261] Ibid.

liberation and AIDS. In *The Folding Star*, it is Korngold's *Die Tote Stadt* —an opera based on Georges Rodenbach's novel *Bruges la Morte*— that serves simultaneously as an artistic projection and a framework for Edward Manner's obsession for his pupil Luc. Architecture is another recurrent artistic form to make up Hollinghurst's novels. As he points out: "All my books have quite a lot about buildings. This happens to be a preoccupation of mine. I love inventing buildings and describing them. I am interested in the atmosphere of [them]."[262] *The Swimming-pool Library* focuses on the surfaces of buildings, while the second concentrates on the interiors. In Bradley's view, this is not just an aesthetic issue, but a symbolic one, which affects the content and characterisation of each novel. Thus, the fact that *The Swimming-pool Library* lays the emphasis on façades is meant to represent "Beckwith's inability to see beyond physical appearance"[263] whereas Manners's "knowing, even essential, psychological self-delusion finds its objective correlative in the interiors of buildings."[264]

Domestic symbolism —Nantwich's and Luc's houses in particular— can also be extrapolated to urban spaces. Both heroes are postmodernist *flanêurs* walking the streets of cities. Will's *Bildungsroman* constitutes a radiography of London whereas Edward's individuation process is set in a crepuscular Bruges. Like Peter Ackroyd's London, Will's London and Edward's Bruges can be considered as characters themselves. The former has witnessed the troubled history of gays during the last century; the latter transmits melancholy to the (rest of the) characters in *The Folding Star*. For Bradley, the interaction between Edward and Bruges is symbiotic: "the city itself, when viewed as a map from above, gives Manners the sense of having all his 'pathetic little circuits laid bare'. The topography of *The Folding Star* is both vague and specific, and the name of the city where it is set is withheld to encourage the idea that it is a symbolic place, a space of the imagination."[265] The hero is thus the traumatic symptom of a much larger belated traumatic scenario, the city itself, which haunts him throughout. Drawing on Beckwith, who foreshadows the traumatic end of his lifestyle, Manners "admits that he is 'having his last fling before age sets in.'"[266] In other words, they announce the onset of adulthood, the demise of a whole generation and the end of an era as a result of AIDS, again a symptom of gays' cultural trauma. Some hints of their traumatic discourses are given from the very beginning. Edward regrets the passing of time and of his promising career (Hollinghurst, 1998b: 5).

Although both novels "come from the tradition of *Bildungsroman*,"[267] this is especially obvious in *The Folding Star*, its protagonist being a teacher. However, it is him, rather than his 17-year-old pupil, who undergoes a "more profound sort of maturation."[268] Indeed, like Hollinghurst's, Manners's individuation process is defective, his life being a compendium of lost opportunities and broken promises. Being a promising writer when a youth, he fails as an adult. Once in Bruges, he accepts Paul

---

[262] In Canning: *Conversations*, 335.
[263] Bradley: "Disciples," 5
[264] Ibid.
[265] Ibid.
[266] Ibid., 8.
[267] Bradley: "Disciples," 8.
[268] Ibid.

Echevin's proposal to complete Orst's catalogue, a symbolist painter and a local celebrity. This inevitably recalls Will's commission to write Nantwich's biography and the impossibility to bring the project to a successful conclusion. That Echevin is unable or reluctant to finish the catalogue adds to the general feeling of failure. And especially it conveys the (im)possibility of writing down AIDS and gay-related traumata. The novel is the evidence of that (im)possibility, the aporia of trauma that must but cannot be told. This is what Bradley addresses in rather optimistic terms: "[Edward] articulate[s] more objectively his own moral and emotional dilemmas […]. It is as though he, artistically speaking, is about to come to his own."[269]

As concerns form, *The Folding Star* features an intradiegetic narrator for two main reasons. Hollinghurst has claimed he wanted his novels to be the product of the narrator's mind.[270] Moreover, writing in the first person produces "a lack of moral heavy-handedness […] because everything's floating and unknown. Everything's responded to very subjectively."[271] Like *The Swimming-pool Library*, *The Folding Star* follows a predetermined size and structure.[272] In a metafictional fashion, the "piecing together and reading [of] the artist's Orst's triptych" reproduces *en abyme* the tripartite structure of the novel itself."[273] It is structured in triangles, most of them around Edward, which mirror each other like fractals. The result is a complex fictional ontology which mirrors itself and refracts other canonical works. André Gide's *The Counterfeiters* is a case in point. Drawing on Gide's novel, the protagonist of *The Folding Star* is a young artist "striving to comprehend a kaleidoscopic reality and turn it into a novel."[274] Like Gide's hero, Edward (and Will) is a young writer (albeit a frustrated one) who comes across the opportunity to rehabilitate gay history and, in consequence, re-define the present of same-sex desire. Yet, the opportunity eventually turns out failed art, another symptom of trauma undecibility.

As concerns AIDS as the trigger of trauma that terminates celebration, *The Folding Star* is set in the nineteen eighties, which makes references to the crisis mandatory, albeit tangential.[275] In the middle of the novel, Edward learns that his friend Dawn has died. Prior to this, during a journey of his friend Edie to Bruges, the hero (and the reader) is indirectly and cryptically informed of Dawn's disease: he has put on some weight and is happier thanks to AZT (Hollinghurst, 1998b: 152). As Woods explains, the acronym makes reference to the most well-known and used drug against AIDS.[276] Thus, although the novel makes reference to Dawn's health problems, only attentive readers and *connoisseurs* can interpret these coded messages. The disease is only mentioned explicitly after the death of Edward's friend;[277] and even then, the novel tricks the disease, since Dawn ironically dies in a traffic accident (Hollinghurst, 1998b: 194).

---

[269] Ibid., 12.
[270] In Canning: *Conversations*, 332.
[271] Ibid.
[272] Ibid., 333.
[273] Ibid., 335.
[274] Bradley: "Disciples," 11.
[275] Woods: *History*, 381.
[276] Ibid.
[277] Ibid., 382.

2.2   The structure of *The Folding Star*

As mentioned above, *The Folding Star* is arranged in mirroring triangles, which affects both its form and content. Characters, episodes or art pieces, as well as a number of intertexts, genres and traditions are thus recast according to this formula. The novel is an overwhelming closed space. Its self-referentiality and obsessive repetitiveness is not only narcissistic, but a symptom of toomuchness akin to trauma. Characters observe and pursue one another in a goose hunt, drawing the state of surveillance and paranoia gays have been compelled to. The symbolic cornerstone of the novel is Orst's masterwork, a modern version of medieval triptychs.

When Edward arrives, Paul Echevin is carrying out the project of piecing together Orst's triptych. This project works as a *mise en abyme* of the tripartite structure of the novel, as Hollinghurst himself has pointed out:

> I think *The Folding Star* was always going to be in three parts. I gradually found myself bringing in other triplets—sometimes rather capriciously: everything started to come in threes. The truth is I've always been involved in and lived a lot imaginatively in arts of different kinds. They seem to me something continuous with and deeply mixed up with the rest of life, so I've always given them quite a significant role in my stories.[278]

The Folding Star is divided into three irregular sections: "Museum Days," "Underwoods" and "A Merry Goose Hunt," thus subverting the regularity of *The Swimming-pool Library* which recalls a symbolic year. The three sections are composed of an irregular number of chapters that apparently follows no logic or symbolic pattern: the thirteen chapters of "Museum Days" form the longest section and set parallelisms between Edward's melancholic desire for Luc, the atmosphere of Bruges, and Orst's paintings. "Underwoods" is made up of a single chapter, a first-person narration with frequent flashbacks to Edward's childhood and youth, just after he learns of his friend and ex-lover Dawn's death. Finally, the eight chapters of "A Merry Goose Hunt" return to and intensify the nostalgic and obsessive discourses of the first section.

Before introducing the triptych itself, Edward makes reference to three pictures representing Orst he comes across at the museum. In the first one, he is still a student whereas "in the second, [...] he was [...] already a cold-eyed dandy [...]. The third, [...] a wash of white light into which the blind old man [...,] seemed almost to dematerialise" (Hollinghurst, 1998b: 67-68). The three pictures work as fragments that make up Orst's identity. As in *The Swimming-pool Library*, the relation between art and reality is a complex and slippery one, where ontological levels —e.g.: Orst's life story and paintings— reflect and affect each other. Orst produces art and can only be interpreted through it: as an aesthete, his life is contained in these three pictures. His ambivalence —tragic and brilliant, half-emerging and half held-back— determines his life story as well as the novel as a whole. He is a painter, a faker, who uses photographs for his pictures, a dandy and a poor invalid. The three-staged revision of Orst's life through art recalls the three-faced Egyptian stele Nantwich shows Will. Like the stele, the pictures show how an individual representation changes according to the viewer's perspective. Hence, Orst's pictures or Hollinghurst's novels can be regarded as constant variations

---

[278] In Canning: *Conversations*, 335-336.

on a limited series of topics. Edward makes reference to the painter's multifarious versions of his muse, the Scottish actress Jane Byron (68-69). Similarly, Orst also scrutinised the Flemish landscape, which adopted multiple forms, depending on the seasons and colours (69), in his pictures. In any case, they always recalled his childhood.

Echevin is obsessed with reassembling Orst's triptych, whose parts were separated long ago. The reconstruction is a symbolic act to give cohesion to the painter's work and, indirectly, to the whole novel. The piece of art, called "Autrefois," is meaningful, for it recalls the retrospective, traumatic, delayed narration of *The Folding Star*. The museum owns just one wing of the triptych representing a woman looking into a mirror and is significantly "cut in half by the edge of the mirror" (89). The other two parts, which Paul knew about from an old photograph, were sold when symbolism became outmoded. Henceforth, he started an obsessive search of Orst's traces, as he tells Manners. Indeed, as in *The Swimming-pool Library*, an older man transmits information to a younger one, a sort of pupil involved in the former's epistemological search. This process of transmission, which with AIDS assumed tragic undertones, is a transgenerational phenomenon connecting gays' traumata, ones hiding and revealing others. Paul travels throughout Europe seeking the two missing wings of the triptych, which he finally finds in Switzerland and Czechoslovakia, a "seascape nearly abstract" (90) and "a deserted gothic town-scape" (92) respectively. The three wings of the triptych are apparently unconnected, but, as Paul argues, they are linked in their difference "like images in a dream" (90). As Edward puts forward, the wings of the triptych formed a complex puzzle (278). Thus, when Edward and Paul try to put it together, they discover that the three pieces do not fit (278).

However, what is really surprising about the assembling process is the subversiveness of the triptych. Orst is a revolutionary, as his art proves. The painter redefines the traditional structure of religious triptychs in a rather unconventional arrangement that shocks Edward (278). Like Nantwich's little treasures, Orst's triptych is a narrative piece, central both structurally and thematically to *The Folding Star*. Its reassembling both precedes and follows the central section of the novel, splitting the novel in two halves. Further, the triptych's triangular pattern is refracted by other tripartite patterns scattered throughout. The three wings share a crepuscular atmosphere which they project onto the rest of the novel and its references to a lost time and space. Drawing on Nantwich, Orst interrupts Edward's first-person narration to describe his childhood in the Ardennes as the inspiring source of his enigmatic pictures, which invariably open little doors "upon mystery, upon the unknown and the unknowable" (278). Like Will or Nantwich, Orst and Edward regress to childhood (278). Indeed, as Orst himself confesses, his paintings are thresholds to the regions of romance and mystery, frequently associated with childhood, and to the ineffable, associated with homosexuality. The sepulchral character of the medieval town, the immensity of the seascape and the erotic version of the virgin are all connected with death and mourning. The three constitute symbolic fragments that represent Orst and Edward's life stories. He recurrently reproduces the Flemish countryside, urban landscapes and the grey tones of the North Sea as metaphors of death and drowsiness. Thus the sunny weather, which *The Swimming-pool Library* links to gays' subversive life styles (particularly Akhenaten's) turns autumnal in *The Folding Star*: the former is a pre-nostalgic text, the latter a fully nostalgic one. The third wing of the triptych —Jane Byron as a mirrored virgin— hides the story painter's obsession for his dead wife and model. The story with Byron mirrors and is mirrored by the deadly town of Bruges and the grey waters of the North Sea where the actress disappears mysteriously. Thus, the triptych makes up a tripartite pattern that, as will be shown, is reflected *en abyme* both within the novel and through its intertexts.

One last aspect worth noting about the triptych, and Orst's other paintings, is its complex relation with reality. Since his youth, the artist could not see very well, and towards 33 —symbolically Edward's age— he lost most of his vision as a result of syphilis. Henceforth, Orst could only paint as part of an optical experiment (279). Paul became 'his eyes' and he started to paint unrecognisable forms. Known as "the white series," these mature works were watercolours mostly in white and grey, which Echevin considers unfinished, like Nantwich's biography or Orst's catalogue. Going on with the pedagogical eros, Paul works as a Pygmalion for Edward, who gets thus involved in rediscovering the bizarre artist: "I [...] had the feeling of some benign plan unfolding in which I played a useful part without knowing" (309). The symbolist painter used photographs as source material (280), which emphasises the problematic character of his art. Photographs are less realistic, or rather, more enigmatic than the paintings themselves. In other words, the artist and the novel as a whole put to the test the taken-for-granted realism of photography. When Edward opens one of the boxes of Orst's collection of photographs —containing, among them, the original of the virgin in the triptych—, he is amazed because of their mysterious arrangement and nature (298). The boundaries between media, painting and photography, or ontologies, fiction and 'reality', are put to the test, or simply erased.

2.3   Specular homosocial triangles

Drawing on Girard and Sedgwick's theories and the example of *The Swimming-pool Library*, the characters in *The Folding Star* have triangular relations, further arranged in a fractal echoic structure. The triangle formed by Orst, Paul and Edward lies in the middle, a number of parallel others orbiting around. In Hollinghurst's first novel, the main tandem, Will-Charles, makes a transgenerational triangle on a third element, which can be traumatic like Lord Beckwith, or celebratory, like Firbank. In *The Folding Star*, Lord Beckwith's role is not embodied by just one character. This is why, unlike Will, Paul is not personally implicated in gay traumatic history, though he is indirectly. Hence, he cannot mourn and is arrested by melancholia instead. He must revise the past and present of mass deaths —Orst's experience of the Holocaust and Dawn's AIDS—, though none of them implicates him psychically and personally, as Lord Beckwith's policy implicated his grandson. The parallelisms between both novels and their male triangles are undeniable, though. Edward also comes across a closeted pre-Stonewall gay, Echevin, who reveals former traumata. Like Lord Beckwith's story and Firbank's camp in Will's case, Edward is confronted with the Nazi invasion of Belgium and Orst's symbolism as trauma and symptom/antidote respectively, though not gay ones. However, although the symbolist artist is a heterosexual at first glance, there are hints which point to his sexual ambiguity. His obsessive desire for his lovers, his camp lifestyle, the specular narcissism of his paintings and their impact on gay characters, like Echevin and Manners, are suspicious. Manners even makes the deliberate attempt to queer Orst's obsessive art thematics and form (292).

Both Orst and Edward (and somehow Paul) are either frustrated or, at best, second-rate artists unable to fulfil their projects. Once again gay stereotypes recur, namely gays' alleged arrested development and, relatedly, their traumatic unutterability. In fact, *The Folding Star* is a novel about lost opportunities and failed promises. Echevin firstly addresses the painter in Proustian imperfect: "Orst was once a famous figure [...]. But that was a long time ago" (36). His nostalgic discourse is trustworthy and unreliable because it is too passionate: indeed, trauma discourse must be flawed to be believable. A forgotten artist, Orst is a rarity that attracts the attention of a decadent group (308). Indeed, the museum is rarely visited except by 'Orstian' queens (308). Drawing on Firbank, *The Folding Star* is a catalogue of second-rate artists. Edward's aunt Tina is a pretentious writer (46). Likewise, his father is a frustrated artist virtually forgotten except for a kitsch revival of a minor hit. Perry Dawlish is also a decadent second-rate poet and aristocrat of relative success long ago in his family circle (215). Finally, Edward proves to be a mediocre artist. In visiting Dewlish to have his writing assessed, the latter can only ironise in campy terms: "You are [... a] born writer" (214). At 33, he is not a famous artist, but a private teacher of English and literature. Paul does not become the renowned researcher and art critic everybody expected, but the director of the Orst Museum. Paul's obsession with the artist explains his incapacity to finish the catalogue and unfold away from Orst's traumatic haunting. Helen, a worker at the museum, tells Edward about Paul's Sisyphus-like task: "For some reason he can't bring himself to finish it" (132). Like Nantwich, Echevin wants but cannot reassemble fragmented memories. And also like Nantwich, he commissions a youth to do it with a similar result. Although unable to finish what he is asked to, Edward, like Will, undergoes his 'maturation' process while us, readers, revise the traces of the past. The traumatic *aporia* —namely the simultaneous necessity and impossibility of writing—he comes across is finally materialised in his dream of poet Gordon Bottomley whose poem remains unfinished after sixty years (373).

Like Will, Edward is also a fatherless hero, whose lack he amends through melancholia, a compulsive return to his childhood with Dawn. Significantly, Edward implicitly assigns his arrested development to their deaths. There seems to be a puritan determinism —that Will confesses, James practises and Edward confirms— in Hollinghurst's novels, as sons inherit the sins, mistakes or frustrations of their fathers and male ancestors. Wilde's Dorian Gray is a case in point, the heir to a long lineage: "One had ancestors in literature, as well as in one's own race, nearer perhaps in type and temperament, many of them, and certainly with an influence of which one was more absolutely conscious."[279] This is an Oedipal ground with psychic, textual and sexual undertones, a narcissistic scenario that frames transgenerational traumata. It is also Edward's point when arguing that 'the sons of symbolist painters' (a metaphor for gays like Echevin) "were teased" (Hollinghurst, 1998b: 294) as social freaks. It is in this sense that, Sedgwick argues, the narrator of Proust's *À La Recherche Du Temps Perdu*

---

[279] Oscar Wilde: *The Picture of Dorian Gray*. http://www.planetpublish.com/wp-content/uploads/ 2011/11/The_Picture_of_Dorian_Gray_NT.pdf, 2018, 185.

regards gays as a *race maudite*.[280] Not being father and son, Paul and Orst problematise parent-child relations. Their allegiance is as strong as traumatic, particularly when Paul's love affair with a pro-German soldier makes Orst's Jewishness challenging. When the painter was murdered by the Nazis, it was "like losing a father" (Hollinghurst, 1998b: 134), but also liberating. The triangle Orst-Paul-Edward works as a sequence of pedagogical eros and surrogate fatherhoods, which Luc closes. Though primarily a master-pupil relation, Edward soon establishes an obsessive desire for the youth, which eventually acquires paternal undertones. In fact, when Luc disappears, the hero goes after him (358).

The narratives of pedagogical eros in *The Folding Star* draw on Michael Cooper's study of Henry James' tales. Cooper coins the term 'erotonomy' to "denote the class of human behaviour to which the discipleship belongs." [281] He emphasises what he considers to be constitutive of that behaviour, namely "a mutual desire of the participants for the personal interaction with each other and a mutually accepted system for exchanging satisfactions"[282] all this he associates with human systems of intimacy such as "friendships, garden-variety sexual relationships, [...] and extreme but not necessarily sexualised relationships of domination and submission." [283] In Cooper's view, these erotonomies are frequently founded on homosocial relations between men. He calls them 'erotonomies of patronage' since they "evoke the relation between disciple and master where an older and wiser character attempts in some measure to enlist and to impart knowledge and experience to a younger, more lively one."[284]

Cooper's erotonomies apply to the triangles of Orst-Paul-Edward and Edward-Luc-Marcel. The former constitutes a chain of discipleship and mastering. Paul confesses the pedagogic significance of Orst in his own life (Hollinghurst, 1998b: 294). Like the narrators of Henry James' tales, Paul is obsessed with his master and devotes his whole life to him. Indeed, after falling in love with a pro-Nazi, Paul owes Orst more than ever; guilt paradoxically ties them together forever. Drawing on James's pupil, Echevin feels "only the young male disciple strives to protect the enfeebled and misunderstood author from the sensory barrage of contemporary life and the threat of objectification by predatory women."[285] The homosocial bond with the disciple grants the artist "the space in which to bear his aesthetic offspring."[286] The second homosocial bond within this triangle —Paul-Edward— is similar to the first. Edward learns about Orst through Paul and, through both, he comes to himself.

The second erotonomic triangle centres on Edward and his two pupils, Luc and Marcel. As Bradley notes, the interaction between master and disciple is more obvious than in the previous triangle. [287] Hence, the critic regards *The Folding Star* as a

---

[280]   Eve Sedgwick: *Epistemology of the Closet*. London 1991, 216-217.
[281]   Michael Cooper: "Discipl(in)ing the Master, Mastering the Discipl(in)e: Erotonomies of Discipleship in James' *Tales of Literary Life*." In Joseph Boone and Michael Cadden (eds). *Engendering Men*. New York and London 1990, 66.
[282]   Ibid.
[283]   Ibid.
[284]   Ibid., 67.
[285]   Cooper: "Discipl(in)ing," 70.
[286]   Ibid.
[287]   Bradley: "Disciples," 8.

Bildungsroman; rather, I would say, it is a chain of *Bildungsromane* arranged like fractals. Orst is Paul's master, who is Edward's, who is Luc's and Marcel's. In other words, almost all characters are both masters and disciples of each other after a narcissistic fashion. As concerns Edward-Luc-Marcel, their relations are not exclusively pedagogic, but also (homo)erotic: a mediator (Marcel) is equidistant between the subject (Edward) and his object of desire (Luc). However, these roles of active voyeur and passive agent are subject to analysis. Cooper's words on Henry James's short story "The Real Right Thing" also apply *mutatis mutandis* to this triangle:

> One person's obsessive involvement in the experience of another [...] eroticizes voyeurism; and as a replication of James' own fantasy of creative direction from his genius [...] eroticizes submission. The story thus makes explicit the erotonomy that underpins the relation between disciple and master. The disciple fantasizes occupying the subject position of the master, literally taking the master's place (at home, in person and social relations, as creator of an oeuvre). Far from assuming conflict between the two persons, this fantasy relies for its erotic value on the master's approval of, compliance with, and even authority over his or her displacement.[288]

The erotic (and later sexual) affiliation between Edward and Luc works as a parodic reversal of James's texts. Obsessed with his pupil, Edward becomes a voyeur. As such and drawing on intertexual referents like *Death in Venice* and *Lolita*, the hero's role is ambiguous, feeling both master and victim (Hollinghurst, 1998b: 27). The hero also erotises submission, though it is finally his own, rather than his beloved's. Thus, unlike Jamesian characters, Luc does not fantasise with occupying his master's place. On the contrary, it is the master who blurs identities with his pupil: he is obsessed with the youth's body, behaviour, friends, home and finally he even wears his clothes (154) to presumably become the other. According to Cooper, disciples (in James's texts) pursue their masters following a "desire for a yet more distant object, namely the intangible and ineffable seat of power that is [...] wisdom."[289] This is Paul's case. However, in the tandem Edward-Luc, it is the master who beholds the disciple as intangible. Luc's beauty arouses the hero's fantasy, which proves to be elusive as the youth finally disappears. Edward's ineffable desire is mediated and witnessed by Marcel Echevin, Paul's bland son. As Hollinghurst admitted in an interview, the fittingly named Marcel echoes the hero and narrator of Proust's *À la Recherche du Temps Perdu*.[290]

Unlike *The Swimming-pool Library*, *The Folding Star* presents truly Girardian triangles with two men negotiating on a woman. The first one is formed by Luc and his two friends, Patrick and Sybille, "the Three!" (Hollinghurst, 1998b: 153), as Edward calls them. Together with Matt —a sinister character akin to Ronald Staines in *The Swimming-pool Library*— the hero goes after the trio in a trip to the beach in the North of France (102-120). Like voyeurs, the two adults scrutinise every movement of the three adolescents during a whole weekend. The teenagers' identities merge in a balletic continuum. Like waves, they overlap one another in a triangular whole in a mystique of their own (153). However, the sophistication and beauty the trio exudes soon turns

[288] Cooper: "Discipl(in)ing," 75.
[289] Ibid., 80.
[290] Canning: *Conversations*, 337.

threatening. Unable to understand the youths' codes, Edward merely catches fragments of their conversations, like the narrators of Firbank's novellas or Jamesian childish focalisers. In Firbankian fashion, Edward, as focaliser and narrator, notices how Luc and Patrick speak about Italy and men (319), which hints at their possible homosexuality. Just afterwards, both Patrick and Sybille leave Luc, who starts flirting with Edward. However, we soon learn, this is just a bet of the youths to test the teacher's obsession for his pupil. In fact, when Luc disappears, Edward strikes up a revealing conversation with Patrick, which disrupts the idyllic image of the triangle so far. Patrick confesses that Sybille is in love with Luc and considers Edward "a great threat" (397). Formerly, Patrick and Sybille had been lovers, and Luc covered up for the couple from the public eye. Yet, following the rules of the classical Girardian pattern, Sybille "had to fall in love with her boyfriend's best friend" (398). Edward feels overwhelmed by "the polymorphous stamina of the Three" (398), which explains his sense of danger and jealousy. The idealised triangle, which the teacher worships, degenerates into a tricky one. Patrick himself points out that nothing fits as it used to because their love relationship has turned one of rivalry (399). As happens in *The Swimming-pool Library*, 'reality' is deceptive because narrators are traumatised and hence unreliable. Through the conversation, Patrick reveals himself naïve and dangerous, enlightening and cryptic. His discourse is also premonitory, announcing Edward's fall under Luc's spell. Edward, he says, is not Luc's first victim. Something similar had happened with Arnold (400) who could not get over the mistake of making love to the *garçon fatal*.

This trio can be read as the specular reflection of another in occupied Belgium. Paul Echevin introduces Edward to the trauma of the occupation both at a political and personal level. His parents were part of the Resistance helping Jewish children (386). They sheltered a couple of these children, Monica and Marcel, when Paul was a child himself. The three made up a cohesive group whose Holocaust-set trauma is raised by Luc, Patrick and Sybille (386-387). After giving some clues, Edward reveals the identity of the two Jewish children. Monica is Lilli (Marcel's surrogate mother) and Maurice is Helene's father. Years after their childhood, the trio keeps close to each other. In fact, the three remain clung to those years, unable to overcome their affiliation under the Nazis. Paul has always worked on Orst's nostalgic painting, and Monica and Maurice have devoted their whole lives to the care of children (388). However, for unknown reasons, their triangular pattern broke down. Their story confirms once more the theory of the Girardian triangle, *i.e.*: the complex relation between two men bargaining on an accessory female. Paul, Monica and Maurice revive the Holocaust for the new generation. Thus, although Edward (like Will Beckwith) resists any involvement in a traumatic past, it eventually strikes back: "I began to be irritated by the ubiquitous power of the unsaid" (388). Edward's is not an evolution from the closet to liberation, but the other way round. He must put to the test post-Stonewall celebration and revise the dark corners of memory to conflate both in traumatic realism and irony.

There are two remaining triangles worth noting. One is intradiagetic and the other overtly intertextual, both focusing on same-sex desire. The former is a tale with Firbankian undertones, which Edward comes across among the *Légendes Flamandes* illustrated by Orst. The medieval story turns around the False Chaplain, a great knight and his beautiful lady. Unable to have a baby, the lady asks the chaplain for help. He advises the knight to go away on the Crusade for God's pardon. Once the knight leaves, the chaplain confesses his love to the lady who, surprised, rejects his advances. In spite of the torments the lady suffers, she remains faithful to her husband. When the knight returns from his mission, the false chaplain asks the lady to conceal his approaches. Faithful to her principles, she argues that no sin is hidden from God's eyes, and his can be no exception. *In extremis*, the churchman decides to poison the lady to keep his secret. The story is a triangle of power and desire in which two men interact through a Griselda-like lady. However, as could be expected, Orst's interpretation is as amazing as subversive, particularly his admiration "of the Chaplain's obsession with the Lady" (177-178).

The last triangle, on Orst and his two lovers, Jane Byron and Marthe, subverts the classic Girardian pattern. The former, a British actress, becomes the model of the painter as well as the object of his obsessions. Once she is drowned in strange circumstances in the North Sea, Orst replaces her with Marthe, a prostitute whom the artist also uses as a model and with whom he experiences a degenerated version of his former affair. This triangle of obsessive desire affects the rest of the novel, especially the also obsessive relation of the hero and Luc. The motif of the replacement of a missing character with his/her *alter ego* or twin is recurrent in Western culture, from the comedies of Plautus, Terence and Shakespeare to Alfred Hitchcock's *Rebecca* (1940) and *Vertigo* (1958). However, the most obvious intertextual reference for Orst's story, as Hollinghurst himself explained in an interview, is Georges Rodenbach's *Bruges-la-morte* (1892). A symbolist novel, *The Folding Star* echoes and challenges it in more senses than one. Set in a sepulchral Bruges, Rodenbach's novel also deals with death and the hero's obsessive desire to overcome it. Like Edgar Orst, Hugues Viane, the protagonist of *Bruges-la-morte*, replaces his dead wife with a new one, thus edifying a complex triangle of desire and death.

2.4   Key-hole narration, the shadow of Proust

The triangular patterns of *The Folding Star* are not incidental. They have a double function, structural and symbolic out of a triptych and orbiting trios. Likewise, the choice of point of view and perspective, though not revolutionary, presents some remarkable aspects. Hollinghurst himself has explained that the use of first-person narration responds to aesthetic, technical and ethical reasons. As concerns the *The Folding Star*, he said that "the book had to be inside the mind and preoccupations of its narrator."[291] Indeed, Manners's self-obsessed, first-person narration has to do "with the moral heavy-handedness [… since] everything's responded very subjectively."[292] Thus, Hollinghurst's own distancing from the narrative voice of *The Folding Star* is in keeping with the postmodernist rejection of one-sided truth and of literature as a tool to convey moral lessons.

Richard Canning also considers there is a link between the novel and French modernism, particularly *À La Recherche Du Temps Perdu*: "There's that playful

---

[291] In Canning: *Conversations*, 332.
[292] Ibid.

reference in *The Folding Star* to a much more self-conscious method of narration, too: Proust. It is in the image of [...] Marcel, sick and in bed."[293] The fact that Edward's second pupil and son of Paul Echevin is called Marcel substantiates the critic's contention. Gregory Woods addresses the narrative techniques used in *À La Recherche Du Temps Perdu* and the complex sexuality they enhance and render. Through these techniques, the novel centres on non-normative desire, particularly homosexuality, which the narrator wears witness to. He eventually becomes an expert voyeur, his final discourse being a mixture of speculation, invention, ignorance and solid information. In Woods's view, Proust heterosexualised the narrator, turning him into a homophobe who identifies gays with Jews as *races maudites*.[294] However, since there is an ironic distance between the author and the narrator, the novel can still be considered a pro-homosexual text, the homophobe making a fool of himself. As Woods notes, Ronald Barthes rejected the traditional version of the novel as a *roman à clef*, on the contention that, if there is a key, the readers are constantly invited to take it out and look through it.[295] The narrative of *À La Recherche Du Temps Perdu* aims at spreading information that one has obtained by poking around. Therefore, information is never complete and reliable.[296] Marcel's discourse is incidental, gossipy and hence fragmented. The narrator gives clues for Marcel and the reader to reach conclusions. This language of uncertainty, Woods notes, helps question characters' sexual orientation.[297] Marcel speculates on the physical appearance, behaviour and use of language in search of symptoms of homosexuality, and he invites the reader to do the same.[298] Proust's style was revolutionary featuring Marcel as an unreliable narrator, whose key-holing discourse points to the capacity of artistic language to represent, construct and deconstruct sexual ambiguity.

Drawing on Proust's narrator, Marcel and Paul Echevin and, to a lesser extent, Edward Manners are voyeurs who look for, listen to and provide fragmented information, especially about Orst. We are told about his two heterosexual affairs; though, simultaneously, some details are given about his ambiguous sexuality and camp behaviour. As happens in Proust's text, the information of the narrator/voyeur is frequently too contradictory to be trusted. Like language, Orst's paintings are referential, doors to meaning that transcend the physicality of the canvass (Hollinghurst, 1998b: 278), which help to decode subterranean stories of his own and other characters. In short, *The Folding Star* proves reality can only be accessed vicariously and defectively through key-holes, photographs, paintings or other media. The main target of key-hole voyeurism in Hollinghurst's novel is not discovering whether a character is a homosexual or a heterosexual, as in Proust's. Edward peeps at Luc through a key-hole to play with sexual ambiguity when gayness is a taken-for-granted reality outside the text. Manners enjoys youth and beauty and vindicates lost innocence, thus resisting, problematising and displacing AIDS-derived traumata. The trope, the pretence and the

---

[293] Ibid., 337.
[294] Woods: *History*, 205.
[295] Ibid., 206.
[296] Ibid.
[297] Ibid.
[298] Ibid. 210.

sublimation that conceal the trauma itself are symptoms of such trauma that help to come to terms with it. When Luc and his two friends go to the beach, the hero goes after them, renting a house nearby to spy on them. Unlike Mann's Ashenbach or Proust's Marcel, Edward is a fully ironical figure (115). Marcel's information feeds the hero's voyeurism as the reader of Proust's novel is fed by its narrator's gossip. As a friend of Sybille de Taeye, Luc's Egeria, Marcel Echevin has privileged information about the young Altidore; especially about an orgy at the *Arctic*, the Norwegian ship where Luc was found when he was just an adolescent (181). However, Marcel gives different versions of the episode. This episode turns a traumatic obsession also for Edward, who syntomatically recasts, fantasises and dreams of it. As the novel advances, the information about Luc turns especially confusing. Edward finds a ticket for a porn cinema and a folded strip of paper with his address written in Luc's pocket (352). Apparently trivial, they lead the hero's own individuation process. He suspects Luc is involved in Matt's —Edward's delinquent friend— sex business, and he learns through Marcel that the paper strip is the address of Luc's psychiatrist (359). Ambiguity increases when Patrick suggests Edward's affair with Luc is merely part of a bet between the pupil and his friends (401) and that Matt and Luc had an affair (421). No information is confirmed and therefore reliable, which leaves the novel and Edward's *Bildungsroman* open. His is the story of obsession as trauma. Luc is as elusive and recurrent as the traumatic event that haunts the victim. Hence, the melancholia of the novel, whose main character cannot introject his own traumata, particularly Dawn's death, sublimates them to Luc, an illusion, en elusion and a void of meaning through a key-hole. *À La Recherche Du Temps Perdu* was seeking a language for a just-born homosexual identity, while Hollinghurst's novel uses a dialogic, intergenerational and intertextual discourse to render the ontological and identitarian crisis of a traumatised community.

2.5   Recasting the aesthetics of obsessive desire through irony

The Folding Star puts forward the aesthetics of obsession intertextually, mostly through *Death in Venice* and *Bruges la Morte*. After Lacan's concept of lack, their protagonists are compelled to repetition and melancholia. Indeed, obsession, beauty and death are the vortices of these novels, which they project onto *The Folding Star*. The folding line of the title is a metaphor of the three vortices, folding repetitively in search of beauty which is eventually akin to nothingness, loss and death. Mann's *Death in Venice* (1912) focuses on the last days of German writer Gustav Von Aschenbach. As a result of a creative crisis, the repressed artist travels to Venice. There, he passes from asceticism to a self-destructive Dyonisian rapture. This process is largely motivated by his infatuation with Tadzio, a fourteen-year-old Polish boy. Aschenbach's obsession with Tadzio increases pathologically. In fact, when the hero learns that Venice is diseased with cholera, he decides to stay to go on admiring the boy. His health worsens dramatically until he becomes delirious, especially when in his last glimpse of Tadzio, "it seemed to him the pale and lovely Summoner out there smiled at him and beckoned; as though with the hand lifted from his hip, he pointed outward as he hovered on before into an immensity of richest expectation."[299] This last epiphany does not guide Aschenbach to a higher life form, but to his self-extinction.

Like *The Folding Star*, *Death in Venice* is controversial; conformist in Woods's view[300] and ambivalent for others who, like James Jones, think the writer "believed the source of his artistic inspiration lay in a realm antithetical to the bourgeois one he achieved in reality, namely, in the erotic, sexual and, in particular, within homosexual desire. [...] Often at the core of that struggle is one male's love for another, an urge that teeters between expression and repression."[301] In any case, *Death in Venice* has become an icon of homoerotic sublimation although, as Woods points out, what lies behind Aschenbach's spiritual worship of Tadzio's angelic appearance is carnality and desire.[302] Woods intends to demystify the novel, a proof of the traumatic excess of same-sex desire: "Tadzio and Aschenbach are respectively, pre- and post-sexual. But far from leaving sexuality out of the reckoning, the story actually frames it: Tadzio is all anticipation; Aschenbach all remembrance."[303] Too soon or too late, about to happen or a memory that recurs, gayness in *Death in Venice* draws on the myth of Narcissus and Echo, impossible, forever delayed and recalled in vain.

For Francisco Ayala, the novel is a poetic journey to death and a spiritual sphere to overcome repressed desire.[304] It is a metaphysical *Bildungsroman* and an exploration of Apollonian and Dionysian elements, as well as a Freudian struggle between the hero's *id* and *superego* (Enotes, 2007: 2).[305] Liberated in Venice, the hero is however haunted. On arriving in the city, he sees a group of young effeminates, among whom Aschenbach soon notices with horror an old man pretending to be a youth. His excessive make-up, jewellery and wig cannot hide his wrinkles; on the contrary, they emphasise his decrepitude.[306] The old man foretells the hero's future abjectly. The man's campy youth has ironic undertones, but also drives the aesthete protagonist to melancholia. He sees himself reflected in anticipation of what will be all remembrance. Aschenbach's melancholia grounds from the city, which is framed between a leaden grey and cloudy sky and sea. Black gondolas turn coffins[307] which take Aschenbach against his will to the Lido. The echoes of Caronthe and the trip of the dead to the Stygian lake are inevitable.[308]

Tadzio's extraordinary beauty recalls "the noblest moment of Greek sculpture"[309] much in line with Socratic identification between beauty and spirit in Phaedrus.[310] Eventually, Venice and the boy become the scenario and object of the hero's suicidal

---

[299] Mann: *Death*, 83.
[300] Woods: *History*, 323.
[301] In Summers: *Gay*, 428.
[302] Woods: *History*, 322.
[303] Ibid.
[304] Francisco Ayala: "Introducción" to *Muerte en Venecia*. Madrid 2005, 11.
[305] Anon: "Death in Venice, Thomas Mann." https://www.enotes.com/topics/death-in-venice/critical-essays/death-venice-thomas-mann, 2007, n.p.
[306] Mann: *Death*, 21-22.
[307] Ibid., 25.
[308] Ayala: "Introducción," 12.
[309] Mann: *Death*, 30.
[310] Ibid., 51-52.

drive, appealing but dangerous. Tadzio is particularly ambivalent, a naïve under suspicion like Navokov's *Lolita* and Miles in James's *The Turn of the Screw*. He smiles, which is for Aschenbach "speaking, winning, captivating, like Narcissus."[311] The boy and the city are as charming as menacing. Indeed, the hero cannot leave Venice although the city is ravaged by an epidemic local authorities silence, as AIDS originally was. Drawing on the link between love and death, back to Elizabethan poetry, as Venice gets infected, the hero is more and more obsessed with Tadzio until death.

The Folding Star draws on *Death in Venice*. Yet, there are some significant differences. Like Aschenbach, Manners is a melancholic expatriate. Venice and Bruges are medieval towns crossed by canals, clung to the past, which work as characters rather than mere scenarios. Indeed, heroes and cities are narcissistic projections of each other, an excess of sameness that leads to and explains the melancholic incorporation in both texts. Manners's exile is due to a personal crisis eventually linked to the outburst of AIDS. Edward's ex-lover and friend Dawn is about to die when the former leaves. Thus, exile is a physical event, as well as an act of withdrawal. The effect of AIDS is intensified and sublimated in/by a sepulchral Bruges in *The Folding Star*, just as Venice intensifies and frames Aschenbach's downfall. However, while Aschenbach's self quest responds to the Freudian struggle between *id* and *ego* and a death drive, Edward's conforms to the Lacanian pattern of regression and lack.

Maurice, Aschenbach and Edward undergo Dionysian processes guided (and attracted) by aristocratic beloveds, Clive, Tadzio and Luc respectively. However, while Aschenbach's obsession remains homoerotic, Edward's becomes overtly homosexual. Besides, as Will does with Arthur and Phil, Manners converts Luc into a fetish (Hollinghurst, 1998b: 154) who, however, torments his admirer with indifference (172-179). If Narcissus was haunted by his reflection, Edward is by his obsessive projection of desire on young Luc. Despite his aura, the novel delves into Luc's local legend of *garçon fatal*. He is marked by a mental disorder that apparently affects the whole family (359-360) and, as Marcel argues in a deterministic fashion, he is a *mauvais sujet* like his father. Unlike presumably naïve Tadzio, Luc is a troublemaker. The fact that he was expelled from school because he "was found on a ship [...] with a bunch of Norwegian sailors" (94) makes up an image that haunts Edward henceafter. The episode possesses the hero as traumatic events do with their victims. Edward dreams of the sailors speaking about Luc in an unknown language (101) or as a painting by gay icon Caravaggio. He speaks about it as an orgy (181), or bears witness to the youth being abused by the sailors also in a dream. Luc was naked (62), ambiguous and elusive (101). Yet, unlike ethereal Tadzio, he eventually becomes flesh and blood. Or so it seems to Edward. He notices overlooked aspects of the youth, "something camp, mischievous" that Edward finds tempting (330). Whether Edward is the victim or, as an unreliable keyhole narrator, he is concealing his own assault on a minor is impossible to say. The fact is that he is or pretends to be traumatised by a *garçon fatal*; he confesses himself to be dissociated between subject and object, actor and spectator: "I saw a phantom me" (331).

Drifting away from *Death in Venice*, Edward and Luc have sex in the end. Even then, however, roles are rather confusing. Like Will Beckwith and some Forster's

[311] Ibid., 58.

characters (and Forster himself), Edward's role is ambivalent, both desiring and hating the subordinate other (337). Once again, sadomasochism is the trope of same-sex desire as driven by power and guilt. As both erastes and tempted, Edward controls and is controlled by Luc, *eromenos* and seducer. When his eyes turn mysterious like "Orst's temptresses'" (337), Edward claims to be unarmed. However, it is obsession as narcissistic self-repetition that explains the protagonist's traumata and its projection on the youth, who thus becomes the passive actor of the interaction. After their brief sexual encounter, Luc disappears mysteriously. Once touched, he proves a metaphysical ephebe who (like Tadzio) lives in the worshipper-punisher's imagination. Desire is lack; that is why it is desire.

In summary, Manners is a flawed version of Aschenbach; from homoeroticism to homosexuality, from Higher to Lower Sodomy, from nostalgia to irony, and from Socratic love to a post-Stonewall interpretation of it. *The Folding Star* is the textual consequence of a sexual politics that has greatly changed in the last century. *Death in Venice* is narcissistically decadent, a crepuscular manifesto announcing the Great War, the epidemic being a metaphor of the end of a world and lifestyle and the beginning of a new one. *The Folding Star* is the textual effect of a crisis in process. Hence, narcissism is aesthetically appropriate and politically relevant, as it is paralysing and ineffective.

Rodenbach's *Bruges-la-Morte* is also a destination "treasured for its antiquity and decay"[312] to better understand *The Folding Star*. In Hollinghurst's view, Bruges and its atmosphere are evoked "not merely as a backdrop, but as an essential character, associated with states of mind, counselling, dissuading, inducing the hero to act."[313] Grey, melancholic, decadent, nostalgic of its medieval golden age, the city assumes the emotions of Hughes Viane, the protagonist. Bruges is made up of different layers that mirror each other. This produces an effect of city-within-the city, which resembles the hero's convoluted psyche and Nantwich's London. Like *Death in Venice* and *The Folding Star*, *Bruges-la-Morte* deals with obsession as futile repetition. Therefore, Viane "finds in the dead city of Bruges a perfect setting in which to grieve for his dead wife."[314] In fact, Viane's discourse of loss reveals he has encrypted his wife's phantom unable to introject it. As Hollinghurst argues, the hero makes a religion of melancholia, "narrowing his aesthetic purpose to his dead wife,"[315] using his house as a chapel, keeping "a cut-off plait, a broken chain, a rope saved from the shipwreck."[316] His obsession grows until the city and the woman fuse into one in the hero's monomaniac imagery. Seductive like deadly Ophelia, the city, "once loved and beloved too, embodied the loss he felt."[317] On a visit to Notre Dame, Viane gets transfixed mistaking the dancer Jane Scott for his dead wife.[318] He follows her and, after disappearing, he finds her at the theatre where she works. There, she is playing the role of nun Helena in

---

[312] Alan Hollinghurst: "Introduction to *Bruges-la-Morte*." In Georges Rodenbach. *Bruges-la-Morte*. London 2005, 11.

[313] Ibid., 12.

[314] Ibid., 14-15.

[315] Ibid., 15.

[316] Georges Rodenbach: *Bruges-la-Morte*. London 2005, 28.

[317] Ibid., 33.

[318] Ibid., 35.

Giacomo Meyerbeer's *Robert le Diable*. Misunderstanding the scene in which the nuns who have died in sin rise from their tombs "into a frenzy,"[319] Viane thinks Jane is his wife resurrected. Therefore, in Faustian terms, "the relationship that follows is shadowed from the start by the idea of a diabolic bargain; though who will pay the price, and how, remains uncertain until the final scene."[320] The amazing apparition of Jane's 'double' is, in Viane's view, "an almost frightening miracle of resemblance that went as far as identity."[321] Henceforth, Viane delusively blends both women in one.[322] He convinces Jane to put on his dead wife's clothes, which transforms her into a parody of the original,[323] a temptress that transcends life. In fact, the hero becomes conscious of his infatuation and consequences: "He had tried to evade Death, to triumph over it and deride it by the specious artifice of a likeness. Death, perhaps, would have its revenge."[324] His words are premonitory since the tension between real women and Viane's idealisation of beauty and femininity can only be solved by death. At the end of the novel, he kills Jane accidentally with his first wife's plait[325] thus achieving his purpose: "The two women fused in one, so alike in life, even more alike in death."[326]

The echoes of Hughes Viane's story resound in Edgar Orst's and, to a lesser extent, in Edward's. Like Viane, the fictional symbolist painter and the English teacher walk the streets of crepuscular Bruges. From the very beginning, the town proves a living character that aspires "to be an artist's impression" (Hollinghurst, 1998b: 11). Thus, Bruges swings between its 'reality' and its artistic representations. Orst's paintings and Edward's perspective as a *flâneur* contribute to making up the city in *The Folding Star*. As happens in Rodenbach and Mann's texts, the decadence of the scenario frames perverse desire. Edward soon describes his dreamlike sensation as if part of "the secret inner life of the city" (13). Bruges is a trigger for Edward to recall his childhood memories, particularly a church tower in Kent and his dead father singing (14-15). Hollinghurst's novel adopts (and adapts) the "universal analogy" and "spleen" of Rodenbach's. The analogies in *The Folding Star* are multiple and narcissistic. Flanders substitutes (Edward's memory of) England; *i.e.*: the hero substitutes (and exiles himself from) his homeland for the unreal city of Bruges to delay post-Oxbridge adulthood. Like Viane, Orst substitutes his dead wife with her exact likeness. Edward also tries to replace dead Dawn with Luc. Like *The Swimming-pool Library*, Hollinghurst's second novel is specular, reflecting itself and a number of hypotexts as fractals after the logic of "universal analogy." *The Folding Star* incorporates melancholia after the Baudelarian "spleen."

Like Will, Edward is a transgenerational effect, Echevin, Orst and (indirectly) Viane modelling his discourse. Edward's first-person narration is interrupted by archival material —fundamentally articles about Orst or his personal objects— which draws the

---

[319]   Hollinghurst: "Introduction," 16.
[320]   Ibid.
[321]   Rodenbach: *Bruges-la-Morte*, 36.
[322]   Agustín Izquierdo: "Introduction" to Georges Rodenbach's *Bruges-la-Morte*. Madrid 1989, 10.
[323]   Rodenbach: *Bruges-la-Morte*, 59.
[324]   Ibid., 90.
[325]   Ibid., 128.
[326]   Ibid., 131.

reader to the past as origin. The first reference to the enigmatic painter is when Echevin shows Edward a photograph of a mature man with "the fastidious ironic look of the heterosexual bachelor" (35-36). The narrator points unnecessarily to Orst's heterosexuality and describes him as a campy aesthete suspicious of his sexual ambiguity to say the least. The relations of Orst and Viane with women are complex, problematic and asexual. Unlike normative heterosexuality, they are sadomasochistic and substitutive; the mysterious death of his first wife gives way to the obsessive search for a substitute. The surrogate is glorified until she turns into a disappointing *femme fatale*. In short, the psychosexual fantasies of Viane and Orst are linked with turn-of-the-century Decadentism, the queerest queers could be at the time. Orst's queerness is a historic framework for Edward's queer obsession with Luc.

The first section of *The Folding Star* closes with the article of an English journalist on Orst's now demolished villa. The past thus speaks directly to the reader. The article describes the fantastic scenario where Orst keeps himself exiled from the world outside. Villa Hermes is a dazzling white sanctuary, a fortress for the "aesthete *par excellance*" (182) crowned by a young deity. Against the journalist's opinion, Orst's work is considered "the art of depravity" (183). Back to the house, the article describes the artist's eccentricities. The door is opened by a young woman in a Greek costume who, like the rest of the servants, is silent (183). Like Nantwich's house and Huysmans's Des Esseintes's, Villa Hermes is both a museum and a magical site. A curtain reveals "an Attic frieze" decorated in the Pre-raphaelite style (184) which leads to an ante-chamber featuring a "figure of Andromeda, chained to her rock" (184). This mythological figure, to which I will return, constitutes an icon of the novel. Finally, Orst's studio can be glimpsed, inviolable like a religious shrine (184). Like a priest, the painter ritualises everyday activities, which thus reach the status of art. Following this camp, mysterious attitude, he zealously keeps secrets in the drawers of his cabinet in "cryptic Hebrew hieroglyphs" (185). In short, everything around Orst and his villa —Catholic imagery, the Cabala, aestheticism, eccentricity, camp, French expressions and his subterraneous lifestyle— points to his sexual ambiguity, not as something to be feared, but as a prerogative of marginality. Hence, closeted gay Paul Echevin recalls how he identified with and imitated the painter's aestheticism (294). Finally, the photograph accompanying the article is significant too, featuring a man who wishes "not to be too intimately known" (186). The parallels between the painter and Nantwich are many and noteworthy: they are virile, stout men who live surrounded by artistic objects in a world of their own. Besides, though they reveal part of their personalities in enigmatic works or in a frustrated biography, both do it cryptically. That is, in line with classic homoerotic literature, these characters play an ambiguous role in a juxtaposing style, narcissistically showing and hiding themselves and their sexual orientation.

The Folding Star plays with the original triangle of *Bruges-la-Morte*. Orst's story is an overtly sexual parody of Viane's and trivialises the Catholic undertones of Rodenbach's novel. When Orst is making the designs for gay-inflected *The Merchant of Venice*, he meets Jane Byron, a red-haired Scottish actress. Obsessed, Orst idealises Jane multiplying her as seer, sufferer, or sphinx (68) in numerous portraits until she drowns in Ostend. Thus, Viane's nameless dead wife becomes Jane Byron in *The Folding Star*, although the latter's name recalls Viane's temptress, dancer Jane Scott. It can be argued that Orst's Jane stands for Viane's two women, which explains her ambivalence in the portraits. Jane Byron is many women in one, from a virgin to a fatal temptress, following turn-of-the-century archetypal interpretations. However, *The Folding Star* goes further. Like the hero of *Bruges-la-Morte*, Orst has a delusive experience in which his first wife returns to life. The painter gets transfixed at church, instead of at the performance of Meyerbeer's *Robert le Diable*. As a pagan, Orst visits the church with curiosity and after a worshipper (289), a young woman with a "dubious reputation" (290). Like Viane, he thinks himself in front of a ghost, the young prostitute, Marthe, and Jane Byron being uncannily similar. Obsessed with Marthe, the painter scrutinises her in search of differences from the original. Like Viane's, his attempt to transcend death through resemblance is fated from the beginning. He considers that Marthe closes the circle initiated by Jane. However, the pattern fails as the differences between copy and original unfold.

As *The Folding Star* approaches its end, drawing on Will Beckwith, Edward is given key information to understand previously overlooked signs. Edward is shown a number of enigmatic photographs of Jane. A photograph of the hotel Andromeda —in front of which she disappeared for ever— stands out. The hotel is symbolically linked with the statue of Andromeda at Villa Hermes. Thus, as Echevin suggests, Orst's idealisation of Jane hides the painter's sadomasochistic fantasy, an Andromeda "with a long and heavy chain" (301). This imagery of Jane echoes not only classic mythology, but also Viane's idealisation and subjection of his two women. *The Folding Star* goes still further with a second group of photographs of Marthe, a parody all this Goddess worship. At first sight, this new collection of images recalls previous ones (303). Yet, after a more detailed analysis, the photographs turn different, a poor and degenerated version of Jane's, as she lacked the latter's "disconcerting power" (303). Edward is shown a last set of photographs, which emphasise the parody of Rodenbach's original story. Next to the paragraphs, he finds a sprig of pubic orange hair (304). Viane's allegorical obsession turns sadomasochistic and narcissistic repetition in Orst. Like Jane Scott in *Bruges-la-Morte*, Marthe is allegedly forced to wear the dead wife's clothes and jewels. In other words, she is compelled to impersonate the dead. However, resemblance soon shifts to parody, the collar and the camera being mere sadomasochistic paraphernalia. Likewise, the plait that Viane keeps like a relic becomes pubic hair in Orst's case. Hollinghurst's novel trivialises Rodenbach's, making obsession into its leit motif, the symptom of trauma.

Drawing on universal analogy, *The Folding Star* recasts *Bruges-la-Morte*: Jane Byron and Bruges, Bruges and Orst, Jane and Marthe. However, it is the obsessions of Orst (apparently heterosexual) and Edward (overtly homosexual) that constitute the main analogy. Edward idealises his pupil as a mythic Aztec king after Orst's idealisation of Jane and Marthe. But Luc is particularly problematic, combining the narratives of pedagogical eros, the perfection of the eromenos, dead wife, and the menace of the erastes temptress. Firstly, Manners imagines his life "consecrated to the image of Luc," (68) just as Orst does with Jane. Soon, however, Luc proves a *garçon fatal* (337). Being Luc a symptom of Edward's narcissistic trauma, the protagonist feels a sadistic desire to punish the youth to redirect his own pain (337). Like the origin of trauma, Luc is elusive and fades away (344), though its traces possess the traumatised.

The Folding Star ritualises melancholia after the Baudelarian "spleen" in a rather ironic tone. In Hollinghurst's view, the nostalgic "spleen" that characterises the discourses of Viane —and, indirectly, of Orst and Edward— recalls Housman's poetry.[327] The nostalgia of a lost world in pastoral poetry is central to *The Folding Star* and its management of gay traumata in the nineties. Drawing on pastoral elegies, Bruges and the Rough Common constitute dreamlike scenarios where the hero retreats from reality. However, what Edward truly escapes and yearns is the sense of a past that haunts him and fades away.

2.6   Arcadia gained, threatened and lost

The elegiac in *The Folding Star* is especially relevant in its second section, 'Underwoods'. When his friend and ex-lover Dawn dies, Edward comes back home for the funeral. This return is not just physical, for it also implies a flashback in time. Manners recalls his early years in the Rough Common in South London (Hollinghurst, 1998b: 189). Edward's reminiscence is doubly nostalgic because he regrets the loss of his childhood and of that England. Drawing on classic nostalgia, before Luc turns it into melancholia, Edward desires what he lacks, a past that is unattainable. For this futile trip back, *The Folding Star* revisits the pastoral elegy and the public school novel.

'Underwoods' is not placed in the centre by chance. The chapter is a retreat of a retreat; in fact, Edward leaves England to come to terms with himself and leaves Bruges with the same purpose. In both cases, Dawn's disease and death respectively drive him forward and backward. And pastoral elegy is the symptom, the trigger and the subterfuge of the traumata of Edward and Dawn's. Traditionally, the poet was moved by the nostalgia of a golden age and space. In this ideal landscape Theocritus placed "the sometimes sad, sometimes comic spectacle of bucolic love."[328] Henceforth, Gifford argues, Arcadia has been "a realm irretrievably lost, seen through a veil of reminiscent melancholy." [329] Pastoral literature is frequently considered a conservative genre, retreating from reality to an imaginary space. However, parallel to escapist versions, there have also been subversive pastorals. As Gifford notes, in *The Fairy Queene*, Edmund Spencer used this framework "to make a social critique of the values of commercial Elizabethan England." [330] English pastoral is and has been especially ambivalent, simultaneously criticising the Establishment and warning "against a radical disturbance of the social order."[331] Georgian poetry has been a main target for its melancholic unrealism. In surviving the Great War, poets like Housman "sought refuge in rural images that did not disturb comfortable reassurance."[332] The pastoral is in these cases an ethical and aesthetic escape to traumata otherwise unnameable. Parallel to nostalgic pastorals, Gifford addresses anti-pastoral and post-pastoral texts. The former reject an idealised rural England and point out its problematic aspects. Thus, the difficulty of anti-pastoral poets consists in finding "a voice that can be celebratory while

---

[327] Hollinghurst: "Introduction," 14.
[328] Terry Gifford: *Pastoral*. London 1999, 17.
[329] Ibid., 21.
[330] Ibid., 28.
[331] Ibid., 52.
[332] Ibid., 71.

corrective."[333] By contrast, the defining characteristic of post-pastoral literature is its eco-centrism,[334] which is much in line with current ecological sensibility.

Hollinghurst himself has admitted the influence of pastoral elegy on "Underwoods." In his view, the novel is an exercise of memory and failed mourning of "all sorts of unhappy things that had happened to me [the novelist]: people dying, my father dying."[335] The inexorable fatalism of the novel is autobiographical, as well as the result of the author's revision of pastoral poetry. As he was writing *The Folding Star*, Hollinghurst was reading Milton and Gerard Manley Hopkins, which influenced on the atmosphere of the novel.[336] Milton's *Comus* and the very end of *Paradise Lost* are two cases in point, in concrete for the "imagery of the woods and lawns [...] in the common in *The Folding Star*."[337] I wonder, however, whether Hollinghurst's pastoral is only aesthetic in purpose, as he suggests. Or the return to mythic England conveys political and/or ethical undertones.[338] Although David Alderson also believes "Underwoods" is essentially escapist pastoral, he finds a pragmatic, political justification for escapism. The narcissistic nostalgia of the novel, especially "its desire to repossess some former moment of pure, unselfconscious sexual being [...,] is enforced by AIDS."[339] Just like Housman's poetry sublimated many English youths' deaths, so the elegiac undertones of Hollinghurst's second novel pay homage to a new generation of young victims at the turn of the millennium. Edward makes reference to this two-waved phenomenon of gay extinction addressing young men's obituaries (Hollinghurst, 1998b: 233). As happens in *The Swimming-pool Library*, old traumata are recalled into new ones, especially AIDS, in a transgenerational textual tradition.

Edward regrets the loss of a mythic England his own narration progressively contests. The first description of his hometown is idyllic, a pre-industrial/Symbolic scenario (189). Like Forster's 'greenwood' and other homoerotic escapist utopias, the Common is not a natural space, but an artificial construction. In fact, the geography of the Common reproduces the English class system, the houses of the different social classes being arranged from top to bottom of the hill in a metaphoric pyramid (189-190). However, as Edward notices, this world, which keeps inalterable in his imaginary, is threatened by progress, crossed by post-roads and by-passes and contaminated by cars (189). Dawn's death and the effects of progress on the Common run parallel and prompt the hero's nostalgia and eventual melancholia. Nostalgia is a complex phenomenon, always swinging between past and present. Indeed, a nostalgic discourse is symptomatic of a problematic present. Therefore, when Edward longs for his youth, he is indirectly pointing to the AIDS crisis and gay stereotyping and marketing of the eighties and nineties, an issue which becomes central in *The Spell*.

---

[333] Ibid., 134.

[334] Ibid., 152.

[335] In Canning: *Conversations*, 338.

[336] Ibid., 349.

[337] Ibid., 359.

[338] José M. Yebra: "Utopia and Dystopia in Homoerotic Territory in Alan Hollinghurst's *The Swimming-pool Library, The Folding Star* and *The Spell.*" *Odisea*, 11, 2010.

[339] Alderson: *Territories*, 38-39.

Edward's memories draw on pastoral poetry and the school novel rather subversively. Like James, Will Beckwith's friend, Edward is a parody of Forster's middle-class Maurice. At public school, Edward's first beloved was the snobbish Lawrence Graves, an aesthete who "clearly resembles Clive in Forster's *Maurice*[340] and Waugh's Blanche in *Brideshead Revisited*. Their homoerotic relationship and camp lifestyle are misunderstood, or simply rejected, by their fellow students. Unlike Oxbridge's virile bonds, theirs are eccentric and affected. This is why they are isolated and make up a language of their own (Hollinghurst, 1998b: 209), a proto-gay code inspired by French *Précieux*. With his friendship with Graves, Edward enters a class-conscious homoerotic system. Edward's true first love, Mark Lyle, is a working-class boy three years older than him. The hero's infatuation with a poorer, stronger and older boy recalls Nantwich's first affair with Strong at Winchester. However, while Nantwich's homoerotic relationship remains identified with a mythic England, Edward's is (despite his efforts) rather ordinary. On leaving school, the narrator says, Lyle becomes an outlaw in his imagination (201). Once more an ordinary 'reality' collides with the hero's nostalgia and poetic imagination, producing an ironic effect. Edward converts Lyle's working-class origin into a moving romantic event (201). Unlike the homoerotic bonds in Arcadia, the hero's infatuation with Lyle ends violently when the latter rejects him while laughing (204). The strict class affiliation in which Edward is instructed and which prevents his life-long affair with Lyle is simultaneously ironic and touching. Irony only increases when the protagonist writes his first book, *The Manners Family of Kent*, a ludicrous account of his family's alleged glory (201).

In spite of the pass of time, Edward still feels clung to Dawn. His death is the trigger of the novel, the one that galvanises Edward's flawed *Bildungsroman* and the traumatic coming to age of gays after Stonewall. Edward's trauma discourse is self-protective, though. Hence, Dawn's death makes gay mortality and marginality conspicuous, but also sublimated through screen memories, especially Edward and Dawn's love affair at public school. An increasingly bourgeois institution, the school encouraged sexual inhibition, although, the hero confesses, it recalled old schools "with [their] real rigour of vice" (234). Yet, rather than the school days, the hero evokes the long summer holidays in a narcissistic fashion (216). Thus, as happens with Will Beckwith's swimming-pool library, the Common and school constitute states of mind, screen memories to refract current traumata, rather than actual places. The void left by these memories reveals, however, how AIDS just triggers a structural trauma haunting Edward throughout. Since his childhood with Dawn, "everything [was] in some way melancholy, frantic or foredoomed" (200). Like Will before, Edward is ironic when he longs for innocence from sexual promiscuity. He recalls Dawn as he is masturbating while looking at a photograph of Luc. Thus, his affair with Dawn can no longer be regarded as naïve. And his obsession with Luc reveals an endemic lack in the hero. That is, once he loses Dawn, Edward tries to fill the void with Luc —a parodic surrogate of the former— just as Orst does with Marthe. In Alderson's view, the bond between Edward and Dawn "is also invested —at least retrospectively— with a sense of loss, prefigured in the very landscape which is the backdrop to their relationship."[341] In their

---

[340] Ibid., 39.
[341] Alderson: *Territories*.

first sexual encounters, they leave the Common for the privacy of the wood nearby. In this scenario, they escape social rules, including being identified with queers (Hollinghurst, 1998b: 219). Drawing on Greek homoerotic tradition, Edward tells apart queers' plain sex and his High Sodomy relationship with Dawn (224).

The interaction and identification between nature, nostalgia and naïve sex is what links *The Folding Star* to prior English gay writing. In Alderson's view, Hollinghurst's analysis of Forster's discourses of desire and loss in his thesis is conspicuous in *The Folding Star*. Homosexual desire, a return to adolescence and the loss of a rural England coalesce in Forster's 'greenwood' and Hollinghurst's novel. Forster's hostility to modernity, particularly "its sense of an irrecoverable past and a present whose freedoms are compromised, very closely anticipates Hollinghurst's response to the development of a self-conscious gay scene."[342] The fact that *The Folding Star* questions post-Stonewall gay culture does not mean that it thoroughly assumes the discourses of predecessors like Forster. Like Maurice and Scudder, Edward and Dawn inhabit their own 'greenwood' (236). In a rather Whitmanesque tone, he vindicates the memory of that pre-(homo)sexual stage of independence and truth (239-240). However, unlike the unrealistic end of Forster's text, the celebration of beauty of Edward's individuation process comes back to trauma. He still dreams of the Common and old England, but when he recalls those years, he does it with a touch of ironic frustration. At a distance, he deconstructs his youth: his family (and the past) was not the eminent he thought or pretended, but rather ludicrous and, therefore, touching. His father was a frustrated artist, like his aunt Tina, his uncle Wilfred was a repressed homosexual, and his parents' marriage simply play-acting. And worst of all, idealised Dawn, we learn, eventually became a sex toy for unscrupulous men. The real trauma is that the past was an empty make-believe possessing its pretenders. Hence, in the aftermath of Dawn's funeral, Edward has sex with a black youth. The rapid, anonymous sexual relationship with a stranger demystifies the landscape and its implications so far and announces "a cold prospect" (256) for Edward and his world.

The trauma of pastoral lies in the transience of Arcadia, as conveyed in elegy. Like *The Swimming-pool Library*, *The Folding Star* is uttered from post-Arcadia: the onset of adulthood, AIDS and related traumatic events erase pastoral celebration and propitiate elegiac melancholia instead. The first (oblique) reference to his disease is made by Edie, a friend of Edward's, when she visits him in Flanders. Drawing on Gidé's *L'immoraliste* (1902), the beauty of Algeria frames a European's recovery (Hollinghurst, 1998b: 152). Instead of AIDS itself, Edie mentions AZT (152), the acronym of the most famous drug against the disease. Moreover, AIDS is also sublimated when Dawn paradoxically dies in a traffic accident (194). Edward starts looking for a piece of elegiac poetry to read at the funeral. Being a poetic lament and celebration of the dead beloved, followed by the consoling discovery of something that transcends death itself, elegy proves to be useful to convey the (im)possibility of homoerotic love. This is so because love for a dead lover is necessarily ideal, which, as Stephen Guy-Bray suggests, makes the genre acceptable in a homophobic *status quo*.[343] The coming of AIDS renewed the aesthetic and political validity of elegy, the

---

[342] Ibid., 40.
[343] In Summers: *Gay*, 205-207.

instrument to sublimate the erasure of a whole generation (Hollinghurst, 1998b: 233). Milton's *Lycidas* and Gray's *Elegy* are Edward's first options (194). The former is a seventeenth-century poem[344] featuring a mythical hero mourning the death of his heroic 'friend'. By contrast, Gray's eighteenth-century poem is a more heterodox version of the genre. As George Haggerty puts it, the lyrical voice speaks about "his own death in intimate terms, looks at his own corpse as it is carried to its grave, and even contemplates the grave itself."[345] The self-lamentation and celebration of Gray's *Elegy* can be applied metaphorically to Edward's dissociated discourse. In fact, "Dawn's death not only symbolises the demise of a whole generation, some of the men [Edward] had slept with […] existed in earlier, close-down precincts of [his] life" (Hollinghurst, 1998b: 231). In a sense, Dawn's death resounds in Edward's narcissistic discourse and metaphoric death. Indeed, he bears witness to the demise of his world splitting himself after the example of Viane after his wife's death. The dissociation from themselves and the projection of their beloved's phantoms into new objects of desire, with Bruges as a funereal scenario emulating a corpse, make up the two-staged trauma of both Viane and Edward.

Edward mourns Dawn's departure with Milton (224) and Luc's with Tennyson (198), turning homotextuality into an instrument against homophobia. Another redeeming feature for gays to cope with trauma and make nostalgia palatable is irony. Like most funerals of AIDS victims, Dawn's reveals gays' double life, the one they left at home and the surrogate family they make up after coming out. The melting-pot of Dawn's two lives during the funeral is ironic, oddly funny (252). After reading an elegiac poem (253-254), the narrator himself feels inappropriately elated. The ceremony reaches its climax when a very old Sir Perry Dewlish —the local celebrity whom Edward visited as a literary promise— arrives. His entrance constitutes a new incursion of old camp in gays' world (255). Dawn's funeral is an encounter, traumatic, bitter, but still campy.

Closely connected with AIDS is *fins de race*, a concept linked with sterility, sexual perversion and decadence. The Beckwiths represent the ideal of aristocratic sexual degeneracy and decadence in *The Swimming-pool Library*, as the Altidores of Bruges, Luc's noble family, do in *The Folding Star*. The lineage is on the verge of extinction since its last member is the ambiguous and self-destroying Luc. Yet, though traumatic, loss is also an ironic re-appraisal of gothic stereotypes, especially *fins de race*. Luc's ancestry represents the spirit of Bruges, impassive to the passing of time (139), as if lethargic. It is Luc himself who tells the narrator the story of his family, which he significantly emplots as "The fall of the House of Altidore" (142), after Poe's gothic "The Fall of the House of Usher." The interest of the gothic for perverse desire and decadent scenarios made it perfect for gay writers to sublimate their sexuality. Edward recalls the history of Luc's family as one of social charm, decline and fall (142-143). The last century of the Altidores runs parallel to the history of gays, made up of ephemeral heights interspersed within longer periods of decadence. Thus, the Altidores lived a last period of apogee in the early nineteen eighties, significantly the last days of

---

[344] Guy-Bray: "Elegy." In Claude Summers (ed). *The Gay and Lesbian Literary Heritage*. New York and London 2002, 206.

[345] In Summers: *Gay*, 318.

gays' golden age before AIDS. Paul and Marcel Echevin complete Edward's knowledge about the Altidores' legend. In their view, the family was always "marked by eccentricity and whimsicality" (179). However, the climax of their family myth goes back to the sixteenth century, when Anthonis Altidore claimed to be realted to Christ's family (180). Such eccentricities ironically anticipate Edward's plot to craft his genealogy tree and book. A middle-class family of frustrated artists, the story and decline of the Manners look narcissistically on the Altidores.

When Luc disappears, Edward and Marcel go after him. This "merry goose hunt" takes the hero to the *Pavillon de l'Aurore*, Luc's grandfather's *château* (364). Although the hero suspects the youth is not there, he panders to a half-hidden desire to explore the site. Significantly, the Pavilion is dedicated to Aurore, the French word for Dawn. Hence, Edward's search for Luc is a re-search of Dawn in the Proustian imperfect tense. The grandest and most ruinous room of the château is especially relevant for its symbolic value with respect to the whole novel because it features enchained Aurora (367). The orientalist painting is symbolic and echoic. It recalls Orst's sadomasochistic abuse of *femmes fatales*. Emulating Andromeda, both Dawn and Rodenbach's female characters are chained up, literally or metaphorically, while being worshipped. This complex interaction of power and desire underlies Edward's self-destroying obsession with Luc. The *Pavillon de l'Aurore* is the hero's last opportunity to find the youth (369). However, it is not Edward that possesses the house to possess Luc vicariously. It is him, a victim of traumatic loss, that is possessed by a monomaniac obsession to return in vain.

Like *The Swimming-pool Library*, *The Folding Star* juxtaposes discourses of display and concealment, since they are simultaneously explicit and circumspect in their approach to sexuality, as concerns the treatment of the disease. Traumata of the present are sublimated through traumatic episodes of the past. In this light, John Bradley argues: "What Manners eventually learns in a more general way is not easy to ascertain. Orst was killed by the Nazis, and so Manners learns about the Nazi occupation of Belgium, but he could have learned about that from a history book."[346] Perhaps the historical episodes narrated do not affect Edward as they affect Will. However, Echevin's first-hand testimony of those times has several implications worth noting. Although Jews were the most numerous victims of the Nazis, many gays also perished in concentration camps. There are no direct references to gay victims of the Nazis in *The Folding Star*: Lilly and Maurice —whom Echevin's parents rescued from the Germans— and Orst are all Jews and, for that reason, they were persecuted. However, Paul Echevin's personal story incorporates a homosexual revision of the Nazi occupation, albeit indirectly. As a child, he formed a homoerotic, Girardian triangle together with the Jewish Lilly and Maurice. He also made up a homoerotic imagery drawing on Tom of Finland, Aryan American soldiers and Fascist virility (Hollinghurst, 1998b: 410). Simultaneously, Paul falls in love with Willem, a Nazi homophobe, which brings about psychic, political and ethical consequences for the hero. Guilt for his illicit desire triggers traumatic dissociation, feeling himself "a kind of double agent" (410); a traitor, like Genet's gay characters, paranoid for lack of sex and ethical justice. When he learns Orst is being watched and kept as a prisoner at home, he warns him. It is too late however, for

---

[346] Bradley: "Disciples," 18.

Willem himself is carrying away the dead artist in his wheelchair (413). This episode becomes a traumatic experience that haunts Paul henceforth and condemns him to revise Orst's artistic production *ad nauseam*. That is precisely the very aporia of trauma, the impossibility to stop uttering the unutterable. Freud contended that "compulsion to repeat traumatic experiences over and over again constitutes an attempt to achieve a retrospective mastery over the shocking or unexpected event that has breached the defensive walls surrounding the psyche."[347] However, as trauma theorists argue, this is unfeasible. Edward, Paul and Orst return narcissistically to images to grant narrative coherence to their traumas in vain. Edward cannot overcome his pre-AIDS youth with Dawn, which he re-experiences in his obsession with Luc. Paul feels guilty about Orst's demise and devotes his life to a never-ending catalogue about the artist. Orst's paintings compulsively repeat a series of motifs, especially his first wife's mysterious death. If, as Pierre Janet argued, "cure is achieved when a patient manages to integrate the fragmentary contents of nightmares or flashbacks, arranging them chronologically and situating them in the past of the individual's life story,"[348] the characters of *The Folding Star* fail. In one way or another, all of them suffer a "collapse of understanding,"[349] which prevents them from verbalising their desire and the circumstances around it. As in Orst's triptych, these characters' stories are supposed to form a whole. However, they do not fit in the end. *The Folding Star* gives voice to traumatised minorities and proposes a pattern first to deconstruct it later.

The Folding Star shows just slight differences with respect to its predecessor. *The Swimming-pool Library* focuses on and revises the history of English homoeroticism during the twentieth century. *The Folding Star* expands the scope, revising Englishness from a European perspective, not only as a geographic space, but also as a literary one. With respect to *The Swimming-pool Library*, Hollinghurst's second novel is more pessimistic and nostalgic; it is equally intertextual, dialogic, self-conscious and specular; and finally, it goes beyond the exclusively homosexual cast of the former. The analysis of his third novel, *The Spell*, will determine whether this basic formula still works, shows signs of exhaustion or is simply overcome.

---

[347] In Onega: "Ethics," 5.
[348] Ibid., 6.
[349] Ibid., 7.

3   Orton meets Shakespeare in a Midsummer night's gay comedy: *The Spell*

After the literary sensation of *The Swimming-pool Library*, his tour-de-force debut, and *The Folding Star*, which was shortlisted for the Booker Prize, Hollinghurst published *The Spell* in 1997. If the first was a comedy of sexual success and the second a comedy of sexual frustration, the third is best defined as an accurate representation of late-capitalist gay life, a comedy of manners meeting romantic comedy. Stylistically, *The Spell* rescues the tone of pre-AIDS coming-out stories as the disease seemed to recede. Despite the differences with its predecessors, *The Spell* still forms part of Hollinghurst's 'sex tetralogy' as long as sexual explicitness connects them all. As in his previous novels, (homo)sexual freedom is not only asserted, but "assimilated to an older tradition of the rake rather than the radical, the libertine rather than the libertarian, *thus further contributing to the novel's representation of the present as merely decadent rather than emancipated.*"[350] In Alderson's view, the protagonists of the first two novels, Beckwith and Manners, are "connoisseurial [...] cultured and rootless"[351] and their discourses are limited to a group of upper-middle-class gay men. The third-person narrator of *The Spell* belongs in the same category. However, despite these and other similarities, his third novel is the odd one out in the 'tetralogy'. As Allan Johnson points out: "The text stands out from Hollinghurst's other works by virtue of its self-removal from an imaginative consciousness built upon images drawn from literature, performance, and visual art."[352] This short-circuiting of gay genealogy is not exactly so, though. *The Spell* is "an elegant and shrewd portrayal of contemporary house music and the mid-1990s London club scene;"[353] but it still draws on hypotexts other than Hardy. Indeed, its attempt to post-trauma narrative is embedded in comedy tradition.

As David Alderson has pointed out, by the year *The Spell* was published, times had changed for homosexuals, the impact of AIDS declining. The critic describes the new gay community as devoid of political commitments, and forming "part of a broader relaxed cosmopolitanism,"[354] since they ceased to be the target of political leaders, but part of their political discourse. As Alderson puts it, in contrast with the first two novels, Hollinghurst's third one has a "relaxed 1990s, 'post-issue' feel."[355] Also, *The Spell* is less ambitious than its predecessors and diminishes their "mood of disenchantment and the[ir] attendant foredoomed desire to transcend the commercialisation and self-segregation of the present by appeal to a supposedly more

---

[350] Alderson: *Territories*, 43, emphasis added.
[351] Ibid., 43.
[352] Johnson: *Alan*, 84.
[353] Ibid.
[354] Alderson: *Territories*, 44.
[355] Ibid.

integrated past."[356] Intertextuality is no longer so focal or the way for dissatisfaction to be redirected to a pre-industrial English Arcadia. With all this in mind, *The Spell* claims for gay celebratory iconography at the expense of trauma discourses. The imaginary rural scenario of Litton Gambril, Dorset, where much of the action takes place, is no longer an idyllic retreat from the city. Focused from an urban perspective, the rural is no longer mythic but "more comic, barely at all inflected by nostalgia."[357] While London allows for personal freedom and interaction, Litton Gambril represents middle-class heteronormative intolerance. *The Spell* also breaks with the paternalism of gay *Bildungsromane* like *The Swimming-pool Library* and *The Folding Star*. The three novels deal with gay genealogy and intergenerational conflicts. However, *The Spell* subverts age-ruled narratives of pedagogical eros. In this case, it is the youth who mentors older characters for them to cope with a new reality. The treatment of AIDS is one of obliteration, rather than proper working-through. The disease is overlooked as if a matter of the past; it is neither "a future which colours our perspective of the past [like *The Swimming-pool Library* n]or part of an elegiac contemplation on desire itself [like *The Folding Star*]."[358] None of the characters suffers or is likely to suffer from the disease, except the hero's ex-lover; an episode only recalled in flashbacks (Hollinghurst, 1999: 30-35).[359] Contrary to Alderson, though, I consider *The Spell* is not a post-AIDS novel, but one that, in avoiding references to the disease, complies with the poetics of trauma as an undercurrent to the poetics of celebration.

The "post-issue feel" about *The Spell* postulated by Alderson draws on Alan Sinfield's 'post-gay', a concept which tries to capture the aftermath of the gay liberation movement. In assessing dissident sexualities at the turn of the millenium, Sinfield still addresses the clash between essentialism and constructivism. In particular, he deals with the complexity of trying to adapt gay identity to non-Western societies and cultures; the impact of queer criticism; and finally, the question of bisexuality and other gender/identity adscriptions.[360] This is the sociological and theoretical context of the 'post-gay', one in which "it will not seem so necessary to define, and hence to limit, our sexualities."[361] Sinfield does not discard gay and lesbian movements from the agenda, as queers do, since he believes that any advance in sexual dissidents' rights must start from the achievement made so far. However, he also reminds the reader that "current identities will never account for more than a proportion of the same-sex passion in our society, let alone in other parts of the world."[362] Assuming gender identities are 'essentially' contingent, Sinfield argues that essentialism cannot be obliterated, but used instead as a starting-point for further developments.[363] This standpoint, which critics like Alderson buttress in recent studies (2016), opens the scope of more orthodox

---

[356] Ibid.
[357] Ibid.
[358] Ibid., 45.
[359] Hereafter all references to Alan Hollinghurst's *The Spell* (1999) will be in the text.
[360] Sinfield: *Gay*, 14.
[361] Ibid.
[362] Ibid.
[363] Ibid., 17.

cultural materialists (Penney, 2013; Lewis, 2016) and queer critics (Halberstam, 2005; Esteban Muñoz, 2009), and helps to understand *The Spell* more comprehensibly.

In spite of queer activism, the definition of gender identities is very restrictive in the 'post-gay' era, due to various social and economic factors, especially the strengthening of neoliberal capitalism, which works to standardise and pigeon-hole them.[364] John D'Emilio was a pioneer in the study of the economic origin of gay identity. In his view:

> Industralisation divested the household of its economic independence and fostered the separation of sexuality from procreation. This eventually allowed the space in which men and women, especially of the middle-class, might organize a personal life around their erotic/emotional attraction to their own sex. Socio-economic conditions, therefore, produced the "social space" in which to be lesbian or gay.[365]

Although capitalism paved the way for homosexual identity formation, it also favoured discrimination. This tendency has apparently changed recently, in particular since capitalism has converted gays and lesbians into "targeted consumers," as Sinfield,[366] Alderson[367] and Liggins[368] have pointed out. As Alderson puts it, this commodification of gay lifestyles has contributed to the birth of the queer chic[369] and the diversified dominant.[370] For the first time, gays do not essentially constitute a marginal or oppositional identity, but rather a group of eager consumers. There are critics, like Mark Simpson and Tony Manning, who particularly disregard the identification of gays with consumerism, and "excoriate the mindless uniformity of gay culture."[371] Yet, ignoring the diversity of homosexuals, Simpson describes gay culture as a monolith, marketed and with no transgressive potential in *Anti-gay* (1996). For Alderson, the increasing normalisation/commodification of gayness under capitalism explains "Hollinghurst's rapprochement between past and present, country and city, innocence and experience."[372] Thus, even the reconciliation of Forster and Firbank with contemporary gay identity and politics in *The Spell* would be part of a marketed intergenerational gay homogenisation.[373]

Despite attempts to open gay "spaces to more diverse audiences,"[374] homosexuals have been commodified, targeted, identified and standardised as consumers. In this process, neoliberal capitalism has promoted promiscuity, youth-worship and sex as gay

---

[364] David Alderson: *Sex, Needs & Queer Culture. From Liberation to the Post-Gay*. London 2016.

[365] In Sinfield: *Gay*, 160.

[366] Ibid., 161.

[367] Alderson: *Territories*, 45.

[368] Emma Liggins: "Alan Hollinghurst and Metropolitan Gay Identities". In Daniel Lea and Berthold Schoene (eds). *Posting the Male. Masculinities in Post-War and Cont   emporary British Literature*. London 2003, 159-170.

[369] Alderson: *Territories*, 45.

[370] Alderson: *Sex*, 91.

[371] In Sinfield: *Gay*, 15.

[372] Alderson: *Territories*, 45-46.

[373] Ibid., 45.

[374] Frank Mort: *Cultures of Consumption: Masculinities and Social Space in Late-Twentieth-Century Britain*. London and New York 1996, 177.

labels. Clubs, pubs and saunas have become sites of socialisation but also of control. This (in Sinfield's terms) 'post-gay' scenario frames *The Spell* and the English TV drama *Queer as Folk*, "which also tackles issues of gay men's reliance on metropolitan models of homosexuality."[375] Like Hollinghurst's novels, the TV series celebrates gay promiscuous lifestyle, and particularly the gorgeous, promiscuous and self-confident super-stud. In *Queer as Folk* Stuart Jones fits this type; a tireless cruiser, postmodernist gay *flâneur* and a fantasy figure in the aftermath of AIDS. However, transgression is not forever in Hollinghurst's texts or *Queer as Folk*. Most characters in *The Spell* leave promiscuity behind, starting presumably stable relationships instead. Likewise, in the second series, Stuart starts a relation with teenager Nathan, adapting gay behaviour to heteronormative patterns. *Queer as Folk* thus proves "some of the difficulties of tackling the promiscuity/monogamy issue whilst appealing to a diverse gay audience, a challenge that Hollinghurst takes up in his fiction."[376]

Opposed to Sinfield and Alderson, Tim Edwards has contended that *The Spell* upholds promiscuity.[377] However, it seems to me, this novel represents a step further, or rather, away from the course initiated in *The Swimming-pool Library* and intensified in *The Folding Star*. *The Spell* still deals with same-sex desire, but it lacks (or, at least, moderates) the nostalgic discourse, the bookishness and the gravity of its predecessors. Moreover, as Colm Tóibín argues, Hollinghurst has mistakenly opted for suspense and unexpected twists while his main skill is at creating mood.[378] Therefore, the final result is a novel of mood "written in a minor key [...] and a good example of how serious these risks can be and how slight the rewards [...]. The book is a comedy of manners in which the comedy is rather better than the manners."[379] Instead of a first-person narrator and protagonist, like Beckwith and Manners, a third-person narrator explores the complex relationships between four gay men in contemporary England. Robin Woodfield, a mature architect who has just lost his lover Simon as a consequence of AIDS, has started an affair with Justin, a campy and selfish would-be-actor. Alex, Justin's ex, is a gentle civil servant who falls in love with Robin's son Danny, a reckless and promiscuous youth. Father and son use their spell —hence the title— to take their new partners to their territories, a cottage in Dorset and London's discos respectively.

In the pages that follow, I intend to find out whether *The Spell* is the post-AIDS/gay novel it aims to, celebratory and no longer traumatic. To this end, I will try to establish (or rather expand on) the way in which it differs from its predecessors, and the identity and sexual politics it endorses. Formally, *The Spell* is a fragmented kaleidoscopic text with various characters-focalisers making up a polymorphous reality. In other words, the voice of the (*a priori* conventional) third-person narrator splits to accommodate the perspectives of the characters. Like *The Swimming-pool Library* and *The Folding Star*,

---

[375] Liggins: "Alan," 159.

[376] Ibid., 163.

[377] Tim Edwards: *Erotics and Politics. Gay Male Sexuality, Masculinity and Feminism*. London and New York 1994, 105.

[378] Colm Tóibín: "The Comedy of Being English," *The New York Review of Books*. 52(1) http://www.nybooks.com/articles/17671, 2005, 4.

[379] Ibid.

The Spell also looks back to the canon with irony but never extensively.[380] Some reviewers contend *The Spell* updates Jane Austen's comedies of manners, marrying her "delicious social asperity with a sly eroticism."[381] Thomas Hardy's imaginary England is also a scenario where *The Spell* revives classic romantic comedies. In sum, Hollinghurst's third novel goes on juxtaposing the discourses of past and present, but with significantly different results. It is still tributary to the (gay) literary tradition, but it keeps enlarging the scope of hypotexts well beyond same-sex desire.

3.1   The novel's structuring of identity

Like its predecessors, *The Spell* proves the difficulty of literature to gain access to (gay) reality. If literary representation is precarious and gay identity is also a matter of debate, finding adequate patterns of queer representation is extraordinarily difficult. Indeed, the question remains whether gayness is an essential trait or a textual effect in Hollinghurst's fiction. As Georges Letissier points out, the writer "draws a subtle distinction between the 'gay novel', in which the homosexual condition and male fellowship are given prominence, and the 'homosexualisation of the novel': an attempt to aestheticise fiction so that it escapes the normative claims of morality."[382] Letissier concludes that Hollinghurst's novels assume an "essentialist approach to gender," thus relinquishing the fluidity of androgyny extolled [for example] by Virginia Woolf.[383] That his characters take their sexual identity for granted apparently proves Letissier's hypothesis. However, the intertextual and autoreferential-narcissistic language and character of the novels these characters inhabit and/or narrate shapes their identity. They are gay because they use camp talk and citationality, they reflect on their own imagery and have "a queer take on 'authentic' and 'represented' utterance" (Harvey, 2002). Gay identity is as essential as well as a construct in *The Spell*, an architectural structure.

Like its predecessors, *The Spell* follows a strict, pre-established pattern, as the writer himself acknowledged.[384] It is his shortest novel, which explains the sketchiness of the plot. As concerns its methodology, Hollinghurst considers *The Spell* as a self-begetting novel because "the form of the book grows much more naturally out of the material; for it must be a study of people and their relations to each other. [...] Things are discovered *en route*."[385] It follows a neat structure, being divided into sixteen chapters, articulated around, and focalised by, four characters in an *a priori* perfect arithmetic. As Hollinghurst points out, we first learn about Robin and his predicaments, and are later introduced to other characters and their perspectives. The effect Hollinghurst firstly intended was that of a refrain-repeating *rondeau*, "with Robin as the first subject" and

---

[380]   Canning: *Conversations*, 346.
[381]   Anon. "Reviews of *The Spell*." http://search.barnesandoble.com/booksearch/isbnInquiry.asp?z =y&EAN=978014028.
[382]   Georges Letissier: "Queer, quaint and camp: Alan Hollinghurst's Own Return to the English Tradition." *Études Anglaises Contemporaines* 60(2) 2007, 198.
[383]   Ibid., 210.
[384]   In Canning: *Conversations*, 333.
[385]   Ibid., 334.

the novel's structure taking the form of "A-B-A-C-A; then Robin's displaced."[386] However, he soon discarded the pattern fearing that reviewers would label it a "ruined rondo of a novel."[387] If the dual narcissism of *The Swimming-pool Library* and the triptych-like structure of *The Folding Star* are conspicuous, the architecture of *The Spell* goes a step further, being arranged as a flawed quadrangle. Indeed, as Nantwich's failed endeavour to repair gay history and Echevin's attempt to assemble Orst's masterpiece, the *rondeau* is doomed to break down.

Besides the quadrangle, the novel features other arrangements. Each chapter has a focal character that attracts the attention of the narrator so that the final effect is a dancing circle with four participants. However, these four characters interact in triangles that complement the overall composition. Robin and Alex are the pivoting vortices in the two main triangles of the novel, being focal characters in more episodes than either Justin or Danny.[388] Justin is the third vortex of the first triangle. The three form a new Girardian triangle, Robin and Alex exchanging Justin as females are in classic homosocial bonds. This triangle is at the core of the novel's quadrangle. In fact, Danny eventually plays the odd one out, leaving the *rondeau* at the end of the novel. As the second main triangle is concerned, it is precisely Danny who becomes the third vortex together with his new lover, Alex, and his father. This triangle is a breakthrough, remodelling father-son relations and the narratives of pedagogical eros, being the youth who mentors the older one. Moreover, Danny not only problematises his role as son and unlikely master, but the roles and interaction between his father and his lover. Surrounding the main triangles, there are similar incidental arrangements in which the characters interact as in circular dances drawing on stereotypes of post-gay promiscuity: Danny-Terry-George, Justin-Terry-Robin, Danny-Alex-Nick, Justin-Gary-Danny to name some of them. Jeanette Winterson's *Gut Symmetries* follows a similar arrangement. As Susana Onega argues, the story of the three protagonists constitutes the basic circular pattern which is repeated in Winterson's "textual macrocosm at large."[389] Onega makes use of the theory of fractals to reach this conclusion:

> Like the measurement of subatomic particles in quantum physics, the composition of this 2+1 triangle is rather unstable, yielding different compositions according to the perspective of the observer; Jove and Stella+Alice, Jove and Alice+Stella; Alice and Stella+Jove. The love triangles formed by the members of the earlier generation allow for similar arrangements [...]. This variability introduces an element of randomness in the 'symmetrical' multiplication of the triangles that brings to mind the multiplication of fractals in dynamic models like the 'zooming Sierpinski [...] or, more appositely, the 'dancing triangles', whose elements move in spirals.[390]

Like the triangles of *Gut Symmetries*, the ones of *The Spell* alternate with a difference, displacing one element each time. These lesbian and gay *rondeaux* draw on Arthur Schnitzler's play *Die Ronde* (1897), which Max Ophuls adapted in his film *La Ronde*

[386] Ibid.
[387] Ibid., 335.
[388] Ibid., 343.
[389] Onega: *Jeanette*, 181.
[390] Ibid., 180.

(1950). Like *The Spell*, Ophuls's film bears an "acid and melancholic view whereby love and passion do not concur, their differences causing dissatisfaction. Indeed, due to lack of love or passion, all characters find reward through impossible relations."[391] Yet, *The Spell* eludes the nihilism of Schnitzler's and Ophuls's to apparently celebrate gayness in three moments that structure the novel; Alex's first visit to the disco, Danny's birthday party and the final scene, with four characters on the cliffs. Fractals, triangles or rondeaux, *The Spell* is about structures, literary as well as architectural. Allan Johnson delves into architectural imagination and its connection with Ecstasy. Johnson's point is foremost, Robin being an architect and his son a drug-user. In their visit to an old house Robin is to refurbish, the narrator recalls that the building "was an attempt to realise the architectural phantasmagoria of an opium dream" (Hollinghurst 1999: 58). However, the connection of architecture and drugs works as a symptom of the contradictory discourses of Hollinghurst's characters, celebratory and traumatic, conservative and radical.

3.2   Architecture, nature and the symbolism of lines

The Spell keeps on Hollinghurst's interest in architecture, Robin Woodfield himself being an architect. The first chapter, a homodiegetic analepsis —in Genette's terms—, frames the story and features the hero in his early twenties while writing his PhD in America. In the course of his research, he finds a "rough piece of sanitary porcelain [...] with the letters SEMPE on it, perhaps a part of SEMPER, forever" (Hollinghurst, 1999: 4). Apparently irrelevant, this piece which Robin keeps at Litton Gambril is highly symbolic. In *The Spell*'s gay world, nothing is definitely closed, but overt. The concept of time is particularly relative in a context where life and relationships are ephemeral. Nothing is forever, as the anonymous epigraph of *The Spell* reads, "happy the heart that thinks of no removes" (1). It is also in this analepsis that Robin learns he is going to be a father (12). In the present of the novel, Robin is in his forties and makes a living as an architect specialised in the reconstruction of old English mansions and manor houses. Robin's job sets connecting lines between past and present, space and time, drawing on British revivalism (Samuel, 1994). Yet, being a gay in a 'post-gay' novel, he sheds light on paradigmatically gay narratives, drawing links between gayness, architecture and Ecstasy. Though Allan Johnson has already addressed this last triple connection, I will focus on its implications on Hollinghurst's celebratory and traumatic discourses.

Tytherbury, the impressive house of Tony Bowerchalke, stands out among the rest. Pesvner (1902-1983), the art historian who wrote the most influential history of English architecture, scorns the appearance of the house (Hollinghurst, 1999: 56). Pesvner is also mentioned in *The Swimming-pool Library* (1998a: 129) and *The Line of Beauty* (Hollinghurst 2004: 48), thus connecting architectural lines through Hollinghurst's fiction. Will Beckwith uses his copy of *Buildings of England* in his visit to an old castle near Winchester, previously visited by Nantwich (Hollinghurst, 1998a: 129). In *The Line of Beauty*, Nick reads Pevsner's humorous comment on Lord Kessler's château

---

[391] Anon: "Críticas film 'La Ronda' (1950)." http://www.filmaffinity.com/es/reviews/1/548137.html, 2008, my translation.

(2004: 48). In the three cases, Pesvner's irony targets the eclecticism, syncretism and "the mixed effect applied also to the mingling of past and present"[392] of three English monuments, enhancing Hollinghurst's ironic tone. Still, Bowerchalke's mansion becomes a symbolic scenario. Like Nantwich's and Orst's houses, this château reconciles present and past, as gay generations meet. The far-off Victorianism of the owner and the turn-of-the-millenium gayness of Danny meet at Tytherbury (Hollinghurst, 1999: 53). Generational differences apart, both characters are gay and belong to the local gentry, like Will-Nantwich-Firbank in *The Swimming-pool Library*, and Manners-Sir Perry Dewlish in *The Folding Star*. Tony Bowerchalke shared the world of Woodfields' ancestors, having once met Danny's grandfather, General Woodfield (54). Whereas Tony is the recipient of anecdotes of the local aristocracy, his mansion constitutes the architectural testimony of a social group fated to extinction.

The most outstanding element of the architectural complex is the Mausoleum, a rarity comparable to Nantwich's cellar, or Orst's mysterious villa Hermes. The Mausoleum, constructed by Thomas Light Bowerchalke, Tony's grandfather, is pyramidal in shape. Despite its decrepit state, the pyramid still produced "its monumental effect" (56). A piece of artistic syncretism, the pyramid is reminiscent of Nantwich's three-faced, Egyptian stele. The mask on top features "a Roman face [...] vandalised into noseless Egyptian flatness" (56), which echoes both the noseless pharaohs and Will's broken nose in *The Swimming-pool Library*. Above the mask, a mysterious inscription in Greek seems codified for all except for Tony (57), as the cryptic messages at Orst's mysterious villa and Nantwich's treasures are only intelligible for both men. Also, Tony's house symbolises the unaccomplished gay work, the piece which cannot be integrated (178). The whole complex stands for in-completeness, a liminal area Hollinghurst's novels address regularly, which defies temporal and special parametres. Allan Johnson explores the complex interaction between time and space in *The Spell*. He does it from the symbolic relation between architecture and drug-consumption in Victorian and nineties gay subcultures. For Tony Bowerchalke, the pyramid was perhaps the "architectural phantasmagoria of an opium dream" (58). The altered states of mind, particularly opium-induced daydreams, have been recurrent in romantic literature, Thomas de Quincey being a paradigmatic example, and fin-de-siècle decadentism. Drawing on Sedgwick, Johnson says of *The Picture of Dorian Gray* it is "an opium narrative that powerfully and playfully correlates [...] the addict and the homosexual" (99). There are several issues worth noting on Johnson's analysis. Firstly, the link between "drug-taking and narrative influence, and between the psychochemical effects of drug use and architectural space" (97); also, drawing on Bloom's idea that opium use "is construed on the language of Freudian fetish" and fosters instead a repetition compulsion, Bloom considers it un-Romantic, for echoic return makes originality unfeasible. Indeed, being under the spell, hence the title of the novel, is akin to be under the influence, and "to narrate is to influence;"[393] finally, Johnson makes a difference between opium daydreaming, which he represents as a buried temple, and Ecstasy use, as an open plane. Johnson places the clash between both metaphors in Bowerchalke's house, which echoes "the castles and

---

[392] Peter Ackroyd: *Albion. The Origins of the English Imagination*. London 2002, 235.
[393] In Johnson: *Alan*, 98, 100.

fortresses to be captured by [opium-induced] poets" and the open spaces gay current culture, especially raves, represent. The imagery of Ecstasy-induced gays on the dancing floor draws on Sadie Plant's conception of this drug to "unpick knotty tangles of problems."[394] However, *The Spell* is a rather nuanced text and this black-or-white reading does not apply. Johnson himself finally argues that both images, buried temple and open plane, "converge in the modern club scene." [395] This convergence of 'opposites' is, however, already conspicuous in the characters' visit to Tony's Mausoleum and particularly so in Alex's encounter with the narratives of Danny's Ecstasy culture. This poetics of celebration of the post-gay is just part of the story. As will be shown later, it all has a traumatic underside that problematises transgenerational architecture.

The Spell has an architectural pattern itself. Divided into sixteen chapters, focalised in their turn by four characters, the novel is split into two contrasting halves in chapter ten. Roughly in the middle of *The Spell*, there is an intertextual reference which constitutes a turning-point. Mrs Hall, a neighbour at Litton Gambril, recalls Shakespeare's *A Midsummer Night's Dream* (Hollinghurst 1999: 122) to describe Danny's birthday, the central saturnalia of *The Spell*.[396] Drawing on Shakespeare's play, along the episode, the relations between the protagonists are reorganised. The relationship between Justin and Robin apparently breaks down at the party. Likewise, Alex and Danny's affair shows signs of a crisis.

The architectural arrangement of Hollinghurst's novels, which deeply affects their narratives and plots, relies on a complex web of lines, which Letissier calls "curved lines of continuity."[397] Although the symbolism of lines, particularly Hogarth's "line of beauty," is especially relevant in Hollinghurst's fourth novel, it is already present in his previous ones. By lines I make reference to a number of patterns, normally symbolic — in reference to gay identity continuum— and occasionally literal —roads or buildings, and male bodies—, that connect discourses, characters and events within his novels, between his novels and between these and the canon. They are somehow related to Johnson's visual images and Hollinghurst's fascination with "rebuilding and renewing a particular vision of history" (3). However, rather than continuity, my reading focuses on disruptions, the short-circuited narratives which are a symptom of the traumatic underside to the celebratory narratives addressed so far. Hence, the lines I propose complement Letissier's. In his view, lines "are used as a special metaphor for lineage"[398] of gay narratives, which is precarious since "Hollinghurst establishes the impossibility of drawing a straight line of kinship between gay men of different generations."[399] Lines in *The Spell* address heteronormative restrictions that characters try to avoid. After visiting Tytherbury, a reckless Robin starts off-road driving, a metaphor of sexual dissidence since "road driving seemed rule-bound and processional" (Hollinghurst, 1999: 62). Robin's Arcadia features open planes, a limitless territory

---

[394] Ibid., 106, 104.
[395] Ibid., 109.
[396] Stella Tillyard: "Interview, Alan Hollinghurst." *Prospect London* 116, 2005: 62.
[397] Letissier: "Queer," 199.
[398] Ibid., 201.
[399] Ibid., 202.

without straight roads to follow. The symbolism of roads, as lines with a meaning, recurs Alex's flashback to the end of the eighties. It is then that he chose an alternative, "gay line" to most people. In the middle of a traffic jam of party-goers, he realises his missing opportunities (115).

3.3   Focalisation, or the ethics of the lines of attention

The shift to a third-person narration in *The Spell* brings about changes in tone, scope and ending. Although the point of view of this novel has been regarded as "omniscient,"[400] Hollinghurst himself discards this label, arguing that his model was Henry James' *The Awkward Age*:[401]

> The idea [was] that each chapter would be seen from the viewpoint of a different character in a changing pattern; that these different viewpoints would illuminate a rather amorphous subject, but there wouldn't be one controlling point of view. Each position would be ironized by the ones that flanked it. That came to necessitate a sort of stylistic change in my writing too. [...] I found myself in *The Spell* writing in a much more spare, detached way [than in The *Folding Star*].[402]

In keeping with this, the story is told by an extradiegetic narrator and focalised alternatively by one of the four protagonists. That each chapter has a focaliser highlights both the novel's subjective and precarious access to reality and the ethics of attention. The fact that the external narrator mostly views through internal focalisers makes his self-imposed limitation of knowledge more programmatic than functional, as in Genette's "variable focalisation."[403] Thus, echoing the key-hole Proustian narration of *The Folding Star*, the restricted internal focalisation in *The Spell*, whereby partial (often minor) details are spotted, challenges narrative hierarchy. Moreover, in paying attention to marginal aspects and to marginal ways of attention, especially Ecstasy-induced, the novel implements a particularly ethical narrative of attention. Socially-irrelevant gay lives are thus given a space; buried or open is yet to decide.

The first analeptic chapter, focalised through Robin's eyes twenty years before the rest of the story and in a different continent, is set as a preamble to the story of the Woodfields, particularly Robin's early fatherhood (Hollinghurst, 1999: 12). Back to the present, Alex focalises the second chapter, mostly narrated in free indirect discourse. His eyes feature Robin and Justin's Dorset home (31-32), approaching Justin from behind (33), seeing a photograph of Robin and gazing an unknown youth, who happens to be Danny (28). In the third chapter, a new analepsis, the narrator recalls Robin's memories of his earlier lover, Simon, and his simultaneous affair with a youth who happens to be Justin (59). Through this analepsis, Justin, we learn, was then living with Alex, a civil servant in the Foreign Affairs office (59), Robin has not met yet (65).

---

[400]   Anon: "Penguin Reviews," n.p.
[401]   In Canning: *Conversations*, 332.
[402]   Ibid., 332-333.
[403]   Gérard Genette: *Narrative Discourse: An Essay in Method*, trans. Jane E. Levin. Ithaca 1980, 189.

Drawing on keyhole narration, Robin starts watching Justin who is having yet a third affair with Gary, a black guy (64) who reappears as a rent boy and friend of Danny's (180). The fourth chapter introduces Justin's camp perspective in the story (70). His shrewd outlook addresses the reader's attention to every nuance, gesture, intentionality in the quartet of protagonists (71-72), from Robin's competitive nature to Alex's involuntary search of Danny's eyes (74). Appearances prove to be deceptive, though, each character and the narrator himself only having access to a fragment of the story. The fifth chapter, mostly focalised through Robin, coincides with the symbolic visit to Tytherbury and its Mausoleum. I say symbolic because, Robin notices, there is "a brief silence of readjustment among the group" (58). This first rearrangement only foreshadows new ones; as the one Danny bears witness to later on: "The four of them set out through the village [...] pairing up in different ways" (225). In chapter six, Alex claims to be "the only watcher" (64), and through him the first signs of exhaustion of his affair are visible (66). Their imminent break-up is rather Alex's 'coming-out'. Though drawing on coming-out *Bildungromane* of the seventies, Alex inaugurates a new type. A Forsterian gay character, he 'comes out' anew, this time to the standardised gay identity of late-capitalism. Thus, Alex passes from the opium-induced buried temple, if at all, to the open plane of Ecstasy and house music (71).

The love affair of Danny and Alex comes to an end in the penultimate chapter. The fact that Danny is the focaliser is, as Hollinghurst himself argues, a wise move.[404] Attention to minor details only forecasts the youth's plan to leave Alex at Litton Gambril, with Justin and Robin as witnesses. Most of the chapter reproduces Danny's mental processes trying to convince himself that their relationship is futile. The gap between both increases when working-class hunk Terry meets them at the beach: the triangle —Danny-Terry-Alex—, like the quadrangle above, cannot hold much longer. Finally, Danny focalises and controls the whole scene, putting an end to his love affair rather subtly announcing he is leaving to the States (Hollinghurst 1999: 233).

The last chapter, focalised by Alex, is a reaction to Danny's focalisation. After his thwarted second coming-out, Alex comes to understand his new role. He intends to reconcile his romantic Oxford years with Nick (240) with Danny's teaching. His individuation process comes to an end very graphically, as if taking the lift from the buried temple to the open plane and back. It is then that he feels "he had just paid a visit to a remote suburb of himself" (248). For the first time, Alex not only focalises, but controls the situation. He becomes the higher vortex in a homoerotic triangle with Justin and Robin, thus reversing the one in the second chapter (253). Put together, the *rondeau* of focalisers serves two purposes: to emphasise the testimonial character of history and the exchangeability of gays in the 'post-gay'. The picture they draw of the nineteen nineties is multifaceted and unstable, never reliable since it depends on the perspective of the focaliser and the point of view of the narrator who filters the information. Moreover, the alternation of focalisers renders the polyhedricity of gay experience and how it is regulated and homogenised.

The alternation of perspectives shaping the structure and chapter-division of *The Spell* recalls again Jeanette Winterson's *Art & Lies* (1994). In her analysis of Winterson's novel, Susana Onega points out: "The multiplication of narrative voices

---

[404] In Canning: *Conversations*, 334.

and perspectives is echoed structurally by the novel's division into eight chapters entitled after the three main protagonists in a sequence of repetitions and inversions (Handel, Picasso, Sappho; Picasso, Handel, Sappho; Picasso, Handel) that suggests both temporal circularity and the complementarity of the characters' life stories."[405] The characters' perspectives rendered by the extradiegetic narrator of *The Spell* complement each other, as the points of view of Sappho, Picasso, Handel and the Bawd do in *Art & Lies*. Onega also argues that these characters' narrations are not "linear and univocal, but rather fragmentary, repetitive and even sometimes contradictory,"[406] and hence "the narrative structure of the novel as a whole may be said to move in ever-closer spirals from dispersion to unification, reaching a climax at the end of the novel."[407] As Mónica Calvo argues, the incompleteness of the spiral is particularly useful as a correlate of lesbians' perception of identity as "diffused and disintegrating."[408] This spiral pattern in Winterson's and other lesbian texts is also used (or inspires similar ones) in gay and Holocaust texts, Claude Lanzman's film *Shoah* being a case in point.[409] Likewise, *The Spell*'s *rondeau* is not a linear or circular pattern, but an open-ended spiral "recoiling upon itself […] in a succession of forays,"[410] which recalls the multiplication of fractals in the "zooming Sierpinnski," recurrent in Hollinghurst's fiction. In the end, the apparently flawless quartet fails when Danny leaves and is replaced by a new character.

The end of *The Spell* remains open. Its final scene, with four men by the edge of a cliff, recalls particularly the end of *The Folding Star*, with Edward scrutinising the horizon at the North Sea vainly searching for Luc. However, Hollinghurst intended *The Spell* to be a sort of therapeutic 'reproach' to the inexorability and fatalism of *The Folding Star*.[411] From its very inception, *The Spell* was to deal with pleasure, which made a happy ending mandatory.[412] However, the novel fails to do so. As Stella Tillyard argues, being Hollinghurst's "sunniest book, AIDS is a penumbral presence."[413] Its ending also recalls *Arts & Lies* and, by extension, the closures of other novels by lesbian and gay writers. In her analysis of Winterson's novel, Onega makes reference to Virginia Woolf's *The Waves* and Richard Strauss' camp opera *The Rosenkavalier*. As she argues, both adopt the motif of the multifoliate rose, a symbol of transcendental unity in Western culture from Dante to Yeats and Eliot.[414] In *Arts & Lies* the motif materialises in a camp scene "with Handel and 'the two women standing together' at the cliffhead, sharing a vision of the World of Art they have just entered" (147).[415] This final reconciliation of fragmented identities, also present in the endings of most of

---

[405] Onega: *Jeanette*, 134.
[406] Ibid.
[407] Ibid.
[408] In ibid., 31.
[409] Saul Friedländer: *Memory, History, and the Extermination of the Jews in Europe.* Bloomington 1993, 121.
[410] Ibid., 121-122.
[411] In Canning: *Conversations*, 338.
[412] Ibid., 338-339.
[413] Tillyard: "Interview," 62.
[414] Onega: *Jeanette*, 146.
[415] Ibid., 147.

Ackroyd's novels,[416] is tellingly similar to that between the characters of *The Spell*. Robin, Justin, Alex and his new boyfriend, Nick, stand close to a cliff looking at the sea (Hollinghurst, 1999: 256-257). The scene places the new quartet together in a rather forced happy ending with obvious ironic undertones. In fact, a few lines above, Alex himself confesses his hatred for Robin whereas Justin is allegedly no longer bitchy. Though the novel attempts reconciliation, it remains an ironic gesture, overtly acknowledging and rejecting the serious attempt of Ackroyd and Winterson to procure their characters a sort of "the transpersonal identity with the writers and artists of the past in a sublime World of Art."[417]

The defective quadrangular pattern of *The Spell* replaces (or rather complements) the dualistic and tripartite structures of *The Swimming-pool Library* and *The Folding Star*. This basic structure is further complicated by the various (re)arrangements of the characters in love triangles and narcissitic specular reflections (144, 161-62, 180-81, 201, 234), which articulate the identitarian discourse of the novel. The shift from first-person autodiegetic narration in the first two novels to extradiegetic narration with variable focalisation of *The Spell* brings about a comprehensive representation of gay realities[418] and a 'post-issue-feel'.

3.4   *The Spell* as an intertextual novel

Hollinghurst himself has pointed out that his third novel is not as self-conscious in terms of literary analogues as his previous ones.[419] He only acknowledges having deliberately planned an "odd joke about Thomas Hardy."[420] Thus, though he does not rule out other literary influences and intertexts, he claims intertextual references to Hardy, Shakespeare and Austen that critics consider unpurposeful.[421] For Colm Tóibín, Hardy is invoked as a tutelary spirit.[422] Only alluded to occasionally, the rural scenario of *The Spell* is inspired by the rolling hills of Hardy's imaginary Wessex. To Carmen Callil, however, Austen is the presiding spirit. Hollinghurst himself recalls Callil's "brilliantly detailed analogy of how *The Spell* is like [Austen's comedies of manners] *Emma* or *Sense and Sensibility*. When characters go to the club, it's like going to London or Bath; both books play with the ambiguous merits of village society, and so on."[423] However, though Hollinghurst admits his indebtedness to Austen and to "that tradition at some level," he considers "the whole procedure of [his] book is so different."[424] In my view, the differences he alludes to regard sexual explicitness rather than point of view and intertextuality.

---

[416] Susana Onega: *Peter Ackroyd*. Plymouth 1998, 46-47; Susana Onega: *Metafiction and Myth in the Novels of Peter Ackroyd*. Rochester 1999, 73, 129-130.
[417] Onega: *Jeanette*, 147.
[418] In Canning: *Conversations*, 334.
[419] Ibid., 346.
[420] Ibid.
[421] Ibid.
[422] Tóibín: "Comedy," 5.
[423] In Canning: *Conversations*, 346.
[424] Ibid.

Though not a bookish novel, *The Spell* is intertextually packed at the generic level. An English pastoral for Tillyard,[425] it draws on two conflicting genres or traditions, namely (Elizabethan) romantic comedy and the comedy of manners. Being the heterosexual genre *par excellence*, romantic comedy seems a priori foreign territory for *The Spell*. Comedy of manners looks a much more natural scenario for gay performance. Eventually, the convergence of both types of comedy explains the ambivalence of Hollinghurst's third novel. Roughly speaking, the differences between each genre date back to ancient Greece. 'Old comedy' follows a dialectical pattern, whereas Menander's "new comedy" has a teleological scope. That is, while the main characteristic of Aristophanic comedy is conflict, or *agon*, the main trait of 'new comedy' is the purposefulness of the plot and its happy resolution. As concerns the English stage, *The Spell* echoes Ben Jonson's 'comedy of humours', via Joe Orton, and Shakespeare's romantic comedies.

Romantic comedies consider matrimony the natural outcome of love and the formula to reassure Greek *diké* or order. In Virginia Wright's view, the compulsory identification of love and marriage is both conservative and contradictory. Yet, as Peter Evans and Celestino Deleyto recall, Wright's analysis of love and matrimony in Hollywood cinema brings to the fore a contradiction between "romantic love as an intense, all-consuming passion that is by its nature short-lived and its status in the modern world as the cornerstone of lifelong monogamous marriage." [426] The genre solves this contradiction making the happy ending coincide with marriage so that passion is frozen in an unproblematic present moment.[427] Although the genre still relies on Shakespeare's formula, synthesised by Salingar as "a process of discovery of a new identity through the vicissitudes of erotic attraction and courtship between lovers,"[428] new elements have been incorporated and identity has been progressively sexualised. As Evans and Deleyto explain, in contemporary versions of romantic comedy, sex has been separated from the sphere of love and marriage and has acquired a self-sufficient status as provider of pleasure. Besides this conflict between love and sex, Evans and Deleyto analyse the relation of both concepts with marriage as an institution in crisis.[429] As they argue, the impact of the feminist and gay/queer liberation movements has had a remarkable effect on social change and, consequently, on romantic comedies. Feminists have denounced marriage as a formula for male domination, whereas gays and lesbians have pointed out how they have been excluded from this and other heterosexual institutions. Hence, in order to survive, the genre was adapted to meet the requirements of these minorities. If it is true that heterosexual love still prevails, subversive messages arise: women's interest in public life, gays' alternative couplings, or even new heterosexual formulas of love/erotic affiliation, to name just a few.

---

[425] Tillyard: "Interview," 62.
[426] Peter Evans, and Celestino Deleyto (eds). *Terms of Endearment. Hollywood Romantic Comedy of the 1980s and 1990s*. Edinburgh 1998, 5.
[427] Ibid., 6.
[428] In Ibid., 3.
[429] Ibid., 7.

The Spell is split in two by Mrs Hall's allusion to Shakespeare's *A Midsummer Night's Dream* (Hollinghurst, 1999: 122). Likewise, Stella Tillyard contends that *The Spell* is an English pastoral, whose "model is not just any old pastoral, but the most famous of all, *A Midsummer Night's Dream*."[430] Also, Hollinghurst himself argues that the novel was supposed "to have some of the elements of Shakespearian romantic comedy. In it, there'd be an older man, but essentially people would be young, attractive, and getting in a muddle."[431] *The Spell* subverts the principles of the genre, replacing (heterosexual) marriage with gay precarious re-couplings. Even Shakespeare's gender-ambiguous plays that feature men playing female roles impersonating boys attracting females — e.g. *Twelfth Night*— eventually finish in heterosexual marriages.

The action of *A Midsummer Night's Dream* unfolds in two parallel ontological levels: the wood, a fantastic fairy world, and the city, the 'real' world of human beings. It all begins with the quarrel between Oberon and Titania, the King and Queen of the fairies, for an Indian boy. In the human realm, conflict also starts when Hermia challenges her father's choice of Demetrius as her husband. Being in love with Lysander, Hermia challenges the rule of the father, and flees to the wood with her lover. The wood thus becomes a carnivalesque scenario where irrational love can triumph, at least before marriage. This middle section deals with sexual love, here associated with women's —particularly Hermia's— desire, against civilisation. Though threatening, the wood is necessary because it brings catharsis by means of fantasy. Indeed, temporary freedom is but a strategy of containment Power enforces. A period of controlled disorder or Bakhtinian carnival is a safety valve for society to keep within its limits (Greenblatt, 1992). Despite Greenblatt's regarding Shakespeare's plays as complicit with power, they show signs of genuine subversion Hollinghurst benefits from. Although the female characters of *A Midsummer Night's Dream* are eventually forced into patriarchy, the important middle section explores their sexuality. In the wood, Oberon's magic potion changes the erotic affiliations between the young lovers. Demetrius does not despise Helena any more, whereas Lysander violently rejects his former lover, Hermia, falling in love with Helena. Everything reversed, males prove to be fickle and Helena and Hermia coherent instead. The carnival finished, the play restores order in rather masochistic terms. Hermia's dream,[432] in which she asks indifferent Lysander (still in love with Helena under the effect of the love juice) to rescue her from a devouring serpent, is a case in point. During the second scene of the Third Act, confusion and masochism between lovers reaches its climax, with Lysander repudiating Hermia. Titania also drinks the love potion, thus sleeping with Bottom disguised as an ass.[433] Hence, the sexual excess of the queen of fairies is punished and exposed. When the effects of the liquor in the wood come to an end, the 'monstrosities' which they have given rise to have to be dispelled. Female sexuality has been constructed as the abject (Kristeva, 1982) to be subdued. Being a conflictive space between conservative and subversive forces, excess and containment, the central section

---

[430] Tillyard: "Interview," 62.

[431] In Canning: *Conversations*, 341.

[432] William Shakespeare: *Four Comedies. The Taming of the Shrew, A Midsummer Night's Dream, As You Like It, Twelfth Night*. London 1994, II, ii, 151-162.

[433] Ibid., III, i, 122-196.

of *A Midsummer Night's Dream* proves to be a sound hypotext for the ambivalent chapter 10 of *The Spell*.

The action in this chapter turns around Danny's 23rd birthday party, a comic saturnalia during the summer solstice, which updates the midsummer night's dream of Shakespeare's characters. I do not mean that *The Spell* is a romantic comedy *strictu sensu*; it just uses one of them to revise the genre. As happens in Shakespeare's comedy, the whole *status quo* is overturned along Danny's midsummer night bacchanalia at Robin's in Litton Gambril. In both play and novel, the difficult relations between father and his offspring are central. Hermia escapes the law of her father, Egeus, and The Father, Theseus, followed by her lover, her suitor and a female friend. In *The Spell*, although Robin is a gay father who organises a party for his gay son —a token of the novel's subversiveness from the outset— he still censors Danny's erotic affiliations, like the hampering fathers of classic comedies. The architect dislikes Danny's flirt George, who, like Wilde's Lord Henry Wotton, attracts, 'instructs' and mistreats youths (Hollinghurst, 1999: 122, 117). Robin's watchful attitude characteristic of the *senex iratus* in classic comedy becomes ironic in his case. Overtly gay and drug-consumer (120), he has no legitimacy to hinder Danny's way of life. His censorious discourse is a parody both of the stereotype he updates and of himself as gay in the post-gay.

Like the wood of *A Midsummer Night's Dream*, the party at Robin's breaks with the novel's 'realistic' ontology. As Tillyard argues,[434] if Oberon's love juice triggers confusion in the lovers, in *The Spell*, drugs and alcohol distort so-called reality. Danny avows that his first experience with drugs in high school was a turning-point in his individuation process (Hollinghurst 1999: 120). Through the party, drug-induced breakage of ontologies fosters the characters' promiscuous interaction. Danny teaches Alex how to snort a line (125); Robin and Lars, Danny's Norwegian ex-boyfriend, flirt while taking some hash, which derives in a "stealthy twist to his thoughts and sense impressions" (132). Robin's focalisation bears witness to the blurring of perceptivity and a new feel of vividness (134). There is a difference, though, between the magic potion that solves the characters' problems in *A Midsummer Night's Dream*, and Danny's party, which sparks off troubles and problematises the foursome stability.

After the Saturnalia, the relation of Justin and Robin goes through a crisis, and Alex and Danny's incipient relationship shows signs of exhaustion. *A Midsummer Night's Dream* is a (heterosexual) romantic comedy and, although love does not always run smooth, it closes in marriage. The novel finishes instead with two couples of handsome, middle-aged bourgeois homosexuals —a rather stereotypical lot— at the edge of a cliff (256-257). This leaves *The Spell*'s sexual *rondeau* overt, in diametrical opposition to the strict closure of classic romantic comedy. Indeed, this happy ending, planned by Hollinghurst from the very beginning, looks unconvincing and rather forced. It is the campy irony of the novel (part of Hollinghurst's subversive programmatic puspose) that explains a scene like this is but a parody of romantic comedy happy endings. How could otherwise bitchy Justin become a romantic lover, or Robin's dislike of Alex turn into empathy all of a sudden?

The country is no longer an Arcadian retreat from the urban/real world. Indeed, mass-marketed urban gayness reduced to "metropolitan muscle and glamour" (122), has

---

[434] Tillyard: "Interview," 62.

finally engulfed the rural myth. Robin prefers Terry Badgett, a sort of Alec Scudder, rather than the city boys (121). Yet, in the end, as Alderson points out, Terry is "a rent boy, rather than a representative of spontaneity,"[435] and Litton Gambril is "characterised by Middle England intolerance."[436] In other words, *Maurice*'s 'greenwood' has turned into a homophobic territory. The Halls are the only neighbours at Litton Gambril who keep on with Robin after his former lover's death of AIDS. Discrimination increases after the party, when residents make formal complaints about the noise, which, as Justin significantly puts it, was annoying because "it was homosexual noise" (Hollinghurst, 1999: 156). For the first time in Hollinghurst's fiction, characters must face the fact that homosexuality may be natural for them, but not necessarily for society at large. This is so because *The Spell* opens the scope of intradiegetic narration in previous novels to others' viewpoints. As if firstly conscious of homophobia, Danny avows "he was so conditioned to a world in which everyone was gay that he found it hard to bear in mind, down here, a hundred miles from London, that almost everyone wasn't" (213). Unlike the forest of *A Midsummer Night's Dream*, Beckwith's swimming-pool and Manners' Rough Common, Litton Gambril is just what it seems, a suburban, homophobic area. Therefore, unlike in classic romantic comedy, the characters of *The Spell* remain alienated and isolated from social codes. They may be assimilated as consumers rather than citizens. Yet, in the end, equality proves casual and the characters are excluded from institutions they can only parody. Thus, whereas older characters are left at the end of the novel looking at the horizon in couples, the youths, Danny and Terry, leave the round. The regenerative logic which informed classic comedy, whereby the old generation was replaced by the new, is upturned by a textual *rondeau*.

While some reviewers have stressed the influence of romantic comedy on *The Spell*, others, like Colm Tóibín, underline its indebtedness to the comedy of manners. "The comedy" in Hollinghurst's text, Tóibín says, "is rather better than the manners."[437] Traditionally, the comedy of manners celebrates and focuses on marital crisis, the Aristophanic *agon*, the dialectic rather than teleological. Being particularly interested in conflict, *The Spell* draws on the comedy of manners. Often related to Restoration comedy main traits, "marriage and sexual intrigue, with their corollaries, adultery and divorce,"[438] the impact of comedy of manners has clearly transcended its origins to become a neatly English literary genre. Indeed, "only in England has there been a continual development of comedy of manners."[439] Being sex and money, wit and intrigue the chief concerns of the genre, it is no wonder it has been indicted for immorality. In fact, as Hirst notes, "the winners are always those with the most style: The sharpest wits, the subtlest intriguers."[440] Many of Hollinghurst's heroes fit in this rake model the writer recasts to the turn-of-the-millenium post-gay.

---

[435] Alderson: *Territories*, 44.
[436] Ibid.
[437] Tóibín: "Comedy," 4.
[438] David L. Hirst: *Comedy of Manners*. London 1979, 7-8.
[439] Ibid., 4.
[440] Ibid., 2.

For Hirst, comedy of manners is "closely related to the social conditions of the time."[441] In particular, the genre has flourished whenever style and camp (which Sontag identified with homosexuality) have succeeded.[442] Appearances prevail over plot in an aesthetically subversive genre that, however, complies with the logic of neoliberalism. This has been the aporia gay literature has been charged with. It is easy to see, in Hirst's view, why the comedy of manners has been "the province of homosexual writers: Wilde, Coward, Maugham and Orton all translated their life-style into their plays, whilst the nature of homosexual relationships features repeatedly in the work of Pinter and Osborne."[443] Obviously, being an heir to them all, Hollinghurst cannot escape the stereotype. If there is a continuum in so-called and much-contested gay sensibility it is camp. Potentially subversive, for it is ironic, parodic and theatrical, camp, as gays themselves, has been rendered politically ineffective. Gay counterculture, of which comedy of manners is a part, has been stereotyped and downgraded as aesthetic, devoid of ethical and political engagement. Gays are considered "the arbiters of good taste, not only in dress, but in behaviour"[444] both within and outside the stage. Yet, in performing, they have raised social satire and exposed the double morality of a system that discriminates them. In a similar vein, Raymond-Jean Frontain argues that, as social outsiders, gays have turned gifted voyeurs and critics of "the hypocrisies of the heterosexual majority."[445]

William Congreve's *The Way of the World* (1700) is the paradigmatic comedy of manners prior to the twentieth century. Instead of the romantic wedding, hero and heroine exchange requirements before accepting marriage in a witty repartee[446] or proviso scene. Moreover, there is no longing for a rural Arcadia, this type of hero representing metropolitan values instead. The genre became more openly gay at the turn of the twentieth century, particularly with Oscar Wilde. Although his plays do not include overtly homosexual characters, they have become symbols of camp and, therefore, of sexual dissidence. Thus, in spite of their apparent frivolity, Wilde's successful plays constitute a harsh attack on Victorian double morality, one far more outrageous than Congreve's.[447] Wilde achieved this through sophisticated camp; *i.e.*: "The disparity between subject and style."[448] After Wilde, Noel Coward, Harold Pinter, John Osborne and, finally, Joe Orton represent camp comedy of manners before Stonewall. Henceforth, gays adapted the genre not only to expose their oppressors, but also to represent their own experiences, particularly derived from the trauma of AIDS. Post-AIDS comedies of manners focused on the new lifestyles available, "living as a celibate male, raising the child of one's heterosexual roommate, siring the child by one's heterosexual best female friend."[449] Terrence McNally's adaptation to a gay

[441] Ibid., 3.
[442] Ibid.
[443] Ibid., 3-4.
[444] Ibid., 4.
[445] In *Summers*: *Gay*, 161.
[446] William Congreve: *The Way of the World*. London 1994, iv: 128-250.
[447] Hirst: *Comedy*, 51.
[448] Ibid., 56.
[449] Raymond-Jean Frontain: "Comedy of Manners," in Claude Summers (ed). *The Gay and Lesbian Literary Heritage*. New York and London 2002, 163.

milieu of "the traditionally heterosexual plot of a weekend in the country —with its resulting misalliances, farcical revelations, and witty banter"[450] is a case in point. *The Spell* recalls McNally's strategy, adapting traditional forms to post-gay needs. Nevertheless, Hollinghurst's third novel is especially tributary to the pre-Stonewall playwright Joe Orton, for he links the rake stereotype with the post-War gay as an antecedent to current post-gayness.

Hirst makes reference to Joe Orton as overtly gay, polemic and revolutionary. His is an extreme version of comedy of manners, frequently farcical, which puts to the test the very bases of the Establishment. Although typical of the sixties, Orton's plays draw on the trends mentioned above. Throughout his short literary career Orton carried farce to its extremes. His sharp campy dialogues subvert bourgeois values and strategies of control over family, sexuality, capitalism, religion and death. His three plays — *Entertaining Mr Sloane* (1964), *Loot* (1967) and *What the Butler Saw* (1969)— joke about and disclose the game of appearances that power has constructed around itself. His characters inhabit a farcical (frequently absurd) and postmoral world where no taboos remain unexplored. Although this view of Orton's production as morally transgressive[451] is widely held, critics like Colin Chambers and Mike Prior regard Orton as a bourgeois playwright. In their opinion, Orton provides the heteronormative Establishment with a countercultural discourse whereby the latter preserves the *status quo*.[452]

As happens in the tradition he recasts, Orton's plays focus on the hypocrisy behind appearances. Thus, although his characters fit in the classic types —especially the truewit, the witwoud, the lawgiver or the *senex iratus*—, they experience irrational, arbitrary and violent ontologies. In *Entertaining Mr Sloane*, which starts as a menace comedy, Sloane is a sort of truewit *maudit* who apparently tricks the middle-aged brothers Ed and Kath, whose father he has previously killed, to live parasitically on them. However, the final proviso scene, in which they share Sloane as a hustler, proves their power over him. *Mutatis mutandis*, it draws on the proviso scene of *The Way of the World*. Yet, Orton's play increases the transgression of the classic with a more violent and overtly homo/bi-sexual story. The subversiveness of *Entertaining Mr Sloane* continues in *Loot*, where the echoes of Congreve's masterpiece resound again. If sex and money are masterly interwoven in *The Way of the World*, so are they in *Loot*. These two factors mould the changing bonds of the characters in both cases. Orton's play focuses on the loot —hence the title— of 140,000 pounds that a couple of gays, Dennis and Hal, steal from a bank and try to hide throughout the novel. The heroine of the play is Fay, a nurse who has killed a Mrs NcLeavy, in the hope of marrying and killing the rich Mr McLeavy, the *senex iratus*. Fay eventually seduces Denis and, therefore, takes part of the loot. Once more, the moral obstacle represented by the *senex* and his generation is discarded, and Fay, the truewit, succeeds in a corrupt society. *What the Butler Saw* is a new example of Orton's zest for the farcical and absurd. The Prentices are a mature couple: Mr Prentice is a prestigious doctor while Mrs Prentice used to

[450]   Ibid., 162.
[451]   Andrew Mayne: "Introduction" to *Loot* by Joe Orton. London 1985, xxiv.
[452]   Colin Chambers and Mike Prior: *Playwrights' Progress: Patterns of Postwar British Drama*. Oxford 1987, 110.

work in a hotel where she was raped being a youth. Out of the rape, she gave birth to twins whom she abandoned. Nick and Geraldine form the second young couple of the play, who finally turn out to be the Prentices' twins. Geraldine is apparently naïve and the victim of her own father's sexual approaches when she applies for a job at the hospital where he works. Nick is a rake who, like Sloane and Dennis, breaks the law[453] and tries to rape his mother. The ignorance of each other's identities leads the play to confusion, including transvestism, violence, and split personalities. All this is in keeping with the phase of *incrementum processusque turbarum* in the classic comedy of errors in Roman literature, which leads to the loss of identity. Rance, a psychiatrist, constitutes the authority figure in the play. As a *deus ex machina*, he favours a *cognitio* scene which recalls the melodramatic ending of Wilde's *The Importance of Being Ernest*.[454] Eventually, order is restored once identities have been recovered. However, the facts of violence and incest throughout cannot be obliterated. Thus, Rance gives the only possible way out in the conclusive line: "You can't be a rationalist in an irrational world."[455] The camp absurdity of the world depicted in the comedy prevents it from going astray and metamorphose into a Senecan tragedy.

The Spell meets the three basic thematic requirements of the comedy of manners, namely sex, friendship and money, added to lack of sentimentalism and moral judgements. Thus, *The Spell* leaves aside the poetic justice in *The Swimming-pool Library* and *The Folding Star*. Justin and Danny are untouched by and immune to moral considerations or schooling. Like the heroes and heroines of Restoration comedy and Orton's plays, these characters know the rules of the game and, therefore, despite their amorality, they win. The four protagonists of *The Spell* fit in recognisable gay types of a late-capitalist, post-AIDS, postmodernist gay comedy of manners. Justin is a truewit; Danny, like Sloane or Dennis, a *bon vivant* and trickster; Alex is a sentimental witwoud; and Robin is the odd one out, belonging in the old generation, though integrated in the new one. Except for Forsterian Alex, the rest are *flâneurs* cruising the streets for casual sex "desacralised and uncoupled from the context of romantic love."[456] Justin and Danny are particularly conspicuous cases. They follow their instincts and fulfil their desires ignoring the consequences. They master the rules, if only to break them.

The second chapter of *The Spell* can be regarded as a parody of the menace scene with which *Entertaining Mr Sloane* and other twentieth-century comedies of manners start. In Orton's play, an intruder breaks into the house of a mature couple menacing their peaceful bourgeois living-room. In Hollinghurst's novel, Alex is the intruder who breaks into the house of Justin and Robin, which he scans "with an Englishman's nostalgia" (Hollinghurst 1999: 15). It is soon obvious that Alex is no real menace to Justin and Robin's parody of the middle-class heterosexual couple. Still, Alex's arrival constitutes a turning-point in their relationship, especially as he eventually becomes Robin's son's lover. Like Orton's mature couples —themselves a parody of Restoration happy couples—, Justin and Robin put forward the arbitrariness and comicity of gender roles and domesticity. Justin updates the role of promiscuous wife who cuckolds his

---

[453]   Juan María Marín: *La tradición de la comedia inglesa en Joe Orton*. Unpublished Ph. Thesis. Universidad de Zaragoza 1992, 217-218.

[454]   Ibid., 251.

[455]   Joe Orton: *The Complete Plays*. London 1976, 428.

[456]   Mort: *Cultures*, 176.

'husband', utters catty remarks and drinks a lot. The narrator uses Ortonian imagery to describe one of their marital discussions and subsequent reconciliations: "Robin said 'I love you', with tears of frustration in his eyes, and Justin, like a secretary briefly disarranged by an importunate boss, smoothed himself" (124). That is, the relationship between Justin and Robin not only parodies conventional married couples, but also other heterosexual couplings and power relationships, from gay camp.

There are two factors which delimit the relation of *The Spell* with the classic tradition of comedy of manners: the effect of AIDS and capitalism. The beginning of the affair between Robin and Justin cannot be dissociated from the simultaneous death of Robin's former partner, Simon. Chapter three is thus a mixture of vaudeville —with Robin hiding behind doors and witnessing Justin's infidelities— and sorrow for Simon's imminent death climaxing in sexual scenes which merge carnality and death (37). As concerns money, Justin represents the cult of capitalism at the end of the century. Like Restoration heroes, he is an intriguer and a sexual dealer, but he does not have to trick others for money. Like Luc Altidore and Ronald Firbank, he is the only son and heir to a very rich and old businessman. Therefore, unlike Dennis and Hal in *Loot*, he does not have to steal a boot. He is a postmodern, late-capitalist truewit who enjoys misbehaving and teasing those around him, just like Stuart Jones in *Queer as Folk*. Although, for Robin, Justin is merely "a devouringly passive lover and a kind of cock-teaser" (38), he usually controls the action. Already in the second chapter, Justin proves his skill as intriguer, introducing his ex-lover Alex to his apparently idyllic life with Robin. Henceforth, Justin establishes a dynamics of desire and rivalry involving his two lovers in a rather Girardian fashion. Thus, as he reflects: "It was satisfactory to bring the two men in his life together, and watch them politely squaring up and backing off" (43).

From the very first pieces of conversation with restrained Alex, Justin shows his mastery of camp and irony. For example, when the former makes up a love affair to conceal that he has no sexual partner, Justin takes the lead in a witty repartee, which recalls Congreve's, Wilde's and Orton's and foreshadows others in the novel. Justin asks Alex to find out his secret story and make fun of him:

> "Is he cute?"
> "Yep."
> "Is he blond?"
> "He is, actually." Alex shrugged. "He's very young."
> "He's another virgin blond like me, isn't he?" Justin made one of his experienced-barmaid faces. "Of course I'm foully jealous." (21)

Like most heroes of comedy of manners, Justin masters autoreferential camp discourse to deconstruct social language and structures. In his campy style, Justin interacts with reality vicariously: through *double entendres* (25); games in which the four heroes must play with language, describing and flirting with each other (45-46); and puns on gender, using feminine names for male characters (155), and on rural life. Like Restoration truewits, he is an urbanite who makes fun of the country, including his boyfriend's name (18) and that of Liton Gambrill (103, 123, 154). After his predecessors, Justin's intriguing is perverse and relentless. Thus, after forcing his lover and his ex to confront each other in chapter two, he fosters the implausible love affair between Danny and Alex (46-47)

Like Emma, the protagonist of Jane Austen's eponymous comedy of manners, Justin acts as a matchmaker. There are, however, obvious differences. Firstly, *The Spell* is set in late-twentieth-century gay London, not in the *beau monde* of *Emma*'s early nineteenth century setting. In consequence, the characters of Hollinghurst's novel rebel against, rather than reinforce, heterosexual institutions like marriage and divorce, as classic comedies of manners (Austen's included) do. They interact more freely, leading promiscuous lives outside hetero-sacramentalism. Despite differences, discos are to Danny and Justin what elegant upper-class balls are to Austen's heroine. That is, Danny works as Alex's Pygmalion and guide to world pleasures as Emma does with Harriet Smith. Alex walks after his young mentor, amazed and confused by the city lights. Meanwhile Danny shows his expertise in flirting and playing with gays in a camp atmosphere along Old Compton street. It is a gossiping ritual he knows all too well: "Danny himself carried one or two [anecdotes] that he heard to the next little group, in an easy pollination of gossip" (74). Danny is in his element in the campy hedonism of late-twentieth-century gay clubs. However, he is also the product of intertextual references. He recalls Austen's heroines and *Vanity Fair* protagonist Vecky Sharp. In fact, although Danny has not read Thackeray's novel (104), when he is sacked from his job, "he wished he could give the place some symbolic insult, like Vecky Sharp" (146). Danny also shares the subversiveness of Firbank's and Proust's upper-class perverts, also *flâneurs* of their respective cities and times. Like the protagonists of these modernist writers, Danny enjoys a life of casual sex, superficiality and witty exchanges, traditionally associated with the aristocracy and (later) with gays. In this light, the metaphor of pollination is very effective: the postmodernist *flâneur* —Danny, Will and Stuart Jones— keeps walking the city, spreading fun, news and disease. Indeed, other than a symbol of *jouissance*, the metaphor of pollination can also be one of AIDS. Inevitably, Danny's pollination brings to mind similar metaphors of gay contagiousness in *The Swimming-pool Library*, though the latter's traumatic discourse is nuanced.

According to Tim Edwards, in line with Quentin Crisp, John Rechy, John Alan Lee and Edmund White, Hollinghurst has constructed "fairly or even very positive promiscuity pieces of work."[457] Like Stuart Jones in *Queer as Folk*, Danny is the super-stud —*i.e.*: an attractive, promiscuous boy— who infatuates Forsterian Alex. Even if they represent different concepts of homosexuality, Alex is soon captivated by Danny's 'queer chic', a model of gayness identified with promiscuous sex, fashion and clubbing. Although *The Spell* celebrates promiscuity, still under the effects of AIDS, it also questions the commodification and standardisation of gay identity and desire furthered by late capitalism. Alex's inability to manage in Danny's world results comic, but it also reveals many gays' anxiety to fit in prescribed stereotypes.[458] In this sense, the discourse of *The Spell* recalls the strategic essentialism of Alan Sinfield and Tim Edwards, demanding "more sites where les/bi/gay people can interact."[459]

---

[457] Edwards: *Erotics*, 105.
[458] Liggins: "Alan," 169.
[459] Edwards: *Erotics*, 3; Sinfield: *Gay*, 199; Liggins: "Alan," 170.

At the beginning of his initiation rite, Alex feels himself a foreigner. He regards gay clubbers as devotees of a foreign "religion" with whom he fails to identify (Hollinghurst, 1999: 82). Indeed, Alex's twofold status, within and outside the gay scene, renders the ambiguity of *The Spell*, celebratory and traumatic; drugs and acid house music are part of a gay subculture overcoming the AIDS crisis. He is a nostalgic English gentleman (15), one who, in a fast-moving world, is remembered as "the one who falls in love" (249). When Alex takes Ecstasy and listens to house music for the first time, he feels transported and looks at 'reality' in a brand new (vivid) way, thus converging the two strands of gay experience the novel conveys. Firstly he feels an outsider, a spectator of a performance: imagining how the chemical components of Ecstasy spread inside the body (81-82), regarding dancers as standardised members of a brainwashing sect (82), or noticing the metamorphosing of music and male bodies (82-83). Later, however, the effect of drugs is reported vividly, firsthand, as a witness to his own self, that later turns into an overwhelming feeling (84). He is still an outsider though, a witwoud who can only imitate Danny and his friends to no avail. He only gets transfixed by music, male beauty and his desire (84) —thus forecasting the line of beauty of Hollinghurst's eponymous novel— when empowered by Ecstasy. Yet, his celebratory experience is not without shadows. The clubs he attends are buried temples as well as open planes that foster transient euphoria. As Johnson points out: "the word 'ecstasy' comes from the ancient Greek *ekstasis*, to stand outside of one self, implying that the body and mind are structures from which one might leave" (86). This, I contend, is related to traumatic dissasociation in *The Spell*. Like the juice of love in *A Midsummer Night's Dream*, Ecstasy fosters a distance within oneself (as actor and spectator) as it does with so-called reality, which may be a state of jouissance and of hallucination provoked by trauma. In repeatedly taking Ecstasy and dancing compulsively, Alex echoes gay stereotypes often furthered by neoliberalism. Other than Ecstasy, most characters use peyote, hash, cocaine and other drugs to go through altered mental states and vivid experiences (134, 138) in Robin's view. Obviously, the novel does not suggest that gays are fond of drugs or that it makes an apology for their consumption. It just forms part of a stereotype that the text represents and deconstructs. Luis Magrinyà considers *The Spell* a commonsensical and brave approach to drug consumption. He regrets that only fiction is able to deal with this contemporary phenomenon straightforwardly.[460] In fact, as with promiscuity, *The Spell* does not make moral judgements about subcultural phenomena.

The novel follows amoral comedy of manners, especially Orton's. If Orton's plays rendered the violent reaction against the Establishment during the nineteen sixties, *The Spell* represents late-twentieth-century (gay) culture without restrictions. Robin Woodfield considers that drugs bring "experiences worth having" (Hollinghurst 1999, 138) rather than ineffectual escapism.[461] His argument points to the potentiality of drugs to convey the blurring of ontological boundaries. Robin's apology of drug draws on *Confessions of a Middle-aged Ecstasy Eater*, an anonymous updated version of Thomas De Quincey's classic *Confessions of an English Opium Eater* (1822), published by

---

[460]   Luis Magrinyá: "Éxtasis para la Madurez." *El País* (29 March), 24.

[461]   The apology of drugs by some characters cannot be confused with the position of the novel and the author.

Granta in 2001. In reworking De Quincey's original, the discourse of some of Hollinghurst's texts and characters demythologises drugs and readjusts inter-generational and father-son relations, thus breaking with (late-capitalist) gay culture stereotypes. De Quincey's confessions are ambivalent as well. He deals with opium-induced pleasures but also with its painful aftermath. Initial euphoria gives way to dreadful dreams and altered states. Other than the moralistic message of a reformed rebel, De Quincey's text forecasts the celebratory and traumatic discourse *The Spell* fleshes out. In Alex's case, for example, his first experience with Ecstasy raises expectations not always fulfilled and a delusive fantasy about his future with Danny. Only when Danny leaves him does Alex realise his drug-induced delusion. However, he keeps in touch with Dave, Danny's drug-dealer (Hollinghurst 1999: 249), so that, once initiated, Alex knows how to survive in Danny's world.

The Spell demythologises and descriminalises AIDS. References to the disease are scarce, the disease thus becoming a "penumbral presence"[462] or rather absence. As a traumatic event, AIDS absence haunts even more than its presence. Thus, although Hollinghurst aims to celebrate gay sexuality and subculture, the underside of AIDS culture is latent and moulds the discourse of celebration as well. Early in the novel, the narrator tells Robin's previous lover, Simon, died of AIDS. However, Simon is soon substituted by Justin so that the disease is sublimated, albeit latent. Very graphically, Robin replaces Simon's dying sighs for Justin's sexual gasps (Hollinghurst, 1999: 38). In overlapping ones and others, the treatment of AIDS, as well as the convergence of celebration and trauma, is very sophisticated. Pleasure sublimates trauma, but it is also its symptom. This is what paradoxically renders gays' historical capacity to overcome tragedy. It is echoed, yet displaced behind narcissistic beauty and campy irony, to be palatable. Thus, in spite of Robin's reaching 'the line of beauty' with Justin, the defeat over the trauma of AIDS is debatable to say the least. The evolution in the treatment of the disease through Hollinghurst's fiction, a future threat in *The Swimming-pool Library*, a fearsome fact in *The Folding Star*, and a matter of the past in *The Spell*, asks for a revision. In fact, AIDS was still a real threat in the nineties, a fact that *The Spell* addresses through penumbral absence. Hence, despite Hollinghurst's claims to suppress AIDS on moral grounds —because it has become a cliché which turns the novel into a moral fable[463] and because "he did not want the disease to determine the truth of gay identity and history"—[464] his discourse says otherwise. Trauma events are too heavy a burden to screen and, in trying to bury them, they resurface to the open plane when recalled.

In designing Danny and Alex's affair only to enjoy their likely break-up, Justin proves to be a master of sexual intrigue and dialectics (Hollinghurst 1999: 234). Yet, as a mercenary rake, when he inherits his father's large fortune, he leaves both Litton Gambril, which he identifies with middle-class narrow-mindedness, and Robin. Based in Musgrove, an exclusive area close to Harrods, time passes fast in his luxurious life style (192). The materialism of comedy of manners and Alderson's 'queer chic'[465]

---

[462] Tillyard: "Interview," 62.
[463] In Burton: *Talking*, 48.
[464] Murphy: *Past*, 72.
[465] Alderson: *Territories*, 44.

converge in Justin. As Sinfield has amply argued, capitalism works towards the standardisation of same-sex identity, trying to transform gays into simulacra of each other, mere impersonators of a marketed stereotype. Hence, Justin's profession as an actor is doubly meaningful: he recalls the rakes of comedy of manners while he also performs the rituals of late-capitalist gay consumers. A passive sexual partner, he is doubly so in asking people to perform, 'do things' for his own consumerist performance, i.e. paying for things (Hollinghurst 1999: 193). With a lot of time and money to spend, Justin starts a ritual of shopping comparable to Alex's disco experience. After visiting the basement of designer Harvey Nichols, he eccentrically decides the prices are too cheap (195). Then, he gets a taxi to the Issey Miyake's boutique, where he spends large amounts of money in a ritual that substitutes spirituality and takes him to "a state of beautitude" (195-196). The use of religious imagery to address Justin's compulsive consumerism is graphic of Sinfield's theory of capitalism and the post-gay.

Justin's time at Musgrove is exciting and pleasurable, but also alienating. Hence, he returns to Litton Gambril. Thus, although the novel avoids moral judgements or taking sides, Justin (like Alex) undergoes a maturation process. *The Spell* is, after all, more romantic and more a comedy of manners than it intends. Moreover, as both characters mature, they reformulate the original four-sided *rondeau* with a new one, now exclusively composed of middle-aged members. This new architecture of desire, which replaces Danny by Alex's new boyfriend, is focalised by Alex "with its momentary sequence of hidden appraisal and denial" (253). Thus, the happy ending characteristic of classic romantic comedy is forced, its final tone being a mixture of decadent frustration and gay brotherhood. The scene with the four characters looking at the sea from the cliffs (256-267) is rather ambiguous and implausible in view of the unfolding of the novel. It apparently celebrates gayness through an idyllic quartet that feels suddenly in communion with nature. The two couples recall the happy ending of Shakespeare's *A Midsummer Night's Dream*. However, if the novel is considered as a whole, this sentimentalism can only be read ironically. Despite appearances, Robin and Alex cannot stand each other (252), Justin has a catty, selfish character, and Nick is a newcomer — almost a *deus ex machina*— with the task of fulfilling the forced happy ending. Thus, unlike the endings of other gay writers' novels like Jeanette Winterson and Peter Ackroyd, *The Spell* longs for and ironises on the final communion and integration of the characters. Instead of a proviso scene, Hollinghurst's novel opts for a parody of heterosexual marriage. If Orton brought the genre to its extremes in order to contribute to the political revolution of the nineteen sixties, *The Spell* does likewise in the nineteen nineties. However, the violence of three decades before is no longer necessary: first, because the vindications of the sixties have apparently succeeded. The climax of the transvestism and comedy of errors of *What the Butler Saw* is replaced by a certain normalisation of sexual dissidence in Tony Blair's England. Moreover, neoliberalism has wiped out the spirit of the sixties. This does not mean that Hollinghurst's third novel does not partake of the satiric and transgressive spirit of (Orton's) comedy of manners; the features are still there, but adjusted to a different age, celebratory but still under the effects of the AIDS trauma. Indeed, *The Spell* proposes a sexual round with no moral restrictions that updates Harriet Hawkins' words on *The Way of the World*: "since the plot hardly moves at all, the movements of the play really are the progressive revelations of the characters into new relationships with each other, and the movements of our progressive understanding of the various characters and their situations."[466]

---

[466] Harriet Hawkins: *"The Audience's Dilemma."* In Harriet Hawkins. *Congreve: Comedies. A Selection of Critical Essays*. London, 1982, 200.

4 The trauma of beauty: The Dionysian assault on the AIDS crisis

4.1 Reception and preliminary considerations

The Line of Beauty is Alan Hollinghurst's fourth novel and his greatest success so far; the winner of the 2004 Booker Prize, it has mostly received good reviews. Anthony Quinn labels it as a "magnificent comedy of manners," one which is alert "to the tiniest social and tonal shifts"[467] from a permanently ironic standpoint. Michael Dirda focuses on style, particularly on Hollinghurst's masterly ability, to choose the right words and make unexpected observations.[468] The title, which makes reference, among others, to Hogarth's treatise on beauty and to Henry James's style, determines the narcissism of the novel, as "every line in this book will be a beautiful one."[469] Stylistically, *The Line of Beauty* keeps on the lyricism of its predecessors' poetic descriptions; in this sense, for instance, James Wood points out, "the twilight in London is exactly described."[470]

There are some objections to the novel, though. Colm Tóibín objects to it being a Jamesian novel out of time. In his view, the writer "has not given up his ambitions to have an old-fashioned plotline, with the tabloid press and lovers discovered and much else. […] It is a sign of his ambition, seeking to merge his own natural talent with another tradition [Henry James'], which is alien to him."[471] Bookishness also informs Don Lee's review. For him, passages on culture are interminable, descriptions are lush and the repartee is always droll, but can be soporific. Moreover, there are too many allusions and names to remember, which are, however, important to the plot. Finally, he argues that some plot lines are not believable.[472] Other than style, Wood considers the moral discourse of *The Line of Beauty* is problematically complicit with Thatcherism. Thus, although

> Hollinghurst's prose has about it an air of Jamesian moral intelligence, one has the uneasy feeling that Hollinghurst is more in love with his gilded world than he can always acknowledge. The novel sometimes surrenders to a kind of yearning, not unlike Waugh's in *Brideshead Revisited*, the yearning that the middle- or even upper-class writer may sometimes feel for thoughtless, graceful aristocracy. So the reader feels that the novel's moral "turn" —the fall from grace into the horror of the 1987 crash— comes not a

---

[467] Anthony Quinn: "The Last Good Summer." shorturl.at/govxA, 2004, n.p.

[468] Michael Dirda: "A Condition of England Novel." https://wapo.st/33q1I88, 2004, n.p.

[469] Tillyard: "Interview," 62.

[470] James Wood: "The Ogee Curve," *The New Republic*, 231, 2004, n.p.

[471] Tóibín: "Comedy," 8.

[472] Don Lee: "Thatcher's London, Sex, Drugs and the Ruling Class". https://bit.ly/3G6z3Tr, 2004, n.p.

moment too soon, because the book needs precisely its moral quickening, that there has
been a little too much gilded drift.[473]

Avowedly, the moral discourse of *The Line of Beauty* is probably problematic,
especially when set against the backdrop of the tough nineteen eighties, with Thatcher's
politics and the outburst of AIDS as the cornerstones of the novel. However, it seems to
me, Wood's argument blends author and narrator. That the narrator and/or hero of the
novel fall in love with conservative circles does not necessarily mean that the author
also does. Whether Hollinghurst feels admiration or despises the Feddens and their
peers is unknown to us. What is more, like many of Henry James's characters and
narrators, *The Line of Beauty* regards the *beau monde* with a mixture of interest and
irony. In this same vein, Michèle Mendelssohn wonders whether Hollinghurst's
"parody-as-critique work[s] and challenge[s] the corrosive forces it thematizes;"[474] that
is, whether the novel is complicit with power and thus, as Wood points out, "the novel
is sceptical of hedonism"[475] and punishes Nick in consequence. As I argued above,
Mendelssohn considers that Wood fails to see that "the novel parodies itself"[476] and also
that he "underestimates the aesthetic and metaphysical counterweight"[477] of the last
scene of the novel.

Narrated in the third person, *The Line of Beauty* is mainly focused from the
perspective of a gay youth, a hybrid of Hollinghurst's former heroes. A middle-class
Oxford postgraduate, Nick Guest is writing his PhD on style in Meredith, Conrad and
James. Having befriended wealthy Tobby Fedden at university, he becomes the
Feddens' guest (hence his surname) in their Notting Hill mansion. Thus starts Nick's
infatuation, which prevents him from noticing what the Feddens really stand for.
Gerald, the *paterfamilias*, is a Tory MP (Hollinghurst, 2004: 3)[478] of Thatcher's second
victory, the landslide of 1983. He is an Oxonian "*bon viveur*" (3) who knows how to get
to the front row and take advantage of his personal charm and his wife's money. Rachel
Fedden, a Kessler —"a Rothschild-like dynasty of Jewish bankers" —[479] is older than
her husband, like Mrs Altidore in *The Folding Star*. Their son and daughter, Toby and
Catherine, complete the family. The former is a "rower with journalistic ambitions [and
the latter] an art student with breakdowns in her past and future."[480] Nick reveres the
first and cares of manic-depressive Cat.

Since his arrival at Notting Hill, Nick's role remains undefined. Despite living with
the family, he is still an outsider, which connects with Hollinghurst's constant idea of
non-belongness. During his long stay, he behaves or is considered as "a friend, pet,
factotum, errand boy, and finally scapegoat."[481] In sum, he is "our guide to the Feddens'

---

[473] Wood: "Ogee," 49.
[474] Menselssohn and Flannery: *Alan*, 46.
[475] Ibid.
[476] Ibid., 47.
[477] Ibid.
[478] Hereafter all references to *The Line of Beauty* (2004) will be in the text.
[479] J. S. Marcus: "Fiction in Review. Alan Hollinghurst," *Yale Review* 93(3) 2005, 181.
[480] Ibid.
[481] Ibid., 182.

rise and fall and, almost incidentally, to his own"[482] and, I would add, to the rise and fall of Thatcher herself. Nick's infatuation and otherness draws on Charles Ryder in Evelyn Waugh's *Brideshead Revisited* or his eponymous Nick (Carraway) in Scott Fitzgerald's *The Great Gatsby*. Failing to identify with the wealthy other, the hero's otherness is boosted, as well as his ambiguous status. In a sense, he seems to be a mere spectator to himself as if traumatically displaced and dissociated from his 'true' self. He bears witness to his own failure at belonging to the dazzling household he reveres. If Ryder is a painter down from Cambridge, Guest performs the family aesthete after graduating at Oxford. Somehow, his cultural connoisseurship offsets his far less glamorous origins, and justifies, at least in part, his staying at Notting Hill. His love affair with the Feddens is extensible to their mansion. Like Nantwich's house in *The Swimming-pool Library*, Orst's in *The Folding Star*, or Tony Bowerchalke's in *The Spell*, the Feddens' is an active scenario that helps mould the novel and the hero. Nick's entrance is very telling of his role hereafter. He falls in love with the house at first sight, which he explores in detail (Hollinghurst 2004: 6). Drawing on Henry James, he "felt that he could 'stand a great deal of gilt'" (6). The beauty of the house is as threatening and mesmerising as that of male bodies' for Nick. Its contours and the surfaces of the art pieces it contains hide the unexpected. Like the novel, the Feddens' house is duplicitous, rococo and curvy, as the pair of gilt-framed mirrors suggest. The specular splendour blinds Nick, who feels secure in what eventually comes out as a hostile territory. Beauty, the novel proves, is tricky and unreliable. It is in this sense that Geoff Gilbert analyses space and particularly the Feddens' residence and gardens. They, Gilbert points out, "are part of a fantasy constitution of space and place."[483] Nick's psychic and sexual investment on this space is revelatory; not only of his libidinal position with respect to the Feddens, but also to his "chronic insider-outsider status"[484] and traumatic end. He invests too much on a fantasy that is especially elusive in a narcissistic/specular fashion, and, therefore, the end can only be traumatic.

Parallel to his romance with the conservative Feddens, Nick is overtly gay. Moreover, drawing on Will Beckwith, he has a predilection for non-white boys: he first blind-dates Leo, a black council worker, at Notting Hill public 'but private' communal gardens (Hollinghurst, 2004: 15). The schizophrenic pairs private-public, conspicuous-invisible accompany the hero's sexuality and gender identity and performance throughout. When Leo disappears, Nick starts a semi-closeted affair with the Lebanese Wani Ourani, the son of a Mohamed Alfayed-like tycoon, owner of a supermarket holding. The equilibrium between the hero's two halves —his adscription to the Feddens' Tory (hetero)normativism and his gay lifestyle— is precarious, eventually breaking to pieces in a dramatic *dénouement*. Indeed, the public exposure of the scandals of his host family —concretely Gerald's white-collar crimes and infidelities— mixed up with his own hastens his downfall.

[482] Ibid.
[483] Geoff Gilbert: "Some Properties of Fiction: Value and Fantasy in Hollinghurst's House of Fiction." In Mendelssohn, Michèle and Dennis Flannery (eds.). *Alan Hollinghurst: Writing under the Influence*. Manchester 2016, 125.
[484] Ibid., 126

4.2   Back to the Traumatic Eighties

The Line of Beauty takes readers back to the nineteen eighties, reprising self-consciously "a number of the plot-lines of *The Swimming-pool Library*."[485] Likewise, J. S. Marcus argues that Hollinghurst's fourth novel picks up "where *The Swimming-pool Library* [urban pastoral myth set in 1983, with AIDS epidemic as a sword of Damocles] left off [...]. What in his first novel was just hinted at is now rubbed in our noses," namely the "telltale pathologies of the 1980s —from AIDS and corporate greed to Tory sex scandals, cocaine and the Merchant-Ivory costume dramas— [...] having the feel of a hangover."[486] Thus, although Hollinghurst claims he "has never wanted to be a spokesman for his generation" (Tylliard 2005: 63), the fact remains that his fourth novel constitutes a retrospective exploration of Thatcher's era after a period of latency to have the trauma allegedly healed and hence utterable. In an interview with Dennis Flannery, Mendelssohn points out, drawing on Gilbert, that "Thatcherism [...] is a libidinal arrangement that structures the characters' lives and loves."[487] Chapter 7 is virtually a pastiche of Beckwith's eighties Corry club, Nick and Wani enjoying the gay golden age just before the outburst of AIDS (Hollinghurst, 2004: 181). As in the Corry, naked males read and swim (181), generations, races and classes meet (182), despite signs of impending AIDS (188) and youths starting to die (182). Meanwhile, those who remain fulfil their "steadiest fantasies" (183), forming a *tableau* of childish sportsmen cruising and "resting in stunned camaraderie" (185). If *The Swimming-pool Library* explored the trauma of an ending, what does *The Line of Beauty* add to that sense of an ending? Kaye Mitchell gives part of the clue to the question when she argues that "the year 1995 might be seen as a 'turning point in the AIDS crisis [...] due to the advent of life-prolonging pharmaceuticals.'"[488] Henceforth, Mitchell continues, "AIDS becomes 'an aspect' of gay literature, 'rather than its main focus or drive or preoccupation.'"[489] This point, which is so conspicuous in the case of *The Spell*, also helps to understand the return to the eighties and AIDS in *The Line of Beauty* with a sense of postness.

Just in the middle of the novel, the narrator makes reference to Lord Beckwith, who inextricably links both novels together. In organising a concert at home for Tory bigwigs —an episode I will return to later— Gerald Fedden attempts to overcome Beckwith's musical *soirée*. As the narrator puts it in ironic terms, in Thatcher's times appearance and competition were two sides of the same coin. As Dolly Kimbolton, a family friend and guest to the soirée, recalls the spirit of the event and the times: "We're all for competition!" (Hollinghurst 2004: 246). Although *The Swimming-pool Library* addresses Lord Beckwith's shameful anti-gay policy, there are virtually no references to Thatcher's politics. Hollinghurst himself claims that "what was significant [...] was its moment in sexual politics, but otherwise ... the 1983 general election was completely

---

[485] Richard Bradford: *The Novel Now. Contemporary British Fiction*. Oxford, 2007, 153.

[486] Marcus: "Fiction," 182-183.

[487] Menselssohn and Flannery: *Alan*, 8.

[488] Kay Mitchell: "Who are you? What the Fuck Are you Doing here?: Queer Debates and Contemporary Connections." In Mendelssohn, Michèle and Dennis Flannery (eds.). *Alan Hollinghurst: Writing under the Influence*. Manchester 2016, 180.

[489] Ibid.

unremarked".[490] *The Line of Beauty*, however, already opens with Thatcher's triumph that year (Hollinghurst, 2004: 3). If Will foreshadowed his (and his world's) downfall in the first pages of *The Swimming-pool Library*, Thatcher's overwhelming victory forecasts the feel of *The Line of Beauty*, its return to trauma after trauma in particular.

In reducing (homo)sexual explicitness and featuring female characters, Stella Tylliard argues that, strictly speaking, *The Line of Beauty* "is not a 'gay novel' at all, just a novel about the unravelling of a family that happens to have a gay man at its centre."[491] However, (gay) sex remains predominant[492] and Thatcher's England is still focalised by a gay hero and homoerotic intertexts. There are overtly gay characters, others who arouse gays' desire and yet others who are identified with homosexual cultural icons: Nick, his lovers Leo or Wani, the young MP Paul Thompson, a fellow-student at Oxford and the two American directors who intend to shoot a filmic version of *The Spoils of Poynton* make up the first group. Gerald, Toby and Catherine's last boyfriend, Jasper, are part of the second. In fact, Jasper tries to seduce Nick during their holidays in France (Hollinghurst, 2004: 311). Likewise, Catherine recalls the possible gay affair between Gerald and Jasper, and insinuates another between Toby and Wani (91). Even heterosexual Gerald and Lord Beckwith are inclined to gay icons such as Strauss (22), a favourite composer of both, and Caravaggio (303).

The Line of Beauty takes up essential issues from its predecessors, especially trauma, AIDS and death, nostalgia, camp and irony, aestheticism, and interracial and interclass desire. Yet again, the convergence of transient (male) beauty and its traumatic underside is conspicuous, if only more intensely. The novel evokes with nostalgia, and a pinch of irony, Oxbridge homoerotic camaraderie, Toby's birthday being a case in point. Surrounding him still in bed, his fellow students recall their childish days without girls (87) to finally mix up in a climax "all of them with their ideas and bow ties and plans and objections" (93). The iconography of the scene, a group of ex-Oxbridge boys homoerotically recalling Nazism (86-87) echoes the naked German soldiers around a bed in Visconti's *The Damned* (1970). The erotic use of Nazi iconography in gay representation is a recurrent issue once more. Unlike Oxford, nineteen-eighties London proves to be an unfriendly territory for a gay youth. However, *The Line of Beauty* is a tragicomedy of manners. As such, in using camp and irony, neo-Victorian morality is dismantled and gay identity and desire are reasserted. What *The Line of Beauty* adds to its predecessor is thus its political satire and revision of the AIDS era from an apparently 'post-traumatic' standpoint, which explains that Hollinghurst himself has assumed the text's reparative character.[493]

---

[490] In Benedicte Page: "Inside the Tory stronghold" *The Bookseller Magazine* (13 February) 2004, 30.

[491] Tillyard: "Interview," 62.

[492] In Page: "Inside," 30.

[493] Laura Fernández: "Hollinghurst narra como era la Inglaterra de Margaret Thatcher." http://www.elmundo.es/ 2006/02/14/catalunya/1930020.html 2006, n.p.

4.3   The specular structure of *The Line of Beauty*: Hogarth's *Analysis of Beauty* revised

The Line of Beauty's main intertext concerning both its structure and, somehow, its content, is William Hogarth's *Analysis of Beauty*. The latter inspires the title of Hollinghurst's novel, and more specifically the lines of cocaine that "spread a beguiling charm over the story's moral and financial subterfuges."[494] Hogarth's withdrawal of moral considerations in favour of aestheticism informs *The Line of Beauty*. For him, objects are reduced to their essential lines, those formed by curves of the *undulating* line (i.e. 'the line of beauty'[495] and the serpentine line[496] being essentially pleasing. Hogarth rejected European *rocalla*,[497] addressing a genuinely British curve: "The waving line, or line of beauty, varying still more, being composed of two curves contrasted [...]. And the serpentine line, by its waving and winding at the same time in different ways, leads the eye in a pleasing manner along the continuity of its variety."[498] To Peter Ackroyd, Hogarth's curves adapt the irregular lines of the English landscape, especially "the allegory of the winding path."[499] All in all, the serpentine line works in *The Line of Beauty* as a metaphor for the (queer) England of the eighties.

The combination of Nick's aestheticism and Wani's money results in a glamorous magazine, *The Ogee*, a celebration of (mostly male) beauty before trauma 'outbursts'. The title of the magazine comes out while Nick is at Wani's flat, as a turn-of-the-millennium recast of Hogarth's style. Indeed, the narrator argues, the publication recalls "the ogee curve [as] pure expression. The double curve was Hogarth's 'line of beauty'" (Hollinghurst, 2004: 200). The line of beauty, which the protagonist links to Wani's back (200), is also the inspiration for a "new *Analysis of Beauty*" (200). These words and moment constitute the core of the novel in more senses than one. Although the narrator argues that the curve is not structural, it recurs throughout the novel. The ogee is a poly-referential serpentine, not only evident in Wani's bed, but in other items: the French rococo furniture that Nick admires and old Pete (Leo's first lover) repairs (106-107); "the double curve of the piano" (240) at the Feddens'; "the Curvilinear tracery of the monks' choir" (268); the rococo treasures of Munich that Nick and Wani visit in search of ideas for their glossy magazine (304); or the "black-and-gilt S-shaped balusters" (467) that Nick admires before being ejected from the Feddens'. The new curve is English and foreign, new and old, simple and baroque, but, above all, unlike Hogarth's, it is shaped after the male body. The serpentine in Hollinghurst's novel is sensual, rather than inert. When Nick tells Catherine about Wani, she quickly draws a Hogarthian caricature (348). Wani is reduced to a few curved lines, yet lines inspiring desire and prospective pleasure. The dip and swell of his back, like the "double curve" of Leo's body (423), update Hogarth's ideal. In projecting Hogarth's line of beauty onto Wani's body tied to the ogee bed (264), the homoerotic narcissism of the double curve,

[494] Tillyard: "Interview," 62.
[495] William Hogarth: *The Analysis of Beauty*. New Haven and London 1997, 41.
[496] Ibid., 42.
[497] Ibid., 47.
[498] Ibid., 42.
[499] Ackroyd: *Albion*, 67.

or ogee, is conspicuous and fated. When Nick witnesses Wani and Ricky, a former Oxford friend, kissing, it is a new example of the specular doubleness of beauty (198). Thus, the narcissistic specularity Hollinghurst's novels convey is also central to *The Line of Beauty*.

The first and last issue of *Ogee* finally comes out, its failure validating the equation silence=death. In other words, although the magazine is complicit with the new Right and neoliberalism, a genuine gay voice is still a mirage, camp and stylish, but bound to extinction. The ogee on the cover is the preamble to the luxury world inside (488). In any case, the first number of the magazine forecasts "the gleam of something that was over" (488-489). AIDS and gays' social ostracism transform the magazine into an event of mourning in and for itself and the generation which conceives it. In this light, Nick's satisfaction for *Je Promets* —a perfume he gets from the Feddens for his birthday (22)— is significant, recalling the lethal talcum powder in *The Swimming-pool Library*. Fragrances work in both cases as metaphors for AIDS, a threat 'in the air' which foreshadows the end of an era.

The serpentine line of beauty and the narrator's artificial discourse also recall Henry James's literary style. There are frequent examples of Nick's appropriation of James's periphrastic style, even to make reference to the most prosaic issues. As a narrator, Nick recalls how he feels attracted to a waiter, particularly to his trouser, which "curved forwards with telling asymmetry" (69), in reference to his penis. Nick's ludicrous updating of the Master's outdated style turns up once and again to confirm that what worked in late-Victorianism does not work in current discourses and cannot address current concerns, no matter how hard Nick tries. The serpentine line also has political undertones, being a metaphor for double morality and grovelling in neo-Victorian neoliberal Thatcherism. Catherine Fedden, who stands for the novel's political commitment and ethical conscience, is very critical with Thatcherism. Unlike her family and Nick, in admiring rococo pieces, she dislikes all this make-believe (305). The metaphoric link between rococo lines and the hypocrisy of Thatcher's England is obvious. The Prime Minister's visit to the Feddens' is a case in point. Thatcher becomes the centre of the house; like a queen bee, she is courted by 'drones' orbiting around her, thus forming curves symbolising social climbing. In other words, out of ambition and sycophancy, crawlers come to redefine Hogarth's serpentine line drawing circles around her. Catherine and Nick cannot help making fun of Thatcher's erotics of power (382). While ambitious men kneel at her feet, it is a cocaine-induced gay like Nick who ironically dares to ask the Lady —whom he reduces in aesthetic terms to a "fusion of the Vorticist and the Baroque"— to dance (384).

As in *The Spell*, drug chemical reactions drive the narrative discourse, dissociating Thatcher from her persona and fragmenting her into a number of geometric and artistic elements. The comic deconstruction/dismembering does not prevent Nick's focalisation from providing an exact impression of her instinctive sense of power. The comic tone only increases when Thatcher, with a couple of whiskies and feeling sexy, dances very fast (385). Their frenetic dance produces curves, encircled in turn by the curves produced by sycophants around the Prime Minister. These are the contours or curves of power and ambition, a late-capitalist parody of Hogarth's line of beauty.

The line of beauty drawn by objects, male bodies, cocaine, Jamesian language and social gestures also affects the novel as a whole and further, Nick, the Feddens and

Thatcher's England. Literature and reality mirror and carve each other; hence, like the
dip and swell of Wani's back, the novel's tripartite structure evokes England's curved
evolution through the nineteen eighties. Michael Dirda defends that the novel interlaces
three different plots: a condition of England, a Jamesian psychological inquiry on social
comedy about the Feddens, and a gay coming-of-age story.[500] In other words, *The Line
of Beauty* delves into the nineteen eighties from national, family and personal
perspectives. Thatcher's England, the Feddens and Nick run parallel processes of
euphoria and trauma, which reach a climax at the end of the decade and of the novel.
The three parts of the novel are in their turn split into six chapters each. Thus, like its
predecessors, *The Line of Beauty* follows a geometric pattern that conveys its content.
The three parts coincide with the years 1983, 1986 and 1987 respectively; i.e., the years
of Thatcher's landslide, the peak of her popularity and, finally, the beginning of her
decline. Likewise, the Feddens and Nick undergo a serpentine three-staged evolution.
As James Wood points out, "in the first section, Gerald Fedden has just been elected to
Parliament, and is clearly in the ascendant, Nick and Toby, and all their chums, have
come down from Oxford with everything ahead of them. Nick loses his virginity to the
comely Leo in the communal gardens."[501] The title of this first section, "The Love-
Chord," makes reference to Nick's infatuation with the Feddens (particularly with Toby
and Gerald), Wani and Leo. His is a leap into the future, unaware but hopeful of what is
going to happen. The swell of this first section reaches its peak in the mid-eighties
section, "To Whom Do You Beautifully Belong?" For Wood, this part "represents the
decade's ripe, wavering acme: parties, cocaine, the swell of money, and sex still
unhaunted by AIDS. But, in Hollinghurst's account, there is little pleasure, there is only
degradation, in this particular line of beauty."[502] Moral considerations apart, the novel
reveals the first symptoms of exhaustion at this stage. Wani becomes a grotesque
parody of himself, his beauty dissolving into AIDS. Exhaustion leads to disappointment
when Nick finds out Gerald's affair with his secretary, which only forecasts the
traumatic resolution of the last part, "The End of the Street." After signs resurfacing and
being repressed throughout, the trauma is belatedly triggered by events that even Nick
cannot ignore:

> Everything unravels, as we knew it would. Leo dies of AIDS, and Wani is now deadly ill;
> his parents continue to maintain that he caught it from a lavatory seat. Gerald Fedden
> narrowly retains his parliamentary position in the general election of 1987. But he is soon
> investigated for financial irregularities. The baying press, now camped outside his Notting
> Hill mansion, discovers that his lodger, one Nick Guest, is the lover of Wani Ouradi, the
> son of the supermarket millionaire and Tory Party donor. Gerald is finished as soon as this
> story is revealed, and the Feddens turn on Nick, who has kept, it seems, so much from
> them.[503]

In a narcissistic fashion, *The Line of Beauty* not only mirrors its predecessors; like *The
Swimming-pool Library*, it also mirrors itself. Episodes and characters recur, producing

---

[500] Dirda: "Condition," n.p.
[501] Wood: "Ogee," 49.
[502] Ibid.
[503] Ibid.

a specular, eventually traumatic, effect. This is especially the case of the hero, who frequently splits himself into performer and witness of his own behaviour. During Toby's birthday party (Hollinghurst, 2004: 89) and in Nick's first sexual encounter with Leo, the extradiegetic narrator describes the protagonist's self-splitting or dis-association: "Just before he came he had a brief vision of himself" (40). In dis-associating from himself and the other, Nick's access to reality is vicarious, traumatic and belated, usually mediated by artefacts or deflectors like mirrors. Hence, the novel recalls Henry James's psychological and labyrinthine discourse, where looking glasses also mould identity.[504] Mirrors serve the novel to bear witness to an "undisclosed crisis" (Hollinghurst 2004: 11) and to Wani's family, "like actors on a set" (211). Yet, they ultimately serve to reproduce but also split and fragment reality and identity for the one looking. Drawing on Lacan's 'mirror stage', the specularity of looking-glasses bears witness and confronts the beholder's precarious self-completeness, of which narcissism is the symptom. Nick's retina works like a convex mirror which catches and projects what he sees. Meanwhile, the mirror itself becomes an active interlocutor to be addressed as well as a space, a stage of the self (255). Being shadowy and glossy, gays' traumatic experiences in Hollinghurst's texts reveal and hide, reflect and deflect. Mirrors echo the beauty of Wani (258) and of Nick's first lover Leo (424) but also the impending lines of AIDS the protagonist fails to identify. Drawing on trauma poetics, beauty and disease are two stages of the same reality in *The Line of Beauty*, the mirror being just the vehicle to render the process. Also, the mirror helps to define Nick Guest as a split character, an outsider, an 'odd one out' to the Feddens. Indeed, his attempts to bridge the hiatus between his lodgers and himself prove to be precarious, his status being an ellipsis in Gerald's discourse. From a literary standpoint, however, his role is crucial, being a privileged focaliser —like Waugh's Charles Ryder, Fitzgerald's Nick Carradine or Proust's Marcel— to Thatcherism.

The dual structure of *The Swimming-pool Library*, the tripartite pattern of *The Folding Star* and the four-angled *rondeau* of *The Spell* constitute an arithmetic progression *The Line of Beauty* completes in a pentangular arrangement: the novel turns around a four-member family focalised by the hero. All structures of Hollinghurst's texts prove to be transient and fallible, though. Nick works as a precarious fifth vortex. And his sexual orientation, together with Catherine's instability and Gerald's scandals, soon ruin Thatcher's neo-Victorian family model and any geometric balance which, like in Hollinghurst's previous novels, also pivots on specular triangles. All these triangles pass through Nick, a fragmented character against his fragmentation. Being many in one, *i.e.* an outsider, a flatterer, an arriviste, a great pretender, a confidant, a Jamesian, a camp aesthete, a surrogate son, a guardian/intruder, a sentimentalist, and finally an outcast and a probable victim of AIDS, Nick ventriloquises himself to disassociate from himself and be someone else. Paradoxically, his narcissism is an act of self-detachment, even self-denial, to elusively disregard his upbringing. A repository of the Feddens' secrets, like a traumatic "sleepy conscience" (369), and a fake surrogate son (4), Nick can only feel "the chill of reality" (369) when witnessing Gerald's extramarital affair. Drawing on the protagonist of Hartley's *The Go-between*, he cannot cope with the scene he considers a treason. In Nick's case, it is even more intense since Gerald's affair

---

[504] Stevens: *Henry*, 24.

comes as an aftermath to the protagonist's witnessing the Feddens' chamber as a powerful metaphor of his personal revision of Freud's primal scene (463). Drawing on Freud, Laplanche and Pontalis address the fact that "the primal fantasies depend on a relation to a primal scene."[505] This is not only what happens with Nick when confronted with the bedroom where his primal fantasy lies. Geoff Gilbert applies it to the experience of reading Hollinghurst as well.[506] Be it as it may, Nick's celebratory aestheticism when he first experiences the Feddens as his own family, space and object of desire, engagement and identification comes to a traumatic end in this last revival of Freudian primal scene.

Before being actually rejected by the Feddens, Nick has vicariously experienced the transition from celebration to trauma when performing Shakespeare's Cerimon in Oxford. The story of the Lord of Ephesus, who must leave the court after having revived Queen Thaissa years before (Hollinghurst 2004: 493), forecasts the protagonist's downfall. That is, Nick's traumatic disassociation recurs when triggering events wake it up. A likely victim of AIDS, because, the narrator hints, "he never lived to find out" (501), Nick can only sentimentalise his life and his problematic cathexis to others. In relinquishing to sentimentalism, he is withdrawing from himself: "It was a sort of terror, made up of emotions from *every stage of his short life, weaning, homesickness, envy and self-pity*, but he felt that the self-pity belonged to a larger pity" (501, my italics). The hero's *Bildungsroman* is dramatically reduced to four traumatic stages, addressing his problematic relations with his parents, his origins, the Feddens and even with himself. Melodramatic sentimentalism, *i.e.* his feeling of irrepressible and universal pity, serves him to convey his sense of loss. Thus, he finally glimpses "The End of the Street," as Margaret Thatcher would do a few years later.

In more senses than one, *The Line of Beauty* reads almost like a sequel of *The Swimming-pool Library*. In both cases, the hero's traumatic destiny is guided by poetic justice (5) due, in part, to their hybris. It is only that *The Line of Beauty* is more politically committed with Thatcherism, and AIDS is no longer an ineffable issue, but one to be addressed belatedly. Indeed, the hero's two boyfriends are infected with the virus whereas an avalanche of catastrophes leads him to an uncertain future. Hollinghurst's fourth novel is narrated by an extradiegetic narrator, who is also a focaliser. However, it focuses on a gay youth who, like Will Beckwith and Edward Maners, is 'the reflector' and, especially, the 'controlling idea'.[507] As the 'controlling idea' or 'centre of interest', the hero gives cohesion to the novel, but also a distance from himself that helps to articulate traumata. Thus, the allegedly celebratory tone of *The Spell* vanishes and *The Line of Beauty* takes the curve started by *The Swimming-pool Library* to its end.

---

[505] Gilbert: *Properties*, 131.

[506] Ibid.

[507] I am using the terminology that Saran Bihari Mathur uses in her analysis of Henry James's theories on point of view (in Martínez-Alfaro, 2003: 300).

4.4   Intertextuality and anti-Thatcherism

The political panorama on the publication of *The Line of Beauty* has nothing to do with that of *The Swimming-pool Library*. In 2004, Thatcher was already history, the impact of AIDS had decreased a great deal, and Blair's government had started a gay-friendly policy. A revision of the exciting but traumatic nineteen eighties in the UK seemed necessary, as American TV series *Angels in America* did with the eponymous play by Tony Kushner (1991, 1992) and André Techiné's film, *Les Témoins* (2007), did to repair the silenced voices of the AIDS era.[508] As a tragicomedy of manners, *The Line of Beauty* recalls the devastating effects of the disease and Thatcher's politics from a satiric outlook, veering to sentimentalism towards the end. The hybrid character of the novel is drawn from the literary voices it recalls. Henry James is the central spirit, but how the satiric tradition of Trollope, Waugh and Hogarth's paintings is recast to edify gayness as a medical, moral and political label in the eighties cannot be overlooked.

The Line of Beauty, Tóibín points out, "invokes the spirit of Henry James and manages this more successfully than in his previous novels."[509] Nick's very surname, Guest, is a borrowing from an early Jamesian story entitled "Guest's Confession."[510] Being Henry James ubiquitous, David Wiegand argues there are traces of other authors as well: "Nick Guest's American cousin could very well be Fitzgerald's Nick Carraway, who is as much an outsider almost admitted to the inner circle of his rich idols as Guest is."[511] Another major influence is Waugh's *Brideshead Revisited* —Guest and Ryder being attracted to a world not their own— and, to a lesser extent, Anthony Trollope. It is political satire, an issue never touched upon by Hollinghurst so far, that makes *The Line of Beauty* tributary to Trollope. According to Tóibín, Trollope "is good on English lords and English MPs and their wives, on the short steps between the London drawing room and the Houses of Parliament. He is very good too on the social and sexual atmosphere which surrounds English power. He can also write well about semi-plausible outsiders."[512] Hence, Tóibín argues, Trollope "would be very proud of some of the scenes in Hollinghurst's novel, some dinner parties at which powerful men are present, where there is much constituted English matter."[513] Trollope's resonances apart, Nick declares himself a Jamesian to Rachel Fedden's brother (Hollinghurst, 2004: 52). James's (written) and Hogarth's (artistic) lines of beauty make up the framework for more contemporary issues, particularly drug-using and male bodies that delineate Nick's individuation process, which turns traumatic (because) it is overaesthetisised.

At the beginning of his career, Hollingurst tried to write a "rather Jamesian novel, set in Venice and about a teenage boy who has an affair with his father's mistress."[514] However, as the writer further explains, "that Jamesian or Proustian disguise of trying to

---

[508]   André Techiné : "Hymne à la vie, interview d'André Téchiné." http://www.evene.fr/cinema/ actualite/interview-andr-techine-temoins-beart-blanc-702php, 2007.
[509]   Tóibín: "Comedy," 5.
[510]   Ibid.
[511]   David Wiegand: "Surface Cracks." https://bit.ly/3AzMtWV, 2004.
[512]   Tóibín: "Comedy," 6.
[513]   Ibid.
[514]   In Canning: *Conversations*, 357.

write about an affair with a middle-aged woman was kind of beyond me […]. Perhaps I could do it now."[515] Although *The Line of Beauty* does not accomplish the original goal, the novel is Jamesian to a large degree. The classic homoerotic affair between a middle-aged woman and a youth is redeployed in *The Line of Beauty* in the affair between Nick and the Feddens. The hero's desire is articulated in all-male gay triangles which, once more, redefine the Girardian triangles that, according to Stevens, also characterise James' fiction.[516] For Stevens, James's standard queer plot "involves a struggle for possession, and ends in a tragic, violent *dénouement*. Rivalry is of course one of fiction's core ingredients, but James consistently turns the screw on the classic rivalry plot, involving a struggle between two men for a woman."[517] Nick's erotic affiliations usually take the form of homo-social/erotic all-male triangles, displacing females as exchange value. He forms a triangle with working-class black Leo and Lebanese millionaire Wani, as well as a utopic erotic triangle with Toby and Wani. The novel recasts James's triangles and oblique language to reveal the inarticulacy and sublimation of (homo)sexual desire in his characters. Even queer critics, like Eve Sedgwick, read the 'blanks' in James's fiction as a sign of (homo)sexual restraint. His discourse on (homo)sexual desire is ambiguous and, therefore, difficult to decode, hence the controversy that makes his fiction so attractive for gay and queer critics alike and so apt to stage the tension between celebration and trauma of gay experience.

According to Stevens, James felt a simultaneous repulsion and fascination for Wilde in the eighteen eighties,[518] which undoubtedly intensified after Wilde's downfall. This would respond to (Sedgwick's concept of) 'homosexual panic', which characterises most turn-of-the-century gay writing. In this light, and with the increasing interest of the medical science and Victorian society in same-sex desire, it is understandable that writers were especially careful about sexual issues. Still, despite (or due to) its obliquity, James's fiction has become part of gay iconography: triangles, ineffable secrets, ambiguous men, strong women, rich American heiresses prey to artful Europeans, aestheticism, and a skilful use of camp make up a literary discourse which, in different degrees, recalls texts by Wilde, Proust or Stevenson. However, unlike Wilde's "loud, flashy, aggressively clever" celebratory camp, that of Henry James is "quiet, self-effacing and subtle […] of the nudging, hinting variety; it is always to say the beautiful and witty thing, and in so doing draw the attention to the utterance rather than the speaker, to the medium rather than to the message."[519] *The Line of Beauty* makes use of this self-enclosed narcissism. For Nick in particular, James's language has become a natural way of seeing and uttering things.[520] However, Hollinghurst's novel adds a political dimension to James's camp, exposing the political and economic excesses and double morality of Thatcherism. It makes use of camp which, despite prejudices, "put[s] to the test [the] theatricality of the political scene."[521] That is, for

[515] Ibid.
[516] Stevens: *Henry*, 90.
[517] Ibid.
[518] Ibid., 129.
[519] Ibid., 168.
[520] Tóibín: "Comedy," 7.
[521] Letissier: "Queer," 203.

Georges Letissier, camp in The *Line of Beauty* reveals the arbitrary character of power and its dramatic consequences.[522] Thus, although the novel takes a narcissistic pleasure in describing upper-class houses, rooms, and gestures in an exercise of auto-referentiality that recalls James's latest fiction,[523] the text is fascinated with the English class system from an ironic standpoint and is in line with a long tradition in English literature, including Austen, Trollope, Galsworthy and Waugh.

Apart from Nick, the most obviously Jamesian character in *The Line of Beauty* is Rachel Fedden. The member of a Rotschild-like family of Jewish bankers, she inhabits an exquisite international world and uses a "code both aristocratic and distantly foreign" (Hollinghurst, 2004: 8). The whole novel is a repertoire of the inarticulacy of Rachel's language and aristocratic poise, and Nick's reverential infatuation. When Gerald's fraudulent business comes out in the tabloids, her serpentine, 'elliptical' discourse points to and eludes her husband's scandal simultaneously: "'Mm …'" and "Well, I suppose they sort of … um …'" (451) is all she says about the matter. Just as Nick does with Henry James, he imitates Rachel's (in turn Jamesian) manners and self-control, particularly "the upper-class economy of her talk" (47), which differs so much from Gerald's disocurse. Rachel's is the position of the self-confident upper-class who, unlike her husband, regards Thatcher as a lower-middle-class and vulgar leader (62). She is a Jamesian prototype, much like Mrs Gereth in *The Spoils of Poynton*, whereas Gerald draws on Trollope's Phineas Finn, which significantly he enjoys reading (302).

In a conversation with Lord Kessler, Nick explains he is working on Henry James's style for his PhD, which he considers particularly elusive (54). After the conversation, Kessler shows Nick two leather-bound albums with Victorian photographs of aristocrats, intellectuals and the King himself (55). Of the whole collection, the hero is especially impressed by a photograph dated in 1903 with the Master in a central position (55). Eighty years later, in a calculated parody, Nick takes the place of his idol at the table of the Kesslers. Like his predecessor, Nick becomes the spectator of surrounding Tories. Without James's insight, the hero starts a noteworthy conversation with Penny, the daughter of Rachel's communist friend, Norman Kent, on James's social insight and how it would apply in Thatcher's England (140). Although, as a whole, *The Line of Beauty* does not imitate James's literary style —only Nick does it— the novel can be read, as Joseph Brooker suggests, as "the answer to Penny's question."[524] If a shrewd Henry James had lived in the nineteen eighties, "he would have had the intimate ambiguities of the dominant class of the age; he would have teased at the relations between money and taste, power and style; he would have used an ostensibly narrow social remit to seek insight into a whole era."[525] That is, *The Line of Beauty* adapts James's psycho-social insight and role of beauty to scrutinise Thatcher's England, frequently through Catherine's censorious discourse and Nick's naïveté. Using aesthetics as an instrument of political satire is one of the novel's main assets. Nick's ex-fellow at Oxford, the promising politician Paul Tompkins, treats Britain's crisis in

---

[522] Ibid.

[523] Stevens: *Henry*, 169.

[524] Joseph Brooker: "Neo Lines: Alan Hollinghurst and the Apogee of the Eighties." London: Birkbeck eprints, http://eprints.bbk.ac.uk/archive/00000470, 2005, n.p.

[525] Ibid.

campy terms addressing the lack of style of MP's wives (Hollinghurst, 2004: 62). The gravity of the country's situation clashes with Tompkins' frivolous analysis of the bad taste of Tories' wives. As Brooker[526] points out, aesthetic poverty is endemic to the conservatives, which provokes hilarious situations. As mentioned above, Catherine uses the Tories' irrational devotion for blue to make fun of her father, having the green front door immediately painted blue just before Thatcher's visit (Hollinghurst 2004: 366). Like Firbank's and James's children, or like the chorus of Attic tragedy, Catherine exposes men's folly, selfishness and hypocrisy. She also points to the ethical and aesthetic deficiency of the New Right (381). All this proves to the novel's satiric potential, the fact that it takes "a more comic view of social activity than either Trollope or James would allow." [527] The narrator also ridicules Lady Partridge, Gerald's Thatcher-like mother, recalling her hilarious comments on a journalist's opinion about racism, which she calls "the *coloured* question" (Hollinghurst, 2004: 78, original emphasis). In delving into Lady Partridge, the narrator resurfaces the precision of James's social insight. Likewise, the Tippers, a tycoon and his wife, and their daughter Sophie, Toby's girlfriend, become the target of the narrator's anti-Tory satire. Sophie's performing the protagonist in Oscar Wilde's *Lady Windermere's Fan* only makes her idiocy conspicuous as long as she argues she loves deconstructing texts, as the director intends to do, when she is unable to understand its meaning (129). Satire climaxes with Maurice Tipper saying he hates Shakespeare because he only recalls being bitten by mosquitoes along a *Pericles* performance (130).

By contrast, the concert of Nina Glaserova at the Feddens' plays a subtle irony on the conservatives' hypocrisy and lack of style. In a funny crescendo, Tory good manners turn into irrepressible impatience, their fake decorum thus being exposed. Gerald hires Nina, the daughter of a dissident from Eastern Europe (237). In front of an ignorant audience (237), the pianist starts her energetic concert, which soon provokes almost general boredom. Bertram Ouradi and Lady Partridge keep in respect (239), the same as Lady Kimbolton, the party fund-raiser, or Gerald himself. When the sonata comes to an end, "a firm applause [breaks] out [...] by the fact of being the end" (241). However, Nina continues with Rachmaninov's Prelude in C-sharp minor and, to the audience's horror, with Bach's Toccata and Fugue in D minor. By then, they have almost completely lost patience and are next to a mutiny (242). The hilarious end comes when the pianist starts playing the third encore, the Sabre Dance by Khachaturian, and Gerald sends Nick to congratulate and stop her (242). Likewise, Hollinghurst recasts Firbank's irony to expose Jenny Groom's (the wife of one of Gerald's political colleagues) ignorance when she argues she read a novel by Henry James under the title *Dr Johnson*. When Nick corrects her saying the novel was written by Joyce Cary, she can only answer: "I knew I had read something by him" (137). Still, in spite of the clash between Toryism and aestheticism, neo-liberalism managed to join both under a common project. For Joseph Brooker, Thatcherism may be old-fashioned and anti-aesthetic; yet, during the nineteen eighties, England lived a period of unprecedented interest for style,[528] which became just a marketable good. Against the backcloth of a

---

[526] Ibid.

[527] Tóibín: "Comedy," 7.

[528] Brooker: "Neo Lines," n.p.

profitable culture industry, Nick —and Henry James— is the worker bee behind the process of marketing of aesthetics that Gerald and Wani represent and control.

Thatcher's politics completely changed the national landscape from a political, ethical and, especially, economic viewpoint. As Julian Critchley argues, there were people who did well,[529] such as the Feddens, the Tippers and the Ouradis. It is this elite that the political and aesthetic satire of Hollinghurst's novel targets. For some critics, the comic treatment of the upper class may not make up for the absence of Britain's real problems in the nineteen eighties. Thatcher's confrontation with —and eventual victory over— the traditionally powerful trade unions, the unemployment rate, the massive privatisation of public services (such as health and education) and its consequences for the underprivileged, are practically overlooked throughout the novel. Only Catherine represents a conflicting voice that claims for social justice against the not-so-concerned narrator. Although mentally unbalanced, as Penny suggests, Catherine is very clever (Hollighurst 2004: 499). Her complex personality is cross-referential, problematic and problematising. Drawing on Flora in *The Turn of the Screw* and, as Flannery argues, on Catherine Sloper, the protagonist of *Washington Square*,[530] Catherine works both as "an agent of crisis and truth."[531] Likewise, she echoes Orton's Hal in *Loot* in her inability to lie, a fact that inevitably brings about funny situations, coming to a climax when she leaks her father's affair to the press. In this context of social masquerade, Nick's justification of Catherine's attitude is particularly funny when he argues her sincerity is the effect of a mania (Hollinghurst, 2004: 481). In a tragicomedy of manners like this one, Catherine's 'mania' for truth serves to disclose the hypocrisy of the conservative circles she belongs to.

Thatcher's politics split the country into two halves: those who made it and those who didn't. Among the former, the novel includes Gerald Fedden, Bertram Ouradi and Sir Maurice Tipper. The three men represent a 'new class' under the auspices of Thatcher's promotion of individualism and ambition.[532] Despite common belief, unlike the class system, the English elite system is scarcely determined by background. Most Thatcher's people "had a great deal more to do with an elite than with the upper classes [...]. Generally they were self-made men."[533] Echoing the pattern of Hogarth's line, her men's trajectories followed the 'ascending' line of (beauty of) the country and its leader. An important contributor to the conservative party, Bertram Ouradi is the self-made man in the novel. As he tells Nick in one of Feddens' parties, he had left a post-war, devastated Lebanon for London (Hollinghurst, 2004: 225), where he made a fortune (227-228). As a pragmatic entrepreneur, Ouradi asks Nick about Gerald Fedden as his passport to the corridors of power at Westminster (220). As the narrator explains, when Ouradi talks about 'our' people, he is quite ambiguous, but interested in any case (220). Be it as it may, it makes reference to Thatcher's sectarian 'one of us', *i.e.* a melting pot

---

[529]   Julian Critchley: *Some of Us. People who Did Well under Thatcher*. London 1992.

[530]   Dennis Flannery: "The Powers of Apostrophe and the Boundaries of Mourning: Henry James, Alan Hollinghurst, and Toby Litt." *The Henry James Review*, 26(3), 2005, 297.

[531]   Ibid.

[532]   John Ranelagh: *Thatcher's People. An Insider's Account of the Politics, the Power and the Personalities*. London 1991, 44.

[533]   Ibid., 42, 45.

of conservatives and neo-liberals. For his part, Gerald is the prototype of the promising Thatcherite: a devoted follower of her politics (243) and of her personality. His devotion turns hilarious when he says he would like to swim in her blue eyes (319). The erotics of power between Thatcher and her young aides (to which Ranelagh makes reference) is nowhere more evident than in Gerald's quasi-religious loyalty. Gerald's career draws on Trollope's Phineas's double morality and political opportunism. On a campaign visit to Barwick, Nick's home county for the 1987 election, the novel lays bare conservative populism. After appealing to English pride and telling stupid jokes, "Gerald was led off on a quasi-royal tour of the fête" (270) and escorted by the mayoress. The gulf between an upper-class man dressed for Westminster rather than for the country (271), and his potential voters, makes the whole scene a political pantomime. Continuing with his mercenary vote-catching performance, he even plays at a tombola as well as welly-whanging (272). The whole pantomime and the gap between Barwick voters and their candidate climax when, in winning a pig, he can only claim in a snobbish tone: "We don't actually eat pork" (275).

A number of scandals soon tarnish Fedden's reputation: his affair with his secretary, his having a gay lodger at home, and the takeover he and Sir Maurice Tipper are involved in make up a troublesome lot. Thus, he soon becomes stuff for the tabloids involving members of Thatcher's government. Before the press makes it public, Nick and Catherine bear witness to Gerald's infidelity with Penny Kent at the Houses of Parliament (460). Once more, Catherine is the *agent provocateur* behind the public exposure of Gerald's peccadilloes. A troubled and heartbroken daughter, the tabloids reveal, "speaks of minister's affair" (462). Catherine's counter-discourse is effective as far as it discloses Tory double morality. Her solid convictions against unethical conservative politics (453) —rather than her mental instability— explain her act of betrayal. Thus, the novel deals with the role of the yellow press as a mechanism of (in Foucault's terms) public surveillance and eventual punishment; a role Trollope's novels already played in the nineteenth century. The yellow press is made into a fetish that freezes people into characters to be morally scrutinised. Hence, a newly naïf Nick feels both "victimized and flattered" (445) as he is yet unaware that photographs, as in *The Swimming-pool Library*, bring about a faint flicker of calamity. The homophobic explicitness and sensationalism of the headlines about the Feddens and their gay friends and AIDS victims (489) only trigger Nick's foreseeable downfall (472). His structural traumatic self-withdrawal is resurfaced when headlines come out. In other words, when the coming-out is no longer a private issue, but socially visible, it must be repressed and trauma symptoms arise. The conflict between freedom and the moral constraints of Thatcherism [534] is conspicuous following the scandal. Sir Maurice Tipper remains virtually untouched because, despite his implication in an impressive takeover, as Wani suggests, has power enough to control the media (Hollinghurst 2004: 442). Tipper is of Michael Ashcroft's type, which revolutionised the economy and society of the eighties. As Critchley points out, Ashcroft was the hero of deal-makers, since "the creation of his empire was largely a one-man achievement,"[535] like his fictional referents in *The Line of*

---

[534] Critchley: *Some of Us*, 177.
[535] Ibid., 98.

Beauty. Take-overs were Ashcroft's main sport.[536] However, the parallelisms between reality and fiction go further. Like Tipper and Fedden, Ashcroft —and Jeffrey Archer (Hollinghurst 2004: 151-161)— passed from the serious press to gossip pages as he combined "money, royalty, *arrivisme* …" (99), and like them, he was mentioned, yet untouched, in high-profile scandals (100).

Chapter eleven is split into six scenes or frescoes on the Feddens' French holidays. The celebratory spirit of these summer days —evocative of Nick, Wani and Toby's Oxford days— breaks down with the Tippers' arrival in the third section. An instinctive Catherine attempts to expose Tipper as a dishonest tycoon who does charity for self-redemption (331). It is obvious that *The Line of Beauty* is not the Communist Manifesto, but it proves some political commitment, at least to lay bare the foundations of Thatcherism and its dubious practices. It is irony, rather than straight condemnation, as usual in Hollinghurst, that highlights the political, ethical and aesthetic mischief the neo-liberal and conservative allegiance conveyed with an incredibly reduced number of ideas.

The fourth section of chapter eleven tackles sexual morality. On the outburst of AIDS, Thatcher's government ignored its effects while 'self-deserving victims' — mostly gays and drug-addicts— died. *The Line of Beauty* displaces the scenario of historical trauma to family level; hence the aforementioned self-withdrawing sentimentalism. When Rachel's friend Pat Grayson dies of AIDS, they all elude the issue (333). James's line of beauty is, in Rachel's discourse, useful to circumvent the traumatic event arguing he died of pneumonia as a result of a trip to Asia (334). However, Catherine dismantles her mother's hypocrisy and tells the sheer truth, that he had a promiscuous life syle and finally: "He had AIDS!" (335). It is not that Rachel suffers from PTSD, as Nick does, but she cannot bear witness to and/or utter the traumatic event unless it is belatedly and vicariously; she does it not out of trauma, but out of a strict aesthetic rather than an ethic code. AIDS is simply not her concern and cannot be uttered because it is as abject as gays themselves for such a conservative elite. Hence, when Nick compares Grayson's death with Tipper's mother's long final illness, the latter is quick to set up a difference, claiming his mother was not responsible for it (339). Tipper draws on a widespread perverse discourse to hold gays morally responsible for their deaths. On the front page of *The Daily Telegraph*, Jeffrey-Poulter recalls, AIDS was labelled as "the prize of promiscuity."[537] This equation, repeated in the press, from the pulpit and elsewhere, converted the disease into "a divine displeasure," "a curse,"[538] "the wrath of God,"[539] and homosexuality into "morally irregular, thus creating a moral panic."[540] *The Line of Beauty* breaks with this moral and political anxiety with irony anew. In this line, Sally Tipper's exchange with Nick on AIDS and sex protection lays bare conservatives' ignorance and gays' risky sexual practices and the dissimilar outlooks on the impending trauma. When Nick suggests oral sex as an alternative to more dangerous anal sex, Sally can only answer: 'Kissing, you

---

[536] Ibid.

[537] Stephen Jeffery-Poulter: *Peers Queers and Commons*. London 1991, 178.

[538] Ibid., 182.

[539] Ibid., 183.

[540] Ibid., 197.

mean.' (Hollinghurst 2004: 339-340). The conversation does not simply reflect the nineteen eighties historically, particularly the decade's historical and cultural trauma. It also reinterprets the decade from a comic, yet ruthless, standpoint, and with a political purpose. Once AIDS has been demythologised, at least in part, and Thatcher's politics have been digested in 2004, irony and camp provide the reader with a new perspective on the crisis.

With the coming of Reagan, Thatcher and AIDS, as Nick's case ascertains, gays' role turned ambiguous, if not directly schizophrenic. They were tolerated if they were discreet. However, simultaneously, they had to be visible enough not to be confused with the rest. Briefly stated, from an essentialist outlook, gays were forced to relinquish the distinctive feature of their identities, namely, their sexual desire to be innocuous to society at large. This is how gay identity itself came to be edified in traumatic terms, its absence and presence being fastidious but necessary for social control, surveillance and (un)utterability. This tension between satire, humour and celebration of beauty, mostly in the first part, and Nick's introspective trauma with Jamesian undertones, mostly in the second, make up the swell and decline of the serpentine, which is as ethic as aesthetic.

4.5   Aestheticism, the trauma of AIDS and Apollonian tragedy[541]

Hogarth's satiric undertones have proved to be convincing to convey Thatcherism. Yet, the Apollonian concept of beauty constitutes the first and foremost key factor of Nick's delusive individuation process, from the narcissistic self-idealisation of Oxford days to the Dionysian rupture of his last days at the Feddens' (Yebra 2011). Drawing on the Corry, the gym where Will cruises in *The Swimming-pool Library*, Nick's is also a very British homoerotic space, "school-like and comfortless" (Hollinghurst, 2004: 181). This is a territory of freedom, celebration of beauty and sexual possibilities, "a floating tableau of men," where, as the narrator describes, identities blur in a continuum of sex and desire (185). Thus, although this Arcadian scenario is plagued with signs of an impending crisis —there is a George who had died very young (182), obituaries and inexplicable weight-losing (186)— it blockages Nick's self-awareness. His infatuation with Toby and the lost *Brideshead-Revisited*-like world he represents is not only a wishfulfilment fantasy. Out of a present stimulus, namely Toby's unreachable muscular body (327-328), the narrator reworks sexual desire as a narcissistic aesthetic experience; one of almostness, lack, problematic cathexis and eventual sentimentalism, drawing on James's heroines'. In desiring and identifying with Toby, Nick is a narcissist; hence his inarticulacy and self-pity, which explains his obsessive yearning for golden days at Oxford (349). This is the trauma of loss, individual, communal and national, the hero attempts to solve evoking James's aesthetic conception of reality.

---

[541] In this section I draw on some ideas from my article: "A Terrible Beauty: Ethics, Aesthetics and the Trauma of Gayness in Alan Hollinghurst's *The Line of Beauty*". In Onega, Susana and Jean-Michel Ganteau (eds.). *Ethics and Trauma in Contemporary British Fiction*. Amsterdam and New York 2011, 175-208.

The treatment of Nick's trauma is necessarily different from that of Will and Nantwich in *The Swimming-pool Library*. Although still a problematic issue, AIDS is not only sublimated intertextually, but an instrument to rework the representation of beauty. Beauty is, in fact, ambivalent, both celebratory and traumatic. Hence, James's *The Spoils of Poynton* (1897) and Thomas Mann's *Death in Venice* will be addressed to prove that Nick's *Künstlerroman* results from Nietzsche's aesthetic conflict between the Apollonian and the Dionysian. Beauty is always under suspicion in Hollinghurst's fourth novel, most often being reduced to a line, a narcissistic trace that is lost and is hard to mourn. That Henry James is its tutelary spirit is not extraneous because, in apostrophising him, *The Line of Beauty* proves recent fiction's increasing concern with loss and mourning.[542] Apostrophe is thus a recurrent figure, particularly in Nick's self-identification through others, particularly James and his sense of beauty. The figure "can be described in terms of its relationship to mourning and the elegiac of how texts (and the emotions they sometimes represent) can derive their power from a capacity to turn from one object or mode of address to another."[543] The event of addressing the dead constitutes an act of mourning in itself whereby the novel establishes a bond with James which permits and encourages "a reconsideration of what mourning can and cannot do."[544] In Flannery's view, James is invoked a) structurally, the plot structure of *The Line of Beauty* hinging on a secret and enveloped in layers of secrecy, as happens in *The Wings of the Dove* or *The Portrait of a Lady*;[545] b) nominally, most names having a Jamesian source;[546] and c) situationally, for it echoes "crucial and painful scenarios in *The Golden Bowl*, "The Aspern Papers," and *The Bostonians*" as well as "The Turn of the Screw" and very especially *The Spoils of Poynton* and *The Wings of the Dove*.[547] James's psycho-social insight informs not only the novel's satiric anti-Thatcherism, but also its discourse on trauma, mourning and melancholia.

The Line of Beauty recasts James's "The Altar of the Dead," as François Truffaut had done in *The Green Room*,[548] to overcome paralysing melancholia and, therefore, make mourning feasible. James's story deals with the protagonist's Freudian melancholia, as there is no available formula to articulate his bond with a dead friend. In "Mourning and Melancholia," Freud had already diagnosed the aetiology of melancholia as frustrated mourning. With Freud's essay in mind, Hugh Stevens argues that to the "inhibition and loss of interest" characteristic of normal mourning, melancholia adds "an extraordinary diminution in self-regard, an impoverishment of ego on a grand scale."[549] As Stevens further explains, this delusional yearning for punishment often affects homosexuals in a homophobic social order.[550] The complex cathexis with the object of desire which characterises queer melancholia is particularly noteworthy in George Stransom, the hero of "The Altar of the Dead." When those

---

[542] Flannery: *Powers*, 294.
[543] Ibid., 295.
[544] Ibid., 296.
[545] Ibid., 296-297.
[546] Ibid., 297.
[547] Ibid., 297-298.
[548] Ibid., 301.
[549] Stevens: *Henry*, 152.
[550] Ibid.

around him begin to die, Stransom decides to transform the small chapel of a Catholic church into a shrine to worship his dead through symbolic flames.[551] However, of them all, Acton Hague constitutes the "greatest blank in the shining page [...]. For Acton Hague no flame could ever rise on any altar of his."[552] The actual relation between both men is virtually overlooked. It is only through some nuanced references that we learn about the unspekability of their friendship and the melancholic inarticulacy of Stransom's mourning. From the narrator's discourse —and the insightful words of Hugh Stevens— it can be inferred that this is a homoerotic relation, beginning at Oxbridge, and broken with the onset of adulthood.[553] After Wilde's downfall, the hero's desire becomes ineffable, except through the altar which Stevens compares to the American Names Project, or the AIDS quilt, "which aims to supplement a lack in American institutional life, to assert the importance of and provide a prominent cultural face for mourning deaths of AIDS."[554] As Queer Nation and similar groups did during the nineteen nineties, "The Altar of the Dead" serves the hero to overcome *non-performative* melancholia through Catholic camp;[555] in fact, Stramson is saved *in extremis* by Hague's spirit in a fantastic end. Truffaut translated Stransom's inarticulate trauma —or Lacanian "kernel of loss"— to First-World-War France.[556] That is, Stransom's personal loss is moved to France's "monumental, public [...], shared traumatic loss."[557] For Flannery, both *The Line of Beauty* and Truffaut's film recast James's story in a new context: "Hollinghurst takes James's animating body of writing with its tantalizingly obscure origins of mournful subjectivity, replicates it, pays tribute to it, uses their own language to confer life on its own vivacity, and in the process repeats Truffaut's reanimating gesture of giving Jamesian mourning 'monumental, public and immediately revealed' causes."[558] More specifically, in Flannery's view, *The Line of Beauty* draws on Truffaut's reappraisal of James's public mourning to invoke the effects of Thatcher's policy and especially "the impact of the then-new phenomenon of AIDS."[559] In my view, Flannery is too optimistic in considering the novel's apostrophe of James as an effective political counterdiscourse[560] and a healing strategy. The political commitment of *The Line of Beauty*, albeit higher than that of Hollinghurst's novels, is still limited and vicarious. Indeed, for Flannery, as Nick's individual trauma is unutterable, it is extrapolated to a communal one. Whereas Truffaut's film sets a parallel between Stransom's pain and First World War France, Hollinghurst's novel sets Nick's pain in the context of "1987 Afghanistan as a place of imperial adventure and sexual danger and the 1982 war in Lebanon."[561]

---

[551] Henry James: "The Altar of the Dead." https://www.gutenberg.org/files/642/642-h/642-h.htm, 1996, np.
[552] Ibid.
[553] Ibid., 3-4.
[554] Stevens: *Henry*, 161.
[555] Ibid., 162.
[556] Flannery: *Powers*, 301.
[557] Ibid.
[558] Ibid., 301-302.
[559] Ibid., 302.
[560] Ibid.
[561] Ibid., 303.

However, I do not think apostrophising James has the healing effect on melancholia that Flannery suggests. Nick's traumatic experiences cannot be extrapolated to communal tragedies such as the wars in Afghanistan or Lebanon, which are marginal to the novel. His trauma is not successfully mourned, as in Stramson's case. On the contrary, in apostrophising James compulsively, Nick is stuck in melancholia, self-withdrawal, denial and sentimentalism. The novel features numerous examples of inarticulacy, almostness and death, the erotic life of the protagonists being "always haunted by the shadow of death."[562] Likewise, Nick's main projects are never fulfilled, namely his Ph. D. thesis on James, his magazine Ogee and the film on *The Spoils of Poynton*. His infatuation with the Feddens also comes to a traumatic end. Yet, although so-called reality seems elusive and impossible to write down, in looking at a photograph of a dying Leo, (Hollinghurst, 2004: 410), Nick cannot help writing a letter to Leo's mother. He does so because, he confesses, it "couldn't be unwritten" (411) as a traumatic testimony of disease and death. Even then, the protagonist articulates death in a Jamesian fashion. Using a Jamesian quote to address a marginal female is not only ironic. It also confirms the inarticulacy of AIDS and yet another irony, that the novel derives "a certain energy from the annihilation of persons and communities."[563]

Besides Nick's complex cathexis with the other and with himself, his most problematic feature —the one that triggers off catastrophe— is his obsession with Apollonian beauty to overcome structural trauma. The protagonist shares with James's characters their ability to make up "imaginary worlds which are 'doomed to collapse when brought into conjunction with the 'facts'. The facts are always that things are different from what a given character had wanted."[564] This structural dissatisfaction, narcissism, self-denial and tension between the Apollonian and the Dionysian draw on James, but especially, on Thomas Mann's *Death in Venice*. Hollinghurst's Nick and Mann's Aschenbach rely on the Apollonian but they eventually yield into the Dionysian because their conception of art as pure form is misleading. In this sense, Nietzsche's *The Birth of Tragedy* is crucial to understand Mann's *Death in Venice*; the "relation between the [Nietzschean] Dionysian corporeal liberation that erupts towards the end of the novel" is inextricably linked to "the hero's repressed homosexuality."[565] The Nietzschean duality between the Apollonian and the Dionysian[566] responds to a principle whereby the Dionysian, which is unconceivable to human understanding, must be adapted to human scale through the *principium individuationis*."[567] Drawing on Nietzsche, the Apollonian conception of beauty, oneness, and selfhood collapse when the tragic hero falls into *hamartia*,[568] or the tragic error.

---

[562] Ibid., 302.

[563] Ibid.

[564] Roslyn Jolly: *Henry James. History, Narrative, Fiction*. Oxford 1993, 37-38.

[565] Vagelis Siropoulos: "The Dionysian (Gay) Abject: Corporeal Representation in *The Birth of Tragedy* and *Death in Venice*." In Ruth Parkin-Gounelas and Effie Yiannopoulou (eds). *The Other Within*. Vol. I: *Literature and Culture*. Thessaloniki 2001, 93.

[566] Fiedrich Nietzsche: *The Birth of Tragedy Out of the Spirit of Music*, trans. Ian Johnston. http://johnstoniatexts.x10host.com/nietzsche/tragedyhtml.html 2017, n.p.

[567] Nietzsche: *Birth*, n.p.

[568] Ibid.

In trying to live according to the logic the *principium individuationis* and Apollonian beauty, Nick, like Aschenbach, is doomed because their non-normative sexuality finally unleashes and everything collapses around. This is related to Nietszche's "return"[569] of the repressed, that is, the unstoppable force of the Dionysian that is at the core of Western civilisation. Non-normative sexual desire brings about disease and death, be it the cholera in *Death in Venice* or AIDS in *The Line of Beauty*. In Hollinghurst's novel, Nick draws on the conception of beauty conveyed by Henry James's literary style and characters. In this light, he intends to make up his *principium individuationis* as he plays the role of aesthete and fears the Dionysian. However, the Apollonian delusion only works for James's characters. Nick, like Aschenbach, suffers from the tension between the celebration of and the traumatic repression of the Dionysian or the abject. His role is thus ambivalent, a liberated gay and a repressed aesthete at the same time. For most of the novel, like tragic heroes, Nick cannot recognise his unstable status. It is only when the Dionysian bursts out in the form of AIDS and when he is expelled from the Feddens' that he undergoes his *anagnorisis*.

Drawing on Nietzsche, Nick's *hamartia* is not a moral failure, but his failure to recognise the repressed Dionysian. The Dionysian is a force of destruction and suffering, as well as of regeneration. Indeed, for Nietzsche, the fact that the tragic hero is destroyed is paradoxically a reason for happiness since "he is just an illusion, and the eternal life of the will is not disturbed by this destruction."[570] Nietzsche deconstructs Schopenhauer's pessimism, and proposes instead the new tragic hero as a mere instrument of the primal Dionysian and as a 'living proof' of its immensity. Nick is ambivalent, drawing on Nietzsche's vitality and its traumatic aftermath. Nick's tragic error also recalls *The Picture of Dorian Gray*. As Margarét Gunnarsdottir contends, Wilde's novel transcends the two ethical responses it usually arises: either it is read as an "outrage for its wicked amorality […], or morality is implicit in the structure, [so] that the plot itself carries with it poetic justice and the hero's punishment." [571] Gunnarsdottir revises the novel's connection between subjectivity and ethics, particularly "through a reconsideration of Wilde's peculiar Hedonism as its theoretical context."[572] Just like Dorian Gray, who "persists in his misrecognition"[573] in front of his portrait, Nick is unable to overcome the aesthetisised version of himself and the world he has constructed around it. In *The Picture of Dorian Gray*, Lord Henry Wotton mentors the hero who, however, is unable to fully understand the scope of the teaching, particularly Wilde's attempt "to upset traditional morality, to subvert categories of common sense and Puritan values."[574] Dorian proves to be a failed choice. Instead of Wotton's "creative transvaluation of the moral life"[575] in art and identity, Gray becomes narcissistically obsessed with his own portrait. The portrait thus becomes a metaphor for

---

[569] Ibid.

[570] Ibid.

[571] Margarét Gunnarsdottir: "Art Mirrors the Spectator: The Field of Otherness in *The Picture of Dorian Gray*." In Ruth Parkin-Gounelas and Effie Yiannopoulou (eds). *The Other Within. Volume I: Literature and Culture*. Thessaloniki 2001, 249.

[572] Ibid., 249.

[573] Ibid., 251.

[574] Ibid., 253.

[575] Ibid., 254.

Dorian's repressed trangressions —the Dionysian, in Nietzsche's terms— while his body remains an Apollonian illusion. Infatuated with this illusion with beauty, the hero challenges Lord Henry's (and Wilde's) conception of art and reality, and becomes a murderer instead. Nevertheless, as happens with Aschenbach, Dorian cannot finally stop the return of the repressed and his tragic end.

Nick Guest must confront a similar *aporia*. His Apollonian ideal turns a mere illusion which eventually breaks up. Like his predecessors, Nick is unable to understand the ironic message of the narrator; like Aschenbach, he misrecognises the function and limits of art; like Gray, he misrecognises himself, withholding his origins, sexual orientation and his addiction to cocaine. Nevertheless, he cannot sidestep his fate. AIDS —not as a moral punishment—, the effect of drugs and the exposure of his sexual lifestyle trigger off traumatic events which result in the hero's final *anagnorisis*. At the turn of the millennium, James's Apollinean aestheticism no longer works, Nick's outdated concept of beauty being worthless to render a new, problematic relation between reality and art.

Like Aschenbach and James's characters, Nick uses aesthetic forms —mostly Hogarth's 'line of beauty'— in reference to male desirability. *The Line of Beauty* even updates the tensions of *Death in Venice*, but transforming Aschenbach's death-driven philosophical *aporia* into an oversexualised *Bildungsroman* of frustration and irony. It is not that Nick's self-negation is not also suicidal. It is only that sublimation gives way to explicitness. As a renowned professor, Aschenbach penetrates Tadzio with the pen appealing to Plato while Nick is simply Wani's "slut" (Hollinghurst, 2004: 387). Much of the magic and gravity of Mann's text is undermined in Nick's story. Thus, the metaphors of oceanic dissolution of the self which close *Death in Venice* are too abstract a picture for Nick's downfall. Following Nietzsche, Aschenbach dissolves, instead of dying, in a final tragic ecstasy, a fact which Dollimore considers a revolutionary "challenge [to] the existing social order."[576] By contrast, Nick is simply expelled from the Feddens' and is likely to confront disease and death after having enjoyed his ivory tower.

In having his heroes pinioned by unfulfilled desire, which often culminates "in drugs, piety, madness and death,"[577] Hollinghurst's novels address (and somehow convey) the equation homosexuality-death as a politically and morally problematic issue. The endemic tension between trauma and narcissism only increased with the coming of AIDS. Indeed, although fantasies of annihilation had been produced before, the disease became the acid test for the gay community to authenticate its liberation movement and reformulate its structural cultural trauma.[578] *The Line of Beauty* does not treat AIDS simply as a moral issue —although some of its characters do— but rather approaches it as a cultural issue. Hence, the collapse of Nick's world does not exactly respond to moral causes, but rather to political, ethical and aesthetic ones.

Nick's *Bildungsroman* is ruled by artistic objects (Hollinghurst, 2004: 6, 13, 18, 66, 94) through which he becomes himself. Henry James's aestheticism is, in this sense, his tutelary spirit, whose way of writing and conception of life and its relation with art

---

[576] Dollimore: *Death*, 300.
[577] Ibid., 302.
[578] Bersani and Foucault have delved into the issue extensively (Dollimore, 2001: 305-311).

explains Nick's trajectory. He even applies Jamesian aesthetics and language to his affairs, to which he refers as "half-hour subordinate clauses of remembered sex" (139). There is, however, a contradiction between his overt sexuality and James's reluctant language. Not by chance is he reading James's *A Small Boy and Others* —James's most elusive novel (312)— when he feels an erection (312). In fact, the contrast between sexual explicitness and the aesthetics of reluctance constitutes a common feature in Hollinghurst's fiction.

Nick is not simply a Proustian/Freudian *voyeur*. He also recalls James's marginal males and vulnerable female characters, such as American heiresses, and poor girls like Fleda Vetcher, who make up self-contained imaginary worlds [579] that eventually collapse. His obsession with the Master thus brings about a catastrophic mimesis of the hero with James's texts and characters, which sheds new light on gays' ambivalence in the era of liberation and AIDS. Like James's marginal males and vulnerable American females, Nick becomes a victim of an equally hostile environment. However, unlike his Jamesian predecessors, he is not only pitiable, but also a laughable character who self-deprecates himself in the name of beauty. That is, while James's characters remain in a limbo of inarticulacy, Nick is the target of irony for this same reason.

Hollinghurst displaces the vulnerability of Jamesian naïve Americans —particularly heiresses— to Nick. Like Milly Theale, the victim of Merton Densher and Kate Croy in *The Wings of the Dove*, Nick is the Feddens' scapegoat, and the recipient of their psychic instabilities and frustrations. In keeping with Victorian medical discourse, which regarded woman as an enigma, Milly Theale represents illness in the novel. Likewise, Nick and his gay lovers are eventually represented as diseased. As Susan Sontag shows in *Illness as Metaphor*, tuberculosis is "the disease of passion, afflicting the reckless and sensual," [580] so that, "susceptibility to the disease stems from fundamental aspects of one's nature."[581] If women like Milly were identified with this type of diseases, gayness has been identified with AIDS. Moreover, being certain diseases considered intrinsic to certain types of individuals, their actual healing is simply unfeasible. Indeed, healing would negate their own identity, since, as Stevens argues, recalling Sontag and Foucault, "disease is a metaphor of sexuality," [582] particularly in the case of women, foreigners and gays. Stevens points to James's refusal to render the hideousness of illness: "Wondering whether the representation of something ugly can be beautiful exposes the tensions between the demands of 'representationalism' and those of 'poetry' which make up [the writer's]' realism."[583] Likewise, Nick's aestheticism reaches even disease. He tries to conceal AIDS when it is too obvious —Leo disappears all of a sudden— or describes it as a romantic disease that emphasises Wani's aquiline features and makes his voice particularly feeble (Hollinghurst, 2004: 430). Despite aesthetic masks, the traumatic effects of AIDS prove inevitable and violent. Both Milly and Nick are subject to the identitarian politics of

---

[579] Kelly Cannon: 1994. *Henry James and Masculinity. The Man at the Margins*. London 1994: 155-160.
[580] In Stevens: *Henry*, 37.
[581] Ibid.
[582] Stevens: *Henry*, 38.
[583] Ibid., 39.

heteronormative patriarchy. As a turn-of-the-century woman and a turn-of-the-millennium gay respectively, they are supposed to suffer from disease, sexual inadequacy and social instability. All this brings them to a permanent state of crisis which, in Milly's case, is "evoked most vividly in the confrontation with the Bronzino portrait at Matcham."[584] The Bronzino portrait represents passivity and stasis, which threatens Milly's "Emersionian self-reliance" and confronts her with her un-originality.[585] Likewise, Nick's and Leo's encounter with Holman Hunt's painting *The Shadow of Death* also has a "proleptically mortal impact."[586] Both Milly and Nick undergo this and other specular epiphanies, through which they are confronted with their fate before they die; the former literally, and the latter metaphorically: the tragedy of *The Wings of the Dove* is that of inarticulacy and restraint. Nick's trauma is more complex and morally dubious. As a gay, he is a victim of Thatcherite homophobia but, simultaneously, he exploits underprivileged youths. Moreover, he masks himself behind aestheticism and self-disassociation. Thus, unlike Nietzsche's final optimism whereby the Apollonian and the Dionysian complement each other for art's sake, Nick's fate is traumatic since he cannot reconcile reality and his idealisation of beauty or, worse still, he confuses one for the other (Hollinghurst 2004: 349). This is his crime or *hamartia*. Nick's encounter with *The Shadow of Death* illustrates his masochism and inclination for dead objects, foreshadowing his end and the annihilation of a whole culture. It is especially in this sense that *The Line of Beauty* recasts *The Spoils of Poynton*.

James's novella focuses on Mrs Gereth's obsession with the furniture and pieces of art at Poynton. Her only son and his fiancée Mona Brigstock, whom Mrs Gereth dislikes, show no interest in the treasures until they learn of their market value. Instead of vulgar Mona, Mrs Gereth prefers poor but exquisite Fleda Vetch as a wife for her son. Owen and Fleda eventually fall in love,[587] but their bond remains inarticulate. The novel's narcissistic prose, characteristic of James's late fiction,[588] matches its subject-matter and (lack of) plot: *The Spoils of Poynton* is essentially the extended description of a treasure that galvanises the psychological confrontation of the characters. Fleda's first encounter with the riches at Poynton is epiphanic, just like Nick's first view of the Feddens' household: "Fleda took a prodigious span. She perfectly understood how Mrs Gereth felt [...] and the two women embraced with tears over the tightening of their bond — tears which on the younger one's part were the natural and usual sign of her submission to perfect beauty."[589] In James's fiction, identity is essentially aesthetic; a view that Nick follows literally. Both Nick and Fleda experience their own romance with an upper-class family to which they are bafflingly and masochistically attached. In fact, drawing on Gilles Deleuze, their pleasure depends "on waiting and delay, postponement and suspense."[590] It is a traumatic move to places and objects rather than to their owners that leads Nick to a feel of possession (Hollinghurst, 2004: 310).

---

[584] Ibid., 41.
[585] Ibid.
[586] Flannery: *Powers*, 298.
[587] Henry James: *The Spoils of Poynton*. London 1977, 150.
[588] Stevens: *Henry*, 169.
[589] James: *Spoils*, 18.
[590] In Stevens: *Henry*, 83.

Further, *The Spoils of Poynton* and *The Line of Beauty* are definitively linked when
Nick intends to adapt James's novella for the screen (213) in a new example of his naïve
'Jamesisation' of (his) experience. For his (once more) unfeasible project, the hero gets
in touch with Brad and Treat, a couple of gay American producers. James's classic
encounter of naïve, rich Americans and sophisticated Europeans after the formers'
money is thus recast. In *The Line of Beauty*, Brad and Treat are fascinated by English
aristocracy (426-427), but unable to appreciate European culture. Thus, though
impressed by Nick's "so British" letters (434), the American producers cannot
understand the hero's plan for the film adaptation. In short, they feel it is too
constrained and lacking passion (435-436). Like *The Spoils of Poynton*, *The Line of
Beauty* is a novel about someone who loves things more than people, and who ends up
with nothing but self-pity and a frustrated aesthetic project. Close to the end, Fleda
receives a letter from Owen offering her the most magnificent piece at Poynton.[591] On
her way, she revives the house in her mind.[592] When she arrives, the station porter tells
her about Poynton's fire and the tragic death of the Gereths while trying to rescue the
riches.[593] Fleda is shaken by the news, "she became limp and weak again; she felt
herself give everything up. Mixed with the horror, [...] with the smell of cinders and the
riot of sound, was the raw bitterness of a hope that she might never again in life have to
give up so much at such short notice. She heard herself repeat mechanically, yet as if
asking it for the first time: Poynton's *gone*?"[594] Like Fleda, Nick disassociates from
himself when he is ejected from the Feddens', a witness thus to his trauma. Although
both Fleda and Nick see how the concept of beauty they have created fades away, the
treatment of the process differs. The crisis in *The Spoils of Poynton* is exclusively
aesthetic, which makes mourning and introjection feasible. Nick's aestheticism is an act
of radical self-denial leading to melancholia. Fleda does not commit a mistake; in
Jamesian terms, she is the inarticulate heroine she is supposed to be. However, Nick's
individuation terminates in a self-annihilating *anagnorisis*.

The *anagnorisis* is traumatic and, as such, experienced in a belated fashion. His
structural trauma is triggered (*i.e.* resurfaced) by the publication of the sex scandal and
unfolds in successive phases. Like many of James's characters, Rachel's passivity and
oblique discourse hide a ruthless violence. Her rejection is particularly dramatic for
Nick, who does not enter a Dionysian state of dissolution of the self, but one of
(self)annihilation. Thus, he reaches the fourth stage of his individuation process
characterised by self-pity, which was part of "a larger pity" (Hollinghurst, 2004: 501).
He perceives Rachel's hard side (465-468) while he paradoxically admires the beauty of
the "S-shaped baluster" at the Feddens' (467), after Hogarth's line of beauty. Rachel's
'coming-out' is as disappointing as unforeseen in the form of "disdain and a hint of a
challenge" (469). Toby's unexpected metamorphosis from a naïve Oxbridge student to a
true Fedden also has the air of traumatic inarticulacy because, as Nick mulls over, it is
"the one utterly unprecedented thing" (471). Reluctant and/or unable to cope with the
traumatic end of his romance with beauty, he focalises his own downfall. Half voyeur,

---

[591]   James: *Spoils*, 187.
[592]   Ibid., 188.
[593]   Ibid., 191.
[594]   Ibid., 192.

half eavesdropper, he first listens to a conversation between Gerald and homophobic Barry Groom in which he is blamed for the Feddens' public shame. Barry shows surprise and disapproves that the pansy, as he calls Nick, is part of the family life (476). Nick's libidinal position concerning Gerald collapses when the latter agrees with his homophobic friend on his bare discourse on Tory prejudices and double morality and the recriminalisation of homosexuality in the eighties. In times of crisis, gays are exogenous, the phantom to be expunged (in Abraham and Torok's terms), the scapegoat of a society in crisis. As Groom recalls, Nick cannot be trusted being gay and aesthete but especially because he is a foreign body in a heterosexual world. Drawing on what Groom considers a "typical homo trick" (477), Nick is a parasite. When Gerald concedes to his friend's accusations against the protagonist, he can only feel disappointed since he still naïvely thinks Gerald "was a friend." (477). After having been denied by Rachel and Toby, the hero is denied yet a third time. Thus, with the coming-out of AIDS, the crudest face of the Dionysian, Nick's traumatic end is exposed and tragedy is accomplished.

Hollinghurst features English culture as being simultaneously homophobic and homoerotic. Gayness is taken for granted, even accepted, whenever it is invisible. Nick is a case in point, particularly with Gerald: "The facts of gay life had always been taboo with him" (479). When (homo)sexuality turns all too obvious, Gerald strips Nick of his identity, even refusing to look at him. The youth's efforts for re-admission and recognition, after being too visible to be repressed, are in vain: "I'm just me. Gerald!" (480). Evoking a whole generation annihilated by AIDS, Nick is ejected from society, denied an identity, criminalised and rendered a self-deserving victim. Gerald's implacability makes up a melodramatic scene which conveys Nick's traumatic consciousnesss-raising and the last two stages of his evolution, envy and self-pity. Eventually, his self-pity turns into a sentimentalism that conceals and demonstrates his self-indulgence as a narcissistic self-defence strategy, especially when Gerald accuses him of having taking revenge against the family out of envy (481). In a rather perverse turn, Nick is accused of using his strategies of a 'pervert' —particularly his mastery of Apollonian beauty— to live on his heterosexual 'victims'. The hero's problematic cathexis with himself and those around him is brought to the fore once more. He is gay and, hence, a perpetual guest to a heteronormative world not his own. Therefore, when he vindicates his presence, Gerald, like Rachel and Toby before, 'comes out', reminding Nick of his absence: "*Who are you?*" (482, my italics). Nick's attitude recalls Leo Bersani's concept of gays' powerlessness, whereby he means, "not gentleness, non-aggressiveness, or even passivity, but rather the positive potential for a 'radical disintegration and humiliation of the self' (217)."[595] This, Dollimore goes on, "is masochism in the sense of a sexual pleasure that crosses a threshold, and which shatters psychic organisation; in which 'the self is exuberantly discarded' and there occurs 'the terrifying appeal of a loss of the ego, of a self-abasement'. A kind of death."[596] Drawing on Bersani and Dollimore, Nick adopts a masochist position, one of submission to Gerald's phallocentrism, which recalls Aschenbach to a certain extent. Ejected from a physical space and from self-respect, like many AIDS victims, his only option as a masochist is powerlessness, self-abasement and death. Thus, this identification of gay

---

[595] In Dollimore: *Death*, 217.
[596] Ibid., 303.

sexuality with submission, AIDS, and an irrepressible sense of loss, which updates the "cultural representation and melodramatic plot lines [of] homosexuals meeting disastrous fates,"[597] closes the penultimate chapter of the novel. The last one is simply a re-arousal of trauma and a withdrawal of celebration: Nick is still reticent and infatuated with the idea of beauty to the very last line (Hollinghurst 2004: 501), but conscious of the end of his wishfulfilment fantasy.

The Line of Beauty closes what I have called Hollinghurst's 'sex tetralogy' or 'AIDS quartet', one in which the principles of the writer's style and main concerns are set up, especially the significance of celebratory and traumatic discourses related to gay identity and sexuality in very explicit terms. In the next section, Hollinghurst's last two novels will be addressed. The main goal in what remains will consist in determining whether his recent literary production has evolved from the 'tetralogy', thus proving the latter to be an exhausted formula. And, if so, what the writer's new concerns are.

---

[597] Stevens: *Henry*, 106-108.

5   Inter/trans-generational blind corners of memory as myth of origins

5.1   *The Stranger's Child*, the celebration and trauma of absence

This final chapter addresses Hollinghurst's last two novels as a redirectioning ensemble that deflects his prior literary patterns. Both memory and scandal come out in the AIDS quartet, but they are the driving force of *The Stranger's Child* and *The Sparsholt Affair*. Memory is not dual, as it is in *The Swimming-pool Library* and *The Folding Star*. It is no longer two protagonists meeting and negotiating the gay discourses and gaps of their respective generations. Hollinghurst's discourse has eventually come to a trans-generational narrative where a scandal, or rather a rumour, passes through and makes up gay experience. Unlike Fedden's yellow press scandal in *The Line of Beauty*, those of Cecil Valance and David Sparsholt haunt gays' lives as if an encrypted body, a traumatic trace whose very origin is lost in time. Gays seem compelled to invoke a narcissistic echo to utter themselves after a transhistorical inertia they cannot control. Rumour has it that Valance had an affair with George Sawles in *The Stranger's Child* and David Sparsholt is allegedly involved in a (homo)sexual and corruption scandal *The Sparsholt Affair* both reveals and conceals. It is not the tabloids that bear witness to these scandals, as happens in *The Line of Beauty*. Hollinghurst, as Theo Tait points out, "has radically cut down on the sex, which is mostly shielded by soft focus or euphemism ('a bit of Oxford style')."[598] Indeed, emotional (rather than sexual) love prevails, Tait goes on. The lessening presence of AIDS and the increasing presence of female characters may be partially responsible for this detour. Yet, AIDS unhealed scars still haunt the novels, and their underlying traumata are juxtaposed with a celebration of male beauty. Also, the story of Echo and Narcissus informs both novels, though Narcissistic protagonists do not so much utter themselves as they are uttered, echoed extrinsically. In being the foci of attention for generations to come, Cecil and David, frozen in a statue and a drawing respectively, turn into auratic presences in their absence. Indeed, it is my main contention that Hollinghurst last two texts delve into the poetics of absence and vanishing aura intrinsic to memory writing. In free indirect style, Daphne Sawle, Cecil's youth beloved, concludes that "memories [are] only memories of memories" (Hollinghurst 2011: 496).[599] Icons of the two world wars, Valance and Sparsholt are as celebrated as loathed, their lives being manipulated to address different anxieties through time. Cecil's poem "Two Acres" and David's draft painting by Evert Dax make up for same-sex desire when it was illegal. From this myth of origins, scandalous at first, the novels convey a continuum of transgenerational allegiances and disengagements. In fact, as Julie Rivkin argues: "What Hollinghurst's *The Line of*

---

[598] Tait: "*Stranger's,*" n.p.
[599] Hereafter all references to Alan Hollinghurst's *The Stranger's Child* (2011) will be in the text.

Beauty did for England in the 1980s […] that is, unmask a triumphalist public narrative and reveal its terrible costs and distortions, particularly in the lives of its queer characters — *The Stranger's Child* does for England over the long span of the twentieth century."[600] This interest in how Cecil's poem or David's affair solidify according to changing circumstances makes the homosexual-gay-queer evolution into a cultural construct. Yet, I do not think Hollinghurst endorses queer deconstructive practices. It is the very fluidity of discourses and terminology used to refer to same-sex desire that these last novels bear witness to and somehow contest. Joseph Ronan aptly makes a point out of this, namely that bisexual camp underpins *The Stranger's Child*[601] and, I would add, *The Sparsholt Affair*. In any case, this move towards bisexuality sanctions and problematises Hollinghurst's juxtaposed discourse, dissolving sex "into the rest of the text."[602] This ambivalent use of absence and presence —the writer himself has argued he is "not writing such completely gay [texts] anymore"—[603] is what Ronan calls bisexual camp, Hollinghurst's ostentatious discretion.

Daniel Mendelsohn addresses this paradoxical excess of absence when labelling *The Stranger's Child* as "an absent penis" novel.[604] While having a look at old pictures by bisexual artist Revel Ralph, Paul Bryant, one of the protagonists of the novel, comes across a series of drawings "of a naked young man, lying, sitting, standing, in a range of ideal but natural-looking positions" (Hollinghurst 2011: 510). The male line of beauty is brought out, yet absent, yet imaginable, yet discarded. Beauty is both celebrated and traumatically repressed to be conceivable. Likewise, David Sparsholt's portrait in Hollinghurst's last novel is an absent-penis type as well, momentous when drafted and a trace of a traumatic episode in the end. The narrator first looks at the picture as ostentatiously discreet. Peter's painting features "a demigod" with a blurred face and sexuality (Hollinghurst 2017: 35).[605] Imagined or suggested, male sex constitutes a present absence in both novels. Thus, although, as Ronan points out, bisexual camp characterises *The Stranger's Child*, it is the male body that is addressed in homosexual, gay, queer or bisexual terms. It is an absent penis that haunts this novel, as well as *The Sparsholt Affair*. Cecil's poem and his reification as a historical and erotic icon and David's corruption and sexual affairs only reverberate as traumatic events do. After Freud's primal fantasy, readers bear witness to both myths of origins. In *The Stranger's Child*, George Sawle is first made into a witness to the kiss of his sister, Daphne, and his best friend Cecil Valance. As the novel advances, it comes out it was Cecil and George that really had an affair. Hence, Cecil's idyll "Two Acres" was possibly not addressed to Daphne, but to George. Bisexual implications apart, Daphne is redundant

---

[600] Julie Rivkin: 2016. "*The Stranger's Child* and *The Aspern Papers*: Queering Origin Stories and Questioning the Visitable Past." In Mendelssohn, Michèle and Dennis Flannery (eds.). *Alan Hollinghurst: Writing under the Influence*. Manchester 2016, 79.

[601] Ronan: "Ostentatiously," 96-109.

[602] Ibid., 103.

[603] In Alice O'Keeffe: "Alan Hollinghurst." www.thebookseller.com/profile/alan-hollinghurst 2011, n.p.

[604] Daniel Mendelsohn: "In gay and crumbling England." https://www.nybooks.com/articles/2011/11/10/gay-and-crumbling-england/ 2011, n.p.

[605] Hereafter all references to Alan Hollinghurst's *The Sparsholt's Affair* (2017) will be in the text.

in the Girardian triangle, both a short-circuit and connector of the boys' homosocial bond. Sparsholt spends all his life engaged, married or having affairs with women. However, it is his affairs with males that give a title to the novel and haunt the rest of the characters' lives. That said, it is a fact that both protagonists, particularly present in their absence and their silences —much of what happened in Two Acres and in David's tabloid scandal remaining unspoken— "would fuck anyone" (Hollinghurst 2011: 456).

I consider both *The Stranger's Child* and *The Sparsholt Affair* as transgenerational narratives of memory because they span the whole twentieth century and the way memoirs have been transmitted. *The Swimming-pool Library*, and to a lesser extent, *The Folding Star* had also characters of different generations in conversation and (dis)engaged with each other. However, whereas Hollinghurst's early novels intend to explore the hardships of prior generations of gays to come to terms with the unspeakability of AIDS and convey the ethical implications of this confrontation, his later fiction focuses rather on the reliability of memoirs and memory to bear witness to the transgenerational transmission of (un)truth. Indeed, these novels are concerned with the (im)possibility of representation as a given, but as a precession of discourses that conflict with each other. Unlike Beaudrillard's simulacra, where referentiality has replaced the referent, these memory discourses follow one another, the old ones haunting the new ones. Thus, although Cecil is a vague remnant of a lost England for years, it haunts generations until gay and queer memoirists resurface him to public interest.

The Stranger's Child and *The Sparsholt Affair* are split into five chapters alike, the former spanning almost a century and the latter covering from WWII to the present. *The Stranger's Child* starts off just before WWI, and the rest of the novel, as Tait points out: "consists of four more sections, set at intervals between 1926 and 2008, while most of the action —deaths, marriages, births— occurs offstage, in the gaps in between."[606] The first chapter of *The Sparsholt Affair* features a memoir by Freddie Green while in Oxford in 1940. Witness to his friends' infatuation with hunky David Sparsholt, then a junior at Oxford, Green sets the homoerotic leitmotif of the whole novel. As for the rest, Laura Miller argues, it "is followed by four sections in the third person taking place at intervals over the next 70 years"[607] and, as in the previous novel, "most of the major events occur offstage."[608] It seems as if Hollinghurst was trying to write and rewrite a story or, at least, a pattern with intervals of roughly twenty years, i.e. a generation, framing the crucial events. Both novels thus refer to the blind corners of memory which make up memoirs. What happens when the narrator does not narrate and the focaliser does not look or bear witness to is what really matters. Absence and secrecy haunt and frame both novels. I am speaking about absence and secrecy not as dialectical forms, but as scenarios of otherness and silence that keep on with gayness as periphery and same-sex desire as a peripheral bond.

In an analysis of Colm Tóibín's *The Blackwater Lightship* and short story "Three Friends" (2015), I deal with this poetics of silence and secrecy and how they convey

---

[606] Tait: "*Stranger's,*" n.p.

[607] Laura Miller: "Rising to the Sunlit Surface." https://slate.com/culture/2018/03/alan-holling hursts-the-sparsholt-affair-reviewed.html, 2018, n.p.

[608] Ibid.

transgenerational traumata. Eventually, Tóibín reworks them to herald a message of renewal in (post)catholic Ireland. In Hollinghurst's last two novels, transgenerational communication is often short-circuited and remains a symptom of failure, though. They address the elusiveness of memory and the dangers of rupturing secrecy for the sake of liberation. When Paul Bryant, a young scholar and biography writer in the eighties, takes Cecil out of the closet, the risks of outing emerge. If memory falters, current (gay) politics makes it up for the void, putting forward alternative readings. Tóibín's "Three Friends" and *The Blackwater Lightship* "exorcise their characters from a (respectively) Oedipal and transgenerational haunting, which explains their introjected discourse, memory and imagery."[609] However, Hollinghurst's novels remain haunted by trans-generational traumata and memory blanks that only confirm such traumata. Hence, characters' discourse incorporates, rather than introjects, phantoms that are somehow encrypted. In other words, characters are unable to come to terms and mourn loss. Instead of integrating the traumata derived from loss, such unresolved loss is encrypted in them and, henceforth, their lives and discourses are determined by trauma. Cecil's story and poem become a phantom generations of both families are bound to. Likewise, the epiphanic infatuation of Green and his mates on semi-naked David makes up the Sparsholt's affair, which thirty years later is further complicated into a corruption case involving fraud and male prostitutes. The affair or, rather, its inscrutable secrecy is incorporated by most characters, particularly David's son and everybody he comes across.

The Stranger's Child has the feel of a family saga. It all starts during a weekend aristocratic Cecil spends at his friend George's. The triangle between the two youths and George's sister Daphne, then only sixteen, and especially Cecil's poem dedicated to one of them, make up the myth of origins the novel relies on. Irony and ambiguity underpin the myth from the very beginning. Not only because the addressee of the poem remains a mystery for generations to come. The fact that narcissistic Cecil writes an idyll on a commonplace middle-class home and that it becomes a national symbol after being quoted by Churchill (Hollinghurst 2011: 162) is ludicrous to say the least. Dead in France in 1916 as a national hero, an ironic upshot of Rupert-Brooke, the novel "tracks the afterlife of [t]his poem, by following the twentieth-century vicissitudes of the two families" (Wood 2011: 86). Cecil's death takes place between the first and the second part when, in 1926, Daphne is married to Dudley Valance, Cecil's younger brother, and has two children, Wilfrid and Corinna. It is during a family meeting at Corley Court, the Valances' Victorian house, that Sebby Stokes, himself a Cecil's lover (Hollinghurst 2011: 157, 197), gathers information to write Cecil's first biography. Stokes's hagiography reveals how the icon is made up: Churchill's speech, the patriotic reification of the poem and Cecil's marble mausoleum, as commissioned by Mrs Valance, ground the myth. The third part, set in 1967, concurring with the decriminalisation of homosexuality in England, features the Valances and Sawles' new generation, as well as a new generation of biographers. Paul Bryant, a young bank clerk working for Corinna's husband, is a gay arriviste who bears witness to the birth of the gay movement and the decline of the Valances and Sawles. When he becomes Peter

---

[609] José M. Yebra: "Transgenerational and Intergenerational Family Trauma in Colm Tóibín's *The Blackwater Lightship* and 'Three Friends.'" *Moderna Sprak* (2) 2015, 122-123.

Rowe's lover, a teacher at Corley Court —now reconverted into a boys' school—, Paul gets fascinated with Cecil. Indeed, the whole fourth part focuses on Bryant's detective work after the track of the poet to write a new biography, an idea he has stolen from his former lover. Tracing Stokes's steps and Daphne and Dudley's biographies of the myth, Paul gets infatuated while trying to 'out' Cecil to the public in his yellowish biography *England Trembles*. Indeed, his 'whodunit' narrative —Stokes being called a clever Monsieur Poirot (174) — condemns ideologically-inflected discourses, particularly when memory is reworked to meet political ends. 'Outing' forcibly is akin to raping memory, Paul being thus exposed as a thief, a sycophant and a 'rapist'. Set in 1980, just before the AIDS crisis, this section lays bare the traumatic scars of memory when it is haunted by forgetting. Daphne is virtually anonymous and Cecil a ghost from the past whom Daphne herself considers an inconsequential teenage flirt. The last chapter works as a coda where yet a new generation turns the screw of the homosexual-gay-queer continuum. Queer theory has become mainstream and, although its practitioners regard Bryant and his likes outdated, they are nothing better. Jennifer Ralph, Daphne's grand-daughter, now a professor at Oxford, bears witness to family decline. Bryant's biography of Cecil has turned from rumour to truth to the public eye, which reveals the novel's concern with the discourses of memory and forgetfulness. Although the Valances and Sawles are no longer publicly relevant, they are still food for some queer critics who, like some gay critics before, 'vulture' around the traces left by the dead. Cecil is regarded as a second-rate artist but, in the era of Grindr, he is still a queer icon, his poems being "a queer manifesto" (541). The novel closes with book dealer Rob, the last queer to trace after the families, still finding new evidences of Cecil's love affairs, the last one being his flirt with Hewitt, a millionaire and special friend of Daphne's grey brother Hudley.

If Will Beckwith represents the paradigm of Hollinghurst's narcissistic character, the mirror always responding in the first person, *The Stranger's Child* disperses the reflection. Cecil is the focal point, a narcissist himself. However, he is blurred in echoic accounts of his persona and desire. According to Bart Eeckhout, in the novel, "desire impels narratives, landscapes, and human interactions alike in ways which afford only passing moments of aesthetic enchantment and provisional insights along the way."[610] Although Eeckhout focuses on this erotics as conveyed in the metonymy of place and architectural change, *The Stranger's Child* addresses transformation as an overall issue, both celebratory and traumatic, Cecil being just a symptom. The ambivalence of the erotics and politics of the novel must be placed in context. Years ago, as Giles Harvey recalls, Hollinghurst himself claimed on the need to do something defiant.[611] He said it in the reactionary climate of the eighties. Yet, his last two novels, conceived in a world "Hollinghurst played his part in creating,"[612] prove how "this isn't a story of straight-

---

[610] Bart Eeckhout: "English Architectural Landscapes and Metonymy in Hollinghurst's *The Stranger's Child*." *CLCWeb: Comparative Literature and Culture* 14.3. https://doi.org/10.77 71/1481-4374.2042, 2012, n.p.

[611] Giles Harvey: "The Cartographer of Sex." *The New York Times Magazine*. 18 March 2018, 29.

[612] Ibid.

forward progress and liberation."[613] That is, neither the past was exclusively traumatic nor the present celebratory as concerns same-sex desire. The echoes of the past, no matter how blurred it is, speak about their transience and dissolution into an equally ungraspable present.

The echoic is far more relational than the narcissistic, particularly when Cecil's persona is dispersed transgenerationally in the form of memory, memoirs and biography. The poet is a focal point, both centrifugal and centripetal, for most of the characters in *The Stranger's Child*. Thus, their relations, sexual desire and identification rely on how young Valance is remembered. Memoirs, by his brother Dudley and his youth flirt Daphne, and biographies, by Stokes and Bryant, galvanise his figure as well as those of his rememberers. In the second chapter, the whole family gathers around Stokes for his first hagiography. From then on, all these documents, more or less valuable and reliable, make up the thread where family and queer erotics merge into a myth of origins that backfires and ends up by demythologising Cecil and the process of memorising itself. In a sense, Hollinghurst is comparing memory, as lived experience, with biography, as a logocentric discourse akin to historiography. Cecil and 'Two Acres' are thus as malleable as memorists, or rather "subjectivities, hybridities, multiple subject positions."[614] Gabriele Schwab's concept of 'haunting legacies' (2011) will prove useful to account for the polyhedral rendering of memory, relationality, absence and grieving in *The Stranger's Child*. Schwab focuses on how "the ineradicable legacies of violent histories"[615] are transmitted through generations of victims and perpetrators in the context of the Holocaust. Hollinghurst's novel does not address such a traumatic episode as the Holocaust, but a more domestic and structural one, namely the loss of Cecil and pre-WWI England. The roles of victims and perpetrators are provisional and exchangeable, depending on whose discourse prevails each time. Cecil and the England he embodies are conceived in different ways along generations. Schwab argues that the violence of haunting legacies "holds an unrelenting grip on memory [and] yet is deemed unspeakable."[616] The unspeakability of Cecil's legacy is his pansexuality (Hollinghurst 2011: 456), which makes his memory unmemorable. In building up a mausoleum for the poet and negotiating the symbolism of 'Two Acres', Lady Valance is grieving her son and celebrating his memory, a victim of the war rather than the fixer and sexual predator he is eventually revealed to be. Back to my analysis of Tóibín's texts and Schwab's theory, the legacies of *The Stranger's Child* are transmitted through generations that are haunted by a double drive to repress and reveal them.[617] The alleged triangle between Cecil, George and Daphne, which incorporates new members as the novel advances, is (un)spekable, as Nicholas Abraham "envisions a crypt" (1). Indeed, the survivors attempt to grieve the dead one, but fail to do so, every time he is echoed.

---

[613]   Ibid.

[614]   Jay Winter: "Notes on the Memory Boom: War, Remembrance and the Uses of the Past." In Bell, Duncan (ed.), *Memory, Trauma and World politics. Reflections on the Relationship between Past and Present*. New York 2006, 55.

[615]   Gabrielle Schwab: *Haunting Legacies. Violent Histories and Transgenerational Trauma*. New York 2011, 1.

[616]   Ibid.

[617]   Yebra: "Transgenerational," 124-125.

Cecil('s loss) is encrypted because it is unmourned and, hence, incorporated in the survivors' psyches. Does the loss of a mythic era deserve to be grieved? Judith Butler has wondered who deserves grieving and who grants that right to be grieved.[618] In *The Stranger's Child*, this dilemma turns crucial. The trauma is entombed in a mausoleum, but also in a compelling drive to rework the myth which paradoxically entombs the myth deeper and deeper as generations transmit and repress it.

The dilemma between trauma representation and repression is rendered in the form of absence. The first section of the novel closes with George claiming to be the actual addressee of Cecil's poem, rather than his sister Daphne. This uncertainty, which persists all over the novel, halts when the second section starts off with a family gathering in 1926 to grieve and celebrate Cecil's memory. A WWI novel where not a single line is devoted to the war proves how absence can be a powerful guiding thread. As James Walton points out, big events, like war, take place offstage in both *The Stranger's Child* and *The Sparsholt Affair*.[619] How Cecil died, Daphne met and fell in love with Dudley and George 'stopped being gay' and married Madeleine are taken-for-granted facts when the second section starts. Wilfrid, Daphne and Dudley's child son, learns that his father had been seriously injured by a German shell; an obvious reference to WWI shell shock syndrome. Moreover, "Uncle Cecil was a cold white statue in the chapel downstairs, because of a German sniper with a gun" (Hollinghurst, 2011: 121). *The Stranger's Child* is about the thwarted transgenerational transmission. Traumata are encrypted when they are coded, hidden or repressed in the characters' actions and memoirs. It is a story of absence, not so much of the penis, as Mendelsohn argues in rather Lacanian terms, but of absence as loss and flawed relationality. Wilfrid is instructed, like the rest of the country, to grieve Cecil as an absent figure. The complex relationality is often due not only to absence because of loss, as is to war casualties. It is a much more complex phenomenon, which has to do with not belonging and denial.

Drawing on queer theorist Sara Ahmad, Harvey recalls the "kinds of experiences you have when you are not expected to be."[620] The traumatic effects of not belonging and denial are particularly conspicuous in Nick Guest' case. His life focuses on the "estranged surreptitiously acquired knowledge about an English high society, generated by the experience of not belonging to it."[621] In *The Stranger's Child*, no character experiences Nick's sheer rejection. Even Bryant, who also scrutinises the Valances and Sawles to prove Cecil's gayness, is never ejected as Nick is. The sense of not belonging is more subtle. Indeed, no character seems to fit in. Daphne's marriages do not work, because she is not an aristocrat, as Cecil and Dudley are, or because she marries a gay man. The same holds for most of the characters, misrecognising their own sexual orientation, their roles or their own sense of truth, when memoirs and biographies conflict with each other. As soon as readers trust a version, a new one contradicts it.

---

[618] Judith Butler: *Frames of War. When is Life Grievable?* London and New York: Verso Books 2016.

[619] James Walton: "Alan Hollinghurst's new novel is dazzling – and just like all his others." https://www.spectator.co.uk/2017/10/alan-hollinghursts-new-novel-is-dazzling-and-just-like-all-his-others/, 2017, n.p.

[620] Harvey: "Cartographer," n.p.

[621] Ibid.

Yet, this queer sense of non-belonging helps rework memory, relationality, absence and grieving. George is a case in point. Despite his affair with Cecil, the absent presence (rather than the death) of the latter stifles him; for instance, when George envisions "a further twenty-four hours devoted to his brilliance, bravery and charm" (Hollinghurst, 2011: 147). It is traumatic, rather than celebratory, to convey his rapport with the dead poet, their love being unspeakable, their social mismatch and George's new status as a respectable married man. His overall sense of non-belonging to himself and his own confusing memory explains that "the man he was hiding from was long dead" (151). A further question arises; is he hiding from Cecil or from his own previous self? The answer is double. George's past is encrypted with secrets, "unpublished, unpublishable [...] now lost for ever" (159). Despite being married to Dudley, Daphne still regards herself a visitor at Corley Court (181); not only because she keeps a secret affair with the dead Valance encrypted, but because she does not comply with the idea her future mother-in-law conveys for her successor as Lady Valance (183).

Drawing on Henry James, Hollinghurst's definite tutelary spirit, Corinna and Wilfrid rework the idea of non-belonging. Like *Maisie* in *What Maisie Knew* (1897), Daphne and Dudley's children bear witness and focalise what for them is incomprehensible, thus defamiliarising children from a context that is both their own, as family members and witnesses, and not their own, as children, at the same time. Wilfrid listens to Sarah, a maid, speaking about Dudley having "another of their wild nights" (Hollinghurst, 2011: 227) with Nanny, whose words about Daphne Wilfrid hated (227). Likewise, the child bears witness to Revel painting his mother and their incipient affair, which obviously he fails to understand. The child's focalisation and thwarted discourse turns especially when he beholds his father's Oedipal conflict with Cecil. Both Dudley and Wilfrid feel dissociated from the dead poet. The former because he feels emasculated by his brother frozen over-presence; he has been a massive redundant presence in his writings in the last times (242). The child because, unable to understand the actual meaning of his father's words, feels confusingly enthralled by "the joy of improvisation [...] as well as the sense of horror that his father's poems always challenged you not to feel" (242). The double celebratory and traumatic character of Dudley's reminder of his brother is alienating, problematising grieving, memorising an absence.

Schwab regards crypts as "the linguistic scars of trauma" (4) as long as they disown mourning. Every time the myth is echoed new scars emerge, not because it is outed, but because it is distorted. Drawing on Caruth's reference to Clorinda's double wound by Tancred, Cecil and the myth he comes to embody is wounded once and again, doubly so when Bryant tries to unravel his 'true' nature and that of his writing. The dead poet is the victim (who does not know) of a repetition compulsion by a number of perpetrators (who know). Back to the idea raised at the beginning of the book, whereby (unwillingly) returning to an unfathomable scenario constitutes a myth of origins that explains the logic of trauma, the weekend at Two Acres is a haunting Arcadia. The scenario is wounded when Cecil dies and every time it is returned to by more or less (un)willing perpetrators. Whenever it is revisited by those haunted it constitutes a literary event, be it a biography, memoir or a collection of edited letters. Hence, being perpetrator a specifically moral or legal term and trauma a diagnostic one, and this book a literary analysis, the concept of perpetrator must be used carefully. As mentioned above, if the victim is the one who does not know and the perpetrator is the one who does know, in literary terms would be related to narrative reliability and access to knowledge. Dudley, Daphne and George know firsthand. They are the actual witnesses to loss whereas Paul and Rob conduct their search through sources and allegedly scientific methodology. Paradoxically though, it is Bryant's account of Cecil and his loss that becomes the so-called truth. After Jennifer Ralph, Daphne's granddaughter, tells her family story, she argues, rather ironically, that in Paul Bryant's view, all her story is false "My aunt wasn't really Dudley's daughter, but Cecil's, Dudley was gay, though he managed to father a son with my grandmother, and my father's father wasn't Revel Ralph, who really was gay, but a painter called Mark Gibbons" (Hollinghurst, 2011: 524). Hence, the perpetrator is not the one who knows, but, like Paul, the one who seems to know and whose truth prevails.

The third section of *The Stranger's Child* leaves mourning behind and explores how its effect merges with literary biography, thus paving the way for a more detached and politically committed account. "Steady, Boys, Steady" features a young Paul Bryant interested through his lover, Peter Rowe, in Cecil and his myth for the first time. Moreover, Corley Court is no longer the Valances' home, but a school for boys, and Cecil no longer a well-known celebrity, but an icon for a gay minority. As mentioned above, the section starts in 1967, when the Wonfelden report, whereby homosexuality was decriminalised in the UK, was put in force. Hollinghurst recalls the atmosphere of the early gay liberation. Still relying on tropes to address each other, Paul, Peter and Geoff look at mirrors to observe men's bodies reflected (247-248). They also exchange and detect secret looks and signs in public places. Thus, Peter glances at Geoff, a visual exchange that Paul perceives and feels threatened (283) as was common before the Wolfenden report crystallised in a more gay-friendly law. Although the fear of pre-decriminalisation anti-gay raids is somehow evident, male masseurs still working covertly (285), the origin of something new is also noticeable. The new political atmosphere these men uphold rehabilitates a whole gay culture which Paul and Peter, like the two Apostles, encapsulate in Cecil, a new Messiah at certain moments of the novel. They even consider the poet a codeword for queerness (340). A public school like Corley Court seems a fitting scenario for queer culture to re-emerge after decriminalisation. Indeed, in free indirect style, Peter ruminates how public schools were the territory where gay erotic affiliations did not fight for relevance as that was their territory (296). Thus starts Peter and Paul's whodunit narrative on Cecil. Already in 1967, they foretell what is about to arrive, particularly a massive gay outing of prior hidden truths, in rather positive terms: "all sorts of stuff's going to come out" (319). Yet, in the retrospect, the prediction also forecasts not only a massive coming-out of gays, but also their massive annihilation by AIDS. That is the (traumatic and celebratory) ambivalence of gay experience *The Stranger's Child* addresses, as Hollinghurst's previous novels had done before.

What starts as a hagiography lady Valance erects in her son's name and that Churchill uses with patriotic ends turns up the seed of a gay subculture Hollinghurst depicts in the last three sections. The pass of the Bill against Sexual Offences is obviously a triumph the novel celebrates. Indeed, the affair between Paul and Peter is endearing at first, a sign of the times when gays learnt to express what they felt, albeit clumsily. Their eyes are unreadable, mimicking each other in an "instinctive, mechanical" way so that "it [is] a sort of triumph just to have kissed another man" (332-

333). However, the novel is not self-indulgent. Cecil is "a second-rate writer," as his tomb (349) and Stokes's biography "almost unreadable" (318). Their zeal for frankness, as recalled in Wolfenden's report and the subsequent law (320), is also intrusive and unethical. The political interest of Paul and Peter prevails over the rights of the individual to conduct his life and memory. To which ethical right can they appeal to 'queer' Cecil, as Peter suggests in a prospective biography intended to amend Stokes's (356-357)? The novel is very critical with appropriation of the other to utter one's political claims. In this sense, gay critics and biographers are voracious, a caricature of themselves. Once Cecil is outed, Paul and Peter lay their eyes on Dudley. He was a devotee to a Billy Prideaux, which, they claim, proves he "seemed if anything the queerer one" (363). Paradoxically, while Peter decides he is going to write Cecil's biography, assuming his queerness and that of his brother out of mere speculation, he concludes the era of hearsay is paving the way for that of documentation (363). Although documentation is obviously more scientifically committed than hearsay, what he claims is still a speculative practice that suspends the right of one to his own memory. That is the polemical status of biography and memory *The Stranger's Child* points out.

When the fourth section of *The Stranger's Child* starts, Paul Bryant regrets the new generation of gays is more concerned about saunas and gyms than old glories like Daphne, Cecil and George (372). In fact, her memoirs on the WWI poet, *The Short Gallery*, raise no interest but in people like Paul, who reviews it for the *New Statesman* (374). Likewise, George's edited *Letters of Cecil Valance*, together with photographs and other memorabilia, and Dudley's autobiography *Black Flowers*, make up a very Hollinghustian gay archive only 'researchers' like Paul delve into. The latter, we learn, has left Peter and intends to publish a new biography on the young Valance reworking the archive Daphne, George and Dudley have left behind. Thus, Bryant calls himself a literary biographer (532), which converts his account of Cecil's life into a biographical novel. This genre, David Lodge argues, "takes a real person and his real history as the subject matter for imaginative exploration, using the novel's techniques for representing subjectivity rather than the objective, evidence-based discourse of biography."[622] Paul's biofiction draws on the popularity of this hybrid genre in the last decades. The whodunit narrative hinted at in Stokes's hagiography gets more complex when it comes to Paul's prejudiced and teleological account of Cecil's life. Cora Kaplan explains there has been a craze for biofiction that is particularly interested in literary figures like Trollope, Thackeray, Dickens, Wilde and James.[623] This trend, she argues, has made such authors into recognisable fictional characters,[624] which is what Paul intends to do with Cecil. In this sense, *The Stranger's Child* is a metafictional account of how fiction reworks so-called real authors. In his analysis of Tóibín's *The Master* (2004), José M. Yebra argues that such fictional biographies "help turn-of-the-millennium readers 'meet' and engage with the authorial figure that early poststructuralism previously withdrew, though not

---

[622] David Lodge: *The Year of Henry James: The Story of the Novel*. London 2006, 8.
[623] Cora Kaplan: *Victoriana: Histories, Fictions, Criticism*. Edinburgh 2007, 39.
[624] Ibid.

always in a reassuring or expected fashion."[625] This is not Paul's case since, rather than reacting to the poststructural crisis of identity, it is his aim to force Cecil into his own identity politics. Drawing on the duality between the 'truth of fact' and the 'truth of fiction',[626] the limits of the biographical discourse and the factuality it allegedly reflects are blurred in texts like Bryant's and Hollinghurst's, but with very different intentions and results. Paul reworks Cecil's life to out him, *The Stranger's Child* reworks it to question factuality. The former claims homosexuality to be a fact to be spotted and forced into being; the latter, by contrast, addresses sexual identity in rather elusive terms, both celebratory and traumatic. As mentioned above, Hollinghurst's fifth novel relies on a disseminated bisexuality rather than on explicit homosexuality, as his previous ones do. The dissemination of sexuality onto the text[627] blurs the limits of desire. Yet, this does not necessarily imply a celebratory outcome. Cecil's pansexuality (Hollinghurst, 2011: 456) is often linked to his social status and supremacy. Moreover, his multiple sexual affiliations are often traumatic and/or secret for the survivors; hence, their need to utter Cecil's effect in a delayed fashion, either in memoirs or edited letters.

Much in line with romances of the archive like *The Swimming-pool Library* and *The Folding Star*, Bryant searches after the traces of gay history. It is only that in *The Stranger's Child*, sexual identity is particularly blurred. Versions contradict each other and one never knows for sure which one is true, if at all. Other than bibliographical references, Paul interviews some of the protagonists for the sake of (his) truth. Theoretically, an interview should put forward the 'truth of fact' because it is not contaminated by the biographer; it is like a guided memoir. However, Paul's biased questions prove that an interview cannot be regarded as necessarily more objective than regular biographies. In interviewing Jonah Trickett, Cecil's valet during his stay at 'Two Acres,' Paul hints at his unsuitable relation with the master. Such a prejudiced start really upsets Jonah, who feels in Paul's behaviour and words there is "some improper suggestion" (403). The rest of the interview is reproduced literally, which intends to make it an objective record. However, even when listening to the recording, it is sometimes inaudible or blurred and, hence, we rely on Bryant's transcription and interpretation. Is Cecil a 'devil', as Paul thinks, Jonah says unclearly (409)? Likewise, when Cecil is referred to as "a horror," is it because a) he was "extremely untidy," b) "he had silk underwear" or because c) "he was very generous" tipping Jonah? (410). The recording leaves more questions than answers. No matter how biased Paul's discourse is, Jonah's answers on Cecil's rapport with him are either inconclusive or inaudible. The same holds for his account of Valance's relations with Daphne and George. When Paul suggests a love affair between Cecil and George, Jonah answers that he cannot see his point (412). However, far from accepting the valet does not recognise a relation between both youths long time ago, Bryant adds a sort of stage direction, "(nervous laugh)" (412), which perversely hints at Jonah's involvement, or

---

[625] José M. Yebra: "Neo-Victorian Biofiction and Trauma Poetics in Colm Tóibín's *The Master*." *Neo-Victorian Studies* 6 (1) 2013, 46-47.

[626] Caroline Lusin: 'Writing Lives and Worlds: English Fictional Biography at the Turn of the 21st Century'. In Nünning, Vera, Ansgar Nünning, and Birgit Neumann (eds.), *Cultural Ways of Worldmaking: Media and Narratives*. Berlin & New York 2010, 269.

[627] Ronan: "Ostentatiously", 113.

complicity, in the alleged 'Two Acres' triangle he claims not to recall (412). All in all, the interview works like a play rather than anything else, Bryant being the script writer, stage director and interpreter, all in one. He uses the rest of the recording to explore another minor character to shed light on the triangle and mainly to prove the gay undertones Cecil's life had. Mr Hewitt, a millionaire and neighbour to the Sawles, had been Hubert Sawle's great friend, as Jonah confirms (414-415). Later in the novel, it turns that the eccentric millionaire tipped the valet, and exchanged letters with Hubert and Cecil. In brief, Paul finds out that most, if not all, men around Cecil were gay or held gay feelings for him (420). And not only that, he assumes there is much more than meets the eye. Jonah, he presumes, knows more than he says and only a sort of covenant with his masters prevents him from uttering the truth. Drawing on the rage for "outing gay writers" (525) at the moment, Paul assumes the truth is secret, (gay) secrecy being the crypt that haunts the Sawles and the Valances and the novel as a whole.

Although Paul intends to find out if Cecil was queer, as he confesses (420), his findings lead him astray. The texts he reads and the interviews he holds prove the gay Arcadia he presumes the Valances and Sawles lived in is as artificial as any other along Hollinghurst's production. The traumatic downfall resulting from confronting the reality of the illusion turns up again in *The Stranger's Child*. When reading Dudley's second collection of memoirs, *Black Flowers*, with Paul, the 'Two Acres' myth is not the celebratory early accounts like Stokes's claimed. It hides instead an underside that, as years pass, resurfaces in Dudley's words. They recall the classic nostalgia for the past as the Arcadian territory before current realities. Yet, Dudley is conscious of how elusive that Arcadian imagery is and how it only represents part of the truth (437). As a side-effect of Paul's unethical outing of gays and straights alike, the novel unveils the layers of pretence that for years have made up an iconography of a man, a poem and a period. The innocence of Stokes's account is dismantled as the Arcadia of early youth love and a kiss cover much more complex bonds. Drawing on trauma theory, half the truth haunts the other half and comes out belatedly. Dudley is thus trying to come to terms with the dissociation between post-war 'actual beings' and pre-war 'foreign beings'. In assuming that former identities were constructed and now absent, his discourse helps to overcome the falsity of the myth. The poem and the kiss, the Arcadia of triangle of naïve youths only collapses. As time passes, Cecil becomes irrelevant in monographs on the Great War. Paul Fussell's book, which Paul considers a referent of the period, only mentions the poet "in a footnote ('a less neurotic –and less talented– epigone of Brooke')" (439). The most compelling drive leading a sycophant like Paul to the myth of 'Two Acres' is its liminality. When the last survivors of that period are about to die, the Great War turns into a cultural product, more or less mythologised, and only accessible through texts. Hence, every time Bryant cannot meet and interview the last survivors in the early eighties, he had a feeling of almostness. It is as if he was about to touch the "greatness" of a past that, however, he could not reach in the end (441). Paul's sycophancy apart, the sense of an ending as well as of elusiveness and liminality the novel recalls is culturally traumatic. *The Stranger's Child* is a text of the absent, of memory that falters. Towards the end, as in a classic whodunit novel, Paul gets closer to the protagonists and hence the truth. First he reaches an aloof Dudley, who demythologises the War generation and its achievements (447). However, the myth resurfaces immediately afterwards when the loss of that generation is regarded as a national trauma that is revived belatedly every time it is echoed in vain, *The Stranger's Child* being the effect and symptom of that sense of loss. To be traumatised is, Caruth argues, "to be possessed by an image or event."[628] This is what happens to Dudley and the rest of the survivors; following Caruth, they are overwhelmingly haunted by an absence that triggers off uncertainty and a crisis of truth (6).[629] In recalling his brother's generation, Dudley is confronted both with Cecil's excessive presence and absence. As WWI heroes were all dead, he says, and even those who remembered them were about to die, "no one remembered the rememberers" (Hollinghurst 2011: 448). As Dudley is uttering one of the main concerns of *The Stranger's Child*, Bryant continues trying to find out the queer 'truth', or rather fitting his personal wish into elusive memory. When he feels close to others' coming-out, his whole body gets excited as he is still a semi-closeted gay man (448). The morbid interest in unveiling the unnameable of Cecil results unethical of the biographer who ignores Dudley's view on his brother's sexual orientation. This takes us to the ethical implications of biography writing.

Mark Llewellyn addresses the problematic appropriation of historical figures in biofiction. Historical fiction, the critic points out, "in many senses ceases to serve one of its primary functions in re-imagining the past, by obscuring or fabricating evidence rather than providing accountable biographical narratives."[630] Although *The Stranger's Child* does not feature real historical figures, the novel points to the process of appropriating others' lives. Bryant's diary is a case in point; the biographer's own biography, whose life he experiences vampirising on others. The entry to April 13, 1980, starts with "Cecil's 89th birthday" (Hollinghurst 2011: 453), as if the poet was still alive. In apostrophising Valance, the biographer puts forward a dissociative disorder resulting in an unethical appropriation of the biographee's life to build up his own identity. As Paul identifies himself as gay, he intends to prove Cecil's own homosexuality to live his own through that of his idol's. With this purpose, after his unfruitful exchange with Dudley, he meets the Sawles, George and Madeleine, as he recalls in his diary. George's discourse is much more convenient to Bryant's purpose. He is the one who met Cecil before the visit to Two Acres, which makes the conversation into a sort of prequel to the myth itself. In Cambridge, George says, starts the Arcadia Churchill later transforms into a national icon. There, Cecil chooses the young Sawle as his son and part of the Apostles (455). George himself feels the unethicality of his unveiling his oedipal bond with Valance, but he eventually concedes to the latter's pansexuality (456), as well as to Revel Ralph's (Daphne's queer second husband) and Mark Gibbons's (her alleged lover). George's hints at fake paternities refers directly to the title, namely to thwarted oedipal affiliations, of which Daphne bears witness to. According to Sawle, most of his nephews and nieces are the children to the men who fathered them; Daphne's daughter Corinna being Cecil's daughter instead of Dudley's, and the son Daphne allegedly had of Revel Ralph being Gibbons's (460-461). Yet, it is the classic Hollinghurstian archive of sepia photographs that paves

---

[628] Caruth: *Unclaimed*, 5.
[629] Ibid., 6.
[630] Mark Llewellyn: 'Breaking the Mould? Sarah Waters and the Politics of Genre'. In Heilmann, Ann and Mark Llewellyn (eds.). *Metafiction and Metahistory in Contemporary Women's Fiction*. Houndmills, Basingstoke 2007, 20.

the way for George's final confession, his sexual affair with Cecil. Although Sawle speaks of his debauchery with Valance, it is Bryant's avidity that is the novel's debauchery. Drawing on Hollinghurst's motif of the camera as an intruder, Paul feels Cecil's further than as a literary subject (464). The latter haunts and comes back belatedly to both celebrate queerness and recall the trauma of his loss. However, if there is a sense of deferral in the novel, it is especially conspicuous in Bryant's final encounter with Daphne.

Paul, the narrator says, had a childish feeling that his interview with Daphne had been postponed for some sort of magical reason (466). Their encounter lies in between Jamesian delay and the characteristic belatedness of trauma discourse. It is a rather liminal moment in more senses than one. Daphne, now Mrs Jacobs, is the last of an era soon to be only recalled in books, the survivor of a long list of dead myths (471). As trauma survivors, she can still bear witness to what really happened in the first person, not vicariously, as second-hand witnesses like Paul can. It is also liminal because he recasts James's pleasure and torment of procrastination and attending the absent that is not to turn up. Finally, the biographer plays with a liminal idea of ignorance and uncertainty about Daphne's sexual affiliations and Cecil's role. Thus, he pretends he does even suspect about Valance's homosexuality in the hope she would come up with it herself (467). What he comes across instead is a lady in the doldrums, living with his son, uninterested in a guest she does not even recognise and whose theory she challenges. Despite Paul's black-or-white questions about the triangle of 'Two Acres', she is elusive; maybe because the myth was much closer to Ronan's bisexual camp than Bryant is ready to accept. Thus, when he hints at George and Cecil being very close, she simply argues their bond was a "hero-worship" (479) one, much in line with classic elegies. In other words, both men's rapport is inscribed in the homosocial, even homoerotic, but not in the homosexual, using Sedgwick's terminology. The biographer's prejudices prevent him from understanding the nature of Daphne and Cecil's affair, which she however acknowledges. As often happens to Hollinghurst's narcissistic characters, Paul fails to see what he has in front of him, let alone the blind corners of calamity when he misses what it takes to intrude other people's lives. The clash between memoirs and biography, witness and second-hand narration, the entitlement and appropriation takes the form of a threatening connection between both (490). Entitled to speak about herself, even poetically reconstructing one's life (497), Daphne censors all those that have 'vultured' around Cecil's corpse and a myth she has been unwillingly compelled to. "They all get it wrong" (490), she cries, as a trauma victim does when her unspeakability is widely accounted for. Bryant's encounter with Daphne serves him well to mull over life-writing as life-stealing, ventriloquising the life that belongs to the other. It is in this moment that he understands that life writing is much more that bringing up what happened but the effects of all that in the present and, further, in the future (490). Echoing the other in writing is thus a contentious, ethically problematic issue. Indeed, generations of gays have tried to make up a culture of their own by reappraising Cecil's figure and adapting it to the political needs and possibilities of their respective moments. The myth, the romance and whatever has been made of 'Two Acres' proves to be a mere construction and subsequent reconstructions owing to Daphne's eventual confession. Unlike the narration so far, it seems Daphne's infatuation with Cecil was transitory and futile, a flirt of her adolescence which she does not even long for with nostalgia (500). As a matter of fact, Dud is not the second best, as one could infer from previous sections of the novel, but the desired side-effect of her encountering Cecil (500).

The last section of *The Stranger's Child* begins with Mick Imlah's words in Tennyson's *In Memorian*, 'No one remembers you at all'. The quotation is, as always in Hollingurst, rather symbolic. Paul attends the funeral of his ex-boyfriend Peter, the man he betrayed to write Cecil's biography himself. Peter's death is thus the demise of a generation (of gays) who made Valance into a codeword for their surreptitiousness and an inspiration for their clumsy liberation. The funeral gathers a new generation, a book dealer, Rob, and Daphne's granddaughter among others, that loathes Bryant's yellowish biographies and resists to forget the 'Two Acres' generation. Jennifer recalls how her grandmother's first husband, Dudley, was once a renowned voice that is "forgotten now" (523). Like the transgenerational crypt mentioned above, the myth goes on trans-migrating in silence to reach the last Valances and Sawles and queer critics alike. Nigel Dupont, already addressed by Daphne in section four, proves to be the latest one-day wonder. A queer critic, Dupont is as much of an arriviste as Bryant before, a vulture around Cecil's corpse; the only difference between both being that, whereas the latter did not hide his unethical appropriation of the myth, the former pretends to an ethically-grounded and minority-oriented interest in the triangle at Two Acres. Narcissistic —he is featured smiling "at the beauty of his own thought" (529) — Dupont's prestige relies on his minimum coterie; so reduced though, that the narrator ironically recalls, virtually no one reads or is interested in his seminal masterpieces on Queer theory (529). Instead, the novel re-values Peter and his peers, a generation of unpretentious gays who were really in the gay trenches before 1967, fighting for new laws to be passed, though without relinquishing gay hedonism and the gay sensibility that Cecil comes to embody in *The Stranger's Child*. In fact, in a clear wink to Nantwich and traumatised peers in *The Swimming-pool Library*, Peter is grieved "under the gilded Corinthian capitals of a famous London club" (535). Grieving consists in trying to forget to continue with one's life, which is a rather celebratory act, but also an attempt to integrate the dead in the survivor, which has more to do with trauma management. Hence, memory is recalled in Peter's funeral, particularly to address the different ways of coming to terms with what is no more.

In 2008, Paul is in his mid-sixties and an easy prey to book-dealer Rob just as Cecil had been for the former years before. In fact, in an exchange between Jennifer and Rob, the biographer turns the biographee. Bryant, Jennifer points out, tried to sublimate his own lack of a father —a story he changed once and again— with his yellowish queer biographies of others (546). It is paradoxical that the one who makes up others' lives is unable to be consistent with his own life story; he, who memorises all, is not able to remember. Moreover, the fact of not having a father seems to explain his appropriation of another's. In this sense, Bryant recalls the case of Nick Guest in *The Line of Beauty* and Hollinghurstian fatherless protagonists in general. Gerald reminds Nick of his parasitism as long as he is unable to have a family of his own. The absence of a father or a household impels both Nick and Paul to be over-present where they are eventually expelled. Gerald and Jennifer accuse them of stealing lives, trust and even money, in Paul's case (546). Unfairly accused the former and justly the latter, Hollinghurst's discourse is never indulgent on account of their homosexuality. Whether their sexual orientation is related to or the cause of their non-belonging or their traumatic compulsion to appropriate others, Guest and Bryant are sycophants not to be acquitted of their acts. Meanwhile, Rob continues the task of resurfacing a story closely related to gay identity but that, unlike in prior Hollinghurst's texts, is rooted in a bisexual event. Two Acres, we learn, has been demolished; Daphne is totally forgotten —her book being sold by a mere pound; and her teenage affair with Cecil —once a national anthem— is now confused with one with Dudley (556). Despite these inaccuracies, the drive to search for traces of the past, as it is obvious in neo-Victorian and retro-Victorian narratives, informs Rob's archival trade. After Wolfenden's report, the liberation movement and queer theory, some gay voices still rework a bisexual triangle to meet their wishes. Thus, *The Stranger's Child* closes while Rob keeps tracing after the myth of 'Two Acres' to explore yet new angles of the story. He delves into some unpublished letters between a new unprecedented triangle made up of Hubert Sawle, Cecil and Harry Hewitt. The latter, a narcissist old queen and neighbour of the Sawles, proves to be a fixer and favouritiser like Nantwich in *The Swimming-pool Library* (245). Hubert, the almost unknown brother of Daphne and George, Rob finds out, held a secret relation with wealthy Hewitt. Reminiscent of nineteenth-century homosexuality, often repressed and spiritual rather than physical, Hubert thanks his friend for his numerous presents and apologises for his restrained attitude. He is not, he says, of "the demonstrative type" (554) feeling reluctant to overtly showing affection. This poetics of gayness as traumatised, encrypted and difficult is however celebrated as a historical rarity by "collectors of Gay Lives" (554) like Rob. The letters between both men soon become food for biography writing in Rob's hands. Hubert's last letters are noted by Harry when the former dies in the war, both voices merging as if in conversation (555). The triangle turns complete when Rob comes across a bundle of six letters between Cecil and Harry. Unlike Hubert, Cecil concedes to a fully-sexualised relation with Hewitt. The romance between the old queen and restrained Hubert thus breaks down with Valance. His last letter dismantles the myth, or rather, puts forward new perspectives on it. As many other writings by renowned artists, his poems are only for the addressee to enjoy in a repressed and repressing England (558). Corley Court is, according to Eeckhout, "outrageous High Victorianism [...] susceptible to queer reading." [631] Yet, I have focused on the camp outrageousness that connects the characters and their different libidinal positions in a context of thwarted relationality, overwhelming absence, non-belonging and liminality between trauma and celebration.

5.2   *The Sparsholt Affair*: Ambiguous beauty through the trans-generational keyhole

The Sparsholt Affair is Hollinghurst's last novel so far. Widely acclaimed like all the previous ones, the last novel coheres with *The Stranger's Child* in more senses than one as they move away from the 'tetralogy' that started off and returned to the nineteen eighties. It could be argued that Hollinghurst's fiction inaugurates the new century with *The Stranger's Child*, a move *The Sparsholt Affair* comes to confirm. However, no change is without transition and in Hollinghurst's case this is doubly so. His discourse is

---

[631] Eeckhout: "English," n.p.

particularly liminal. Moreover, his last two novels delve into the twenty-first century, but they do so by coming back almost a century, to the WWI the former and the WWII the latter. In this way, the writer still addresses myths of origins —the two world wars being turning-points in British history and culture— to 'hinge' his discourse into complex processes of memorialisation. In a public reading of *The Sparsholt Affair* aired at *Talks at Google*, Hollinghurst was asked about his evolution as a writer and, more specifically, on how his interests have changed, if at all. His answer is illuminating because the writer elucidates how his last two novels differ from his previous ones, mostly because, in his view, there is now no longer the same urgency. By urgency,[632] I take he means the political scenario of the nineteen eighties and nineties that engendered his 'tetralogy'. Thatcher, AIDS and the recent decriminalisation of homosexuality bestowed these novels with a feeling of urgency, somehow absent in current narratives. He started writing *The Swimming-pool Library* in 1984 (published in 1988) as a book about gay life,[633] a reaction to the *status quo*. He intended to broaden the social canvas in *The Spell*, he concedes. Yet, the sense of urgency still made the novel mostly a fresco and celebration of gay lifestyles. The broadening process increased in *The Line of Beauty* where most of the characters, Hollinghurst states, were not gay.[634] However, it is in *The Stranger's Child* and *The Sparsholt Affair* that the scope is greatly magnified, focusing on memory, displaying large time gaps and reducing eroticism. However, it is the increasing ambiguity of Hollinghurst's discourse, much in line with current post-identity politics, that is particularly remarkable.

In talking about new lifestyles and post-identities, the writer argues "Rather than defining themselves as we used to in the past, there seems to be so much more elasticity about the idea of sexuality now. And I think that is, perhaps, in a way, been reflected in what I have been writing myself and been much more interested in sexual ambiguities."[635] This necessarily calls back Ronan's article on bisexuality and camp. Far from queer theory, which Hollinghurst parodies in *The Stranger's Child*, his last two novels respond to an elasticity that breaks with and yet reworks the very idea of identity. Indeed, it is freedom to explore one's own sexuality that prevails. Una, a minor character in *The Sparsholt Affair*, has a relationship with another woman while she asks the protagonist, Johnny Sparsholt, for his semen to have a child. It is in this new scenario where sexual identities are more blurred than ever that Una claims for non-binary sexualities. Hollinghurst is not clearly for queer theory, but his writing responds to new realities. Likewise, the fact that he "isn't experimental doesn't mean that he doesn't experiment. He has recently begun a new structure for his books, one that allows him to move more freely through time."[636] In other words, the evolution of social mores, especially sexuality and the family, is the key factor of the writer's narrative experiments. The unambiguous discourse of, let's say, *The Line of Beauty* on family

---

[632] Alan Hollinghurst (reader): "Alan Hollinghurst's *The Sparsholt's Affair*." In *Talks at Google* (video). https://www.youtube.com/watch?v=H69iLEK8nUo, 2018a.

[633] Ibid.

[634] Ibid.

[635] Ibid.

[636] Alexandra Swchartz: "A novel of sex and secrecy." *The New Yorker,* https://www.newyorker.com/magazine/2018/03/19/a-novel-of-sex-and-secrecy, 2018, n.p.

matters is nuanced in *The Sparsholt Affair*. Thus, whereas Gerald Fedden refuses Nick arguing the latter is a gay parasite playing an "old homo trick" on the Feddens because he is unable to make up his own family, his last novel "with its numerous variations on the theme of family, 'real' and otherwise, could serve as Nick's belated response."[637] Giles Harvey also regards *The Sparsholt Affair* as an answer to the new panorama. A world neatly different from the one that engendered *The Swimming-pool Library* and *The Folding Star*, "in which gay rights are increasingly recognised and sexual-truth-telling is ubiquitous is one Hollinghurst played his part in creating. What kind of literature it might demand is a question that *The Sparsholt Affair* tries to answer."[638]

Like *The Stranger's Child*, *The Sparsholt Affair* is a "lengthy epic, straddling generations and major historical events while charting the course of gay history in British society from criminality to acceptance." [639] Also, like its predecessor, Hollinghurst's last novel is split in five parts in which the narration leapfrogs from WWII to 2012, thus rendering a transgenerational account of the Sparsholts and their satellites. Reluctant, the writer himself has confessed,[640] at first to repeat the same structure (for he planned a shorter novel) he comes back to it in the end. In trying to establish a difference with *The Stranger's Child*, Hollinghurst points out that *The Sparsholt Affair* does not rely on an only event described at first and glossed over in the other four sections, as happens in the former.[641] In the latter, he continues, the different sections are "connected to each other more indirectly."[642] He has even argued that the novel can be read as a collection of short stories. This is true to a certain extent, though. In fact, although the primal event that gives structural cohesion to *The Stranger's Child* is not so conspicuous in *The Sparsholt Affair*, David Sparsholt's affairs work as a recurring leitmotif, albeit in a blurred fashion, to which I will come back later.

Part one, 'A New Man' makes reference to David, a 17-year-old down in Oxford for a few months just before joining the Royal Air Force during the Blitz. The section is narrated years later by Freddie Green, an allegedly straight student surrounded by gay friends, especially the painter Peter Boyle and writer Evert Dax. Written in the first person and drawing on the literary style of the nineteen forties, Freddie himself recalls Sparsholt's first affair, which constitutes the myth of origins and "best place to start this little memoir" (Hollinghurst, 2017: 3). Although David is engaged to Connie, he soon awakens the interest of Dax and Boyle. The fact that the first section is set in Oxford during WWII, a scenario virtually unexplored except for books like Larkin's Jill —as Hollinghurst has recalled—[643] renders Green's testimony a blurred, liminal tone. It was, Green says, "that brief time between sunset and the blackout" (Hollinghurst, 2017: 5). Hence, from the very beginning, *The Sparsholt Affair* reveals the liminal, key-hole account of absence. In reducing the narration to a few moments throughout seventy

---

[637] Ibid.

[638] Harvey: "Cartographer," 29.

[639] John Boyne: "*The Sparsholt's Affair* Review: A Blitz of Gay Longing." *Irish Times*. https: //bit.ly/3o68Iyx, 2017, n.p.

[640] Hollinghurst (reader): "Alan Hollinghurst's," n.p.

[641] Ibid.

[642] Ibid.

[643] Ibid.

years, the novel relies on the absence of the unsaid, that which remains in the shadow. That is why the blackout of War Oxford is not only a historical fact, but especially a metaphor for gay surreptitiousness. It is as if the most significant and traumatic could not be uttered, even witnessed to, directly. Neither Green's "style of fine writing, in which the rarefied pleasures of euphemism and indirectness concerning sexual matters still had a certain currency"[644] nor the rest of the narrators' allegedly post-Wolfenden accounts bear witness to key episodes of the novel. The Second World War is just mentioned, though David is alleged to make a hero; likewise, the scandal that gives the title to the novel is just hinted at, never addressed directly. Thus, the poetics of absence and non-belonging of *The Stranger's Child* keep central to *The Sparsholt Affair*.

The second part of the novel features Johnny, David's 14-year-old son, spending his holidays in Cornwall with his parents and his French exchange friend Bastien. The tone of the narration, now in the third person, moves away from Green's dullness and accuracy. Drawing on the changing times, the section takes place in 1966, the narrator addresses Johnny's infatuation with the French guy in rather forthright terms. In free indirect style, we learn they had some sex the year before while Johnny's stay in Southern France. However, Bastien has turned a precocious attractive guy now interested in girls, which frustrates the expectations of the young Sparsholt. During the holidays, the Sparsholts meet the Haxbys, a well-to-do couple. Particularly intense is the relationship between David and Clifford Haxby. When they sail with the two boys, the homoerotic undertones in the constraining space of the boat is conspicuous. However, whereas the rapport between both youths recalls the homoerotic innocence Hollinghurst's texts yearn for and parody, the relationship between the two adults is much more awkward. There is "a clandestine affair going on,"[645] one involving crooked business and a commodification of sex and beauty. The section closes in a rather mysterious key-hole focalisation (Johnny's father) that bears witness to secrecy. Just before homosexuality is decriminalised in the UK, Sparsholt and Haxby are holding a secret meeting that leaves many more questions than answers in the reader. It is not Green's writing, but the truth, whatever it is, that is still unutterable.

'Small Oils', the third section, is set in 1974 in an atmosphere of liberation where the old and new generation of gays meet through Johnny's keyhole viewpoint. Now twenty-something, the young Sparsholt opens the door to the mores of gay London as soon as he arrives at Evert Dax's, which has become a hub of gay subculture. Ironically, when the youth arrives, the group of old Oxonians are holding a meeting of their memoir club. As usual in Hollinghurst, hazard and intentionality merge uncannily. One never knows whether Johnny meets his father's Oxford partners by chance or on purpose. Be it as it may, like Will Beckwith in *The Swimming-pool Library*, the former is confronted all of a sudden with his father's generation and with secrets encrypted transgenerationally, particularly David's incarceration. Thus, the youth turns the recipient of a trauma that haunts and infatuates the gay community belatedly, a sexual and business affair in which Sparsholt was involved with Haxby and MP Leslie Stevens

[644] James Lasdun: "*The Sparsholt's Affair* by Alan Hollinghurst review – passion and folly, beautifully observed." *The Guardian*, https://www.theguardian.com/books/2017/oct/05/the-sparsh olt-affair-by-alan-hollinghurst-review, 2017, n.p.

[645] Ibid.

soon after the family holidays in Cornwall in 1966. Drawing on the precedent of *The Swimming-pool Library*, one expects the narrator will give full account of the affair that gives title to the novel. Indeed, "the questions of what exactly happened and how the disgrace of the father is going to play pout in the destiny of the son loom large, and seem to promise tremendous revelations."[646] Yet, the 'truth' is never fully revealed, just hinted at, as often happens in trauma cases. The traumatic event is only captured belatedly and defectively.

The last two parts of *The Sparsholt Affair*, 'Losses' and 'Consolations', feature a mature Johnny, in 1995 and 2012 respectively. There are two sides of the same coin, namely the trauma of loss and its subsequent mourning. Hollinghurst himself has addressed his optimistic celebratory ending, for consolations stand for new possibilities of happiness after a period when losses are as frequent as parties.[647] This ambiguous liminality between death and its overcoming is part of the new ambiguity critics claimed and Hollinghurst has granted. The death of Jill, Freddie's first love while in Oxford, only announces Freddie's. Their deaths symbolise the demise of a generation. This is obvious when the survivors come across the dead's belongings, particularly so in Freddie's case, whose memoir writing has borne witness to gays' lifestyles since the nineteen forties. Moreover, the fact that Lucy, Johnny's seven-year-old daughter, focalises the chapter in a clear What-Maisie-Knew fashion, gives it a sense of time past, as incomprehensible for the reader as it is for the child. 'Consolations' comes as a coda to demise. Johnny, a reasonable well-known portraitist is commissioned a family portrait by Bella Miserden, a major television star, and a new concept of celebrity the artist loathes. He is a widower now. However, his story is one of survival despite circumstances. The Sparsholt's affair being almost a shadow no one can figure out accurately, Johnny can reconstruct himself, using dating apps and "setting up a profile, sort of a self-portrait" (Hollinghurst 2017: 410). Thus, he meets Michael, a young occasional lover who takes David's affair for a film (411). It is this new generation of gays that, despite their cultural gap, help Johnny to bereave his late husband and father. Beauty and sex, as often in Hollinghurst, prove to be the redeeming features during or after trauma processes. However, this time, the focus is eventually on the celebratory rather than on the traumatic, thus reformulating the poetics of absence and memory.

John Boyne has argued that Hollinghurst's work "has been defined by his preference for finding joy rather than trauma in his youthful characters' exploration of their homosexuality."[648] As I have contended along this book, there is a tension between trauma and celebration underlying his novels. Gay lifestyles are recalled and celebrated, particularly sexuality, very especially in his early fiction. *The Spell* is perhaps the most conspicuous case. When criticising Hollinghurst's novels for being "relentless gay" — nobody so far has been accused of writing relentless heterosexual texts–, John Updike is especially judgemental about *The Spell*, for, he claims: "nothing is at stake but self-gratification."[649] The underlying message under Updike's judgement is twofold: self-gratification is annihilating because it breaks with compromise and hetero-

---

[646] Ibid.
[647] Hollinghurst (reader): "Alan Hollinghurst's," n.p.
[648] Boyne: "*Sparsholt's*," n.p.
[649] In Harvey: "Cartographer," 53.

sacramentalism. Hollinghurst's characters update and sexualise the motif of the *fins de race*, thus reifying the idea of pleasure as an end in itself. Moreover, he contends that focusing on gayness is self-limiting as an artist. Harvey shrewdly responds to this indictment claiming that Hollinghurst's conception of homosexuality is a democratising force, bringing "people together across boundaries of race and class and age."[650] It is true that women are either absent, as is the case of *The Swimming-pool Library*, or play ancillary roles, as in most of the other novels. It must be admitted though there has been an evolution to more ambiguous gender positions, particularly bisexuality, in his last two novels. Thus, the celebratory tone underlying Hollinghurst's texts has been much more inclusive recently. However, celebration of sexuality has always been under threat, trauma poetics constantly thwarting fulfilment. Indeed, longing, postponement and belatedness have often distressed or cancelled most of Hollinghurst's protagonists' pleasure. The threat of AIDS was the ghost that terminated the subculture Will Beckwith, Edward Manners, some characters of *The Spell* and Nick Guest inhabited. The belatedness with which the AIDS virus developed and affected its victims was itself a metaphor of the characteristically delaying discourse of trauma. And hence, trauma poetics became a common feature of Hollinghurst's writing. However, in *The Stranger's Child* and especially *The Sparsholt Affair*, it is not the disease, but the pleasurable metaphor of belatedness that justifies its nostalgic undertones. Post-ponement inflates the homoeroticism of Hollinghurst's latest novel in Oxford, Cornwall or London when men 'keyhole' on other men. This is particularly the case of David Sparsholt, whose beautiful body is worshipped, commodified, exposed, criminalised, memorialised and absent throughout the novel.

David's first appearance in the novel is in the form of a male model Evert, Peter and Freddie admire through the window of their Oxford room during the blackout. A shadow at first, his body comes soon "a figure in a gleaming singlet, steadily lifting and lowering a pair of hand-weights" (Hollinghurst 2017: 5). His muscular body is however dematerialised into a fantasy that transcends his corporeality. Indeed, he turns up the mere effect light his beholders just fantasise with (6). David comes to represent male beauty, a model for Peter's painting, an inspiration for Freddie's memoir and a dream for Evert. Drawing on Platonic tradition, as we saw in *The Death in Venice*, and more down-to-earth muscular homoeroticism, Sparsholt is an abstraction, a group of lines which make up a shape, as Hogarth's line of beauty. He is an elusive illusion, like Luc in *The Folding Star*; the effect of light and shadow, a pictorial image himself, like a succession of stills from a black-and-white film on early male nude models. It is as if his very essence was not physical, so to speak, and extremely physical at the same time. Indeed, the result of the abstraction made up of light beams proves to be palpably corporeal and triggers a neatly bodily reaction of his admirers. As an idealised Greek or Roman statue, Sparsholt seems not to suffer from effort. However, echoing his most obvious referent, namely Michelangelo's David, Hollinghurst's character is both deeply human and idealised. He may be glorious, but also a mere sportsman lifting weights, as his prominent veins confirm. Thus, David's first impression haunts the rest of the novel, as Peter's painting does. Indeed, as if frozen in the picture, Sparsholt remains young, beautiful and abstract forever as a twentieth-century version of Dorian Gray. All the

[650] Ibid.

depravities, suffering and humiliation David is alleged to undergo, being imprisoned and socially ostracised, contrast with the timeless effect he produces on his obsessed admirers and Goyle's subsequent painting. As mentioned above, Peter drafts David as a demigod, yet faceless and the genitals hidden, drawing on Greek statues. The effect, as that of his affair when the three Oxonians look at him weighting lifts, is perturbing. As uncanny as his predecessors, Michelangelo's David, Wilde's Dorian, Mann's Tadzio and Hollinghurst's prior *hommes fatales*, Sparsholt is unfathomable.

The painting, however, bears witness to the pass of time, delaying his comprehensibility and meaningfulness along time. David's worship is not without irony, though. The youth is a liminal figure, as uncanny as void. Freddie suggests that where others find beauty, he sees a blank (68). In fact, as Freddie's narration advances, he proves to be a square-faced hustler in the guise of a demigod, an arriviste who does not hesitate to seduce Evert to get his goals, a calculator, tactician (80), and planner (81). Goyle's painting of David's torso, a mere few lines deluding the viewer, becomes a testimony of an era that, however, bears witness to gays' changing attitudes trans-generationally. Freddie hands it over to Evert in the conviction that nobody is "likely to value it most" (93). After the fashion of Dorian Gray's portrait, Goyle's draft gives itself and its owner away. Thus, Evert's reencounter with it is Faustian: "The red chalks [...] made the drawn image [...] a little satanic" (93). The scene of Dax holding the dammed picture forecasts another still, this one much more cinematographic, of the young Sparsholt moving forwards towards a future which is and is not his own: "A figure so unstoppable was alarming as well as splendid" (93). The iconography of the moment is very graphic of what is to come, enormous success and failure. Like Wilde and Nantwich, David cannot be accounted for in a single narrative. The poetics of trauma and belatedness, hence the doubleness of the two gaps, bear witness to his simultaneous pragmatism and elusiveness. The red chalk drawing recurs in the third section of the novel, when Johnny goes to Evert's by chance. Paradoxically, this piece of old porn mixes the two generations together around. The naked man, the young Sparsholt observes, features a muscled man "with a high-minded blur where the cock and balls should be" (170). Looking, without knowing, at his own father's portrait is quite of a Hollinghurtian game; particularly ironic when Johnny feels it part of London's bohemia and far from his father's pre-Thatcherite neo-Victorian morality (170).

The draft of Sparsholt's body proves a simultaneously transient and lasting commodification of male beauty. Johnny, himself a painter, ruminates on the palimpsestous elusiveness of the canvas in free indirect style. He thinks of the surface of a painting whose varnish "darkened [...] what it was meant to protect" (199). He comes to understand that art works in layers conversing with each other and reaching out for meaning despite the pass of time (226). It is in this sense that *The Sparsholt Affair* addresses a poetics a postponement. Old layers always come out in a palimpsestuous fashion. The new painting is haunted by the underlying one that, drawing on trauma theory, re-surfaces belatedly. Goyle's painting of Sparsholt is a case in point, the novel's leitmotif so to speak. When Freddie dies, Evert and Johnny mull over his things, Goyle's draft being a focal point yet again. Lucy, Johnny's 7-year-old daughter, focalises the moment when her father comes across the painting, or rather, the reddish drawing of a man in the nude "with no head and cut off above the knee" (368). Rather symbolically, Evert intends to bequeath it to Johnny and thus close the circle. Although in 'Consolations', the last section of the novel, dating apps and mobiles update self-portraits into web profiles (410), "endless selfies" (412) and porn iconography, Goyle's draft remains central. In 2012, the painting hanging at Johnny's, it has become a symptom of absence. Indeed, David being dead, the piece of art is like a traumatic aftermath. When Bella Miserden gets a glimpse of it, Johnny confesses that, only after years seeing the portrait, he has come to guess it is his father (449). Thus, the circle Evert intended to close in bequeathing it to Johnny finally does so with the latter's self-recognition.

Like *The Stranger's Child*, *The Sparsholt Affair* leaves many unspotted events in the epic family saga it features. David's painting is a proof of the relentless absence of the protagonist and the scandal that gives title to the story. Indeed, rather than being thoroughly detailed, as happens with Nantwich's incarceration and downfall in *The Swimming-pool Library* and Gerald Fedden's tabloid-aired scandal in *The Line of Beauty*, Hollinghurst's sixth novel keeps it almost a secret, only eavesdropped, seen through a keyhole, echoed defectively and drawn in a blurred painting. It takes place off-stage, in a liminal, in-between space, which ascertains the novel's focus on unrealiability and unknowability of the other. This double feeling also underscores David's sexual scandal. The "deliberate obliqueness" it is addressed with grants the novel a fascination "at the risk of slowing its sales."[651] For critics like Lasdun, however, Hollinghurst's cryptic rendering of the central trauma of *The Sparsholt Affair* is a "slight letdown."[652] This twofold reading of the novel's poetics of denial only confirms the classic understanding of gayness as too visible or too invisible. Time leaps amount to an echoic narration that recalls but is neatly different from that of *The Stranger's Child*. Hollinghurst himself has addressed such differences, arguing that the interlocking sections of his last novel are related more indirectly than those of his prior novel. There is no single episode that focalises the attention throughout and is always retrieved, like Cecil's myth. However, the Sparsholt's affair is recalled in the form of seismic replicas moving forwards and backwards. That is, the keyhole account of the business and sexual affair that takes David to prison is pre-empted by his being painted at Oxford also addressed as the Sparsholt affair and recalled by Johnny's painting of the Miserdens, which they also label the Sparsholt's affair. This dispersion of the central event, rather than the nostalgic yearning of the myth of origins of *The Stranger's Child* makes a difference. The first reference to David's affair with Clifford Haxby, MP Leslie Stevens and, we later know, male prostitutes, is as hazy as vivid. Details are scarce, but enough to make up the classic Hollinghurstian momentum. In an apparently closed bungalow at Greylags, the Haxbys's summer house, Johnny can eventually notice some movement that gives away those who are inside in a clandestine meeting (Hollinghurst 2017: 152-154).

Johnny's heyhole narration is at its utmost, pointing to his excess and lack of seeing. He bears witness to one of the novel's momentums without him knowing. He just stares

---

[651] John Powers: *"The Sparsholt's Affair* Confirms Alan Hollinghurst's Status as a Literary Master." *Npr Books*. https://www.npr.org/2018/03/12/592868267/the-sparsholt-affair-confirms-alan-hollinghurst-s-status-as-a-literary-master?t=1530086438599, 2018, n.p.

[652] Lasdun: *"The Sparsholt's,"* n.p.

at a house that looks as well as it is looked at. The allegedly absent residents are, Johnny guesses, gone to the lookout, a vantage point whose main purpose is looking; in this case staring back at the protagonist/focaliser and indirectly at the readers. The windows reflect the light, which makes the house more subject than an object, impenetrable to the foreign eye. Moreover, rather disturbingly, the Venetian blind, which both prevents and allows to see and to be seen, eventually moves as if automatically. A proof that the viewer in control is not Johnny, but the one(s) inside is particularly disconcerting, leaving the narrated events overt to speculation. The whole second section is a lookout, as its title advances, from where to spy on the affair to come out. Not only are the sexual innuendos between David and Clifford constant while sailing in the (aptly named) Ganymede. Both men's meeting MP Leslie Stevens is, in Norma Haxby's words, a proof that "they're cooking something up" (138); whether sexual or businesslike she never says. When a young Johnny gets acquainted with Evert's troupe in 1970s London, the affair is a scandal that, though never fully explained, fascinates the then rising gay community. Thus, in meeting the young Sparsholt, his surname raises these men's interest and sheds some light on the scandal barely hinted at at the end of section two. Evert's lover Ivan cannot help recalling his infatuation, particularly the pictures that tabloids published of the threesome between David, Haxby and a third unknown man in the bungalow (194); the same scene Johny was a witness of. The early infatuation with the event, involving male prostitutes and taking three prominent figures to the headlines, paves the way for forgetting or, rather half-forgetting; that is, the liminal stage where events are blurred with imagination. A scandal is a major event that, with time becomes "a blurred image or two, the facts partial or distorted, the names eluding memory" (194). Like Goyle's painting, the affair becomes a draft, a few lines, nodes of meaning turning hollow as time passes. Hollinghurst himself has addressed the question of veracity and scandal as something "just half remembered, a lingering stain."[653] Thus, at the end of the novel, Alan Miserden only recollects there was a long-time-ago scandal on the name Sparsholt he must 'google' to fully recall (Hollinghurst 2017: 406).

It is Bastien who bears witness to what the novel sees first-hand of the scandal. Moreover, the second section constantly refers to David as Johnny's father, as if Bastien was narrating or, at least, focalising the Cornwall holidays. It is also surprising that the scandal takes the name of its less relevant protagonist. An MP and a wealthy businessman are a priori much more suitable for the tabloids front pages than an anonymous man like David, no matter how enigmatic and disturbing he is. However, among other things, *The Sparsholt Affair* commodifies beauty, Bastien and David being its main instruments. Beauty is celebrated in the shape of Sparsholt's body and enigma and of Bastien's attitude of *garçon fatal*, drawing, as mentioned above, on Mann's Tadzio or Luc in *The Folding Star*. But beauty usually has an underside in Hollinghurst. The celebratory hides and is fuelled by a much more traumatic underside of beauty which, as seen in *The Line of Beauty*, is related to the Dionysian. Nevertheless, the Dionysian in *The Sparsholt Affair* is not so intense because it all takes place offstage.

Beauty is not only an abstraction, like Hogarth's line. It is informed by postponement and evasiveness. No matter how frustrating eluding so-called truth is

---

[653] Hollinghurst, Alan (reader). 2018b. "Alan Hollinghurst on *The Sparsholt's Affair*." In Shakespeare and Company (video). https://www.youtube.com/watch?v=4JQuPJjTNbs.

for readers,[654] the novel invests most of its erotic and narrative promise on these principles. Few words are more repeated along *The Sparsholt Affair* than delay. This again is related to the novel's twofold celebratory and traumatic nature. Delaying is both the necessary belatedness a traumatic event must undergo to be first acted out and eventually worked through.[655] In other words, postponement may be the symptom of a trauma that is yet to be uttered, if at all. However, postponement can also be a willing attempt to delay a pleasurable outcome. In this case, it is paradoxically the promise of an end that makes suffering worth it. Celebration thus involves a traumatic undergoing in *The Sparsholt Affair*. Infatuation is a case in point: Evert's fascination with David, and Johnny's with Bastien, prove what I say. Despite evoking Connie, Evert cannot help the erotic investment of David's delayed presence in an Oxford bedroom (Hollinghurst, 2017: 45). Likewise, after Johnny is kissed by Ivan Goyle, the latter holds Sparsholt's hand "delaying whatever might happen next" (179). Later on, there is a new sense of excitement when Johnny feels "the coy delay in whatever was staring to happen" (281). The liminality linked to postponement recurs when Johnny meets Colin, yet a new would-be lover. As the narrator recalls, the delay in the moment only intensifies the force of desire (202); that is, the longer the delay, the higher the suffering and the pleasure. Johnny's procrastination, like that of James's characters, is both related to a restrained sexuality, as his sexual encounters above evince, and a longing for beauty. Other than male beauty, though related to it, the novel addresses the beauty of things. Like Nick in *The Line of Beauty* and its Jamesian hypotext, *The Spoils of Poynton*, the young Sparsholt feels a sort of thwarted desire for beautiful objects. They are, moreover, commodified as part of their categorisation as beautiful. It is at an auction, where the sense of postponement (until the object is sold) and commodification of art is especially conspicuous, that Johnny feels the anxiety of almostness. His waiting for the picture to be shown for sale triggers his "impatience for what was mixed with a nervous longing for delay" (221). There is also a sense of delay in the final encounter between David and Evert long after they first met in Oxford; the former a twice-married closeted bisexual and the latter a gay subculture pioneer who is losing his memory (383) in a novel memory is crucial. Hollinghurst is somehow holding the mirror of one against the other and, indirectly, of Nantwich against Lord Beckwith in *The Swimming-pool Library*. The old generation is confronted to itself and the phantoms that have been haunting around for years. In *The Sparsholt Affair*, the encounter is not one of poetic justice, as it is in Hollinghurst's first novel. Both Evert and David have been victims of a homophobic politics, being stigmatised and criminalised respectively. Hence, their meeting is somehow Johnny's homage to a lost world where, Hollinghurst likes calling back, homosexuality was a coded way of desire. It is also an act of beauty because the circle is closed; more in an echoic fashion, since they recall the past, than in a narcissistic one, both men having experienced their non-normative sexualities in dissimilar ways. In joining them in a room, Johnny "realized what he'd done for Evert and his father was just what Freddie had done for them" in the past (385). Unknowing why Freddie had done it, he concedes he is unable to explain his aim (385). Once again,

---

[654] Schwartz, "Novel," n.p.
[655] Cathy Caruth (ed): *Trauma: Explorations in Memory*. Baltimore MD and London 1995, 9.

it is in this liminal space of elusiveness that beauty lies in *The Sparsholt Affair*. It is, however, the interstitiality of memory that looms large along the novel.

Memory is elusive, but stubborn, along the novel since it relies on an absence that, as happens in *The Stranger's Child*, is haunting and ever present. Hollinghurst himself has confessed *The Sparsholt Affair* is about the pass of time and the working of memory. Indeed, it is memory that links up (at) bleak angles (2018 n.p.) thus making up the five-staged narration of the novel. The traces of memory in Hollinghurst's fiction in general and his last two texts in particular fade away. In this way, they turn into scars the biographer or memoirist recalls with nostalgia to guide the reader. This return to the past does not guarantee resolution, as it does in his early fiction. Unlike the detailed accounts of Lord Nantwich's prosecution and incarceration in *The Swimming-pool Library*, Orst's fated end in *The Folding Star* and Guest's ejection from the Feddens' in *The Line of Beauty*, the Sparsholts' saga remains open. References to the scandal are always vicarious and oblique, glimpsed through a Proustian keyhole, an issue of the past that resists signification. Only in the retrospect is David's downfall vaguely addressed. Seven years have passed and his misbehaviour with a Tory MP becomes just a provincial affair in the tabloids for a while (182). Surprisingly, however, the MP has been forgotten by public opinion whereas Drum becomes a hero thanks to "his beauty and wartime glory" (182). A family saga like its predecessor, *The Sparsholt Affair* is made up of memory fragments that complement each other, negotiating the reliability and forms of memory itself. The novel starts off with Freddie's memoir, "written for, but never read" (94). Green's circuitous phrasing which, as Olivia Laing recalls, is hallmarked by Hollinghurst's devotion to James and Firbank shifts in the next sections.[656] The first-person Oxonian narration of Freddie moves forward to third-person accounts that recall the Sparsholts' family history against the backcloth of almost eighty years of sexual dissidence in England. Unlike Green's incisive use of memory to recall the Sparsholt's affair at Oxford clashes with the much more detached viewpoint of the third-person narrator of the second section. As I pointed out above, the fact that David is addressed as Johnny's father implies the narrator is next to the young Sparsholt; Bastien is quite a tempting option. Indeed, it is the French boy that, in noticing a suspicious closeness between David and Clifford at the latter's house, "glimpses something through the window".[657] However, Bastien himself is addressed in a rather detached fashion, Johnny's object of infatuation and frustration. Be it as it may, the narrating voice recalls a number of "disjointed scenes,"[658] proving a limited viewpoint and memory.

Drawing on the cinematographic stills of the Feddens' holidays in France, "The Lookout" bears witness to the Cornwall vacation of the Sparsholts as if through a keyhole or a camera. Also, as it always happens when something momentous and traumatic is about to occur in Hollinghurst's texts, the narration is prophetic and blurred, mixing a present and a past equally elusive to Johnny. He starts the section

---

[656] Olivia Laing: "Alan Hollinghurst's *The Sparsholt's Affair Feels* like looking through a Keyhole." *New Statesman.* https://www.newstatesman.com/culture/books/2017/10/alan-hollin ghursts-sparsholt-affair-feels-looking-through-keyhole, 2017, n.p.
[657] Schwartz, "Novel," n.p.
[658] Laing: "Alan," n.p.

drawing people whose intentions he is unable to foresee. Like Firbank's characters, the youth only bears witness to something beyond his comprehension. Yet, his drawings, no matter how much of a draft they are, and the narrative voice serve the reader to decode what is going on. The truth of traumata, like the one about to dismantle the Sparsholts, can never be simply uttered. That is the aporia of traumatic (un)speakability. The narrative of trauma must be thwarted for it to bear witness to the traumatic event and be credible. If one is under the effect of trauma, truth can never run smooth, but defectively. Literature is a privileged scenario for traumatic realism, 'troping' reality into fiction. The homoerotic drive of Haxby towards David is only hinted, mostly in the form of tropes. The sailing scene is as apparently inconsequential as dramatically relevant to the novel's unfolding. The boat is significantly called after Ganymede, Zeus's beloved. And there, all being men (Hollinghurst, 2017: 109), Clifford is attracted to David while Johnny feels attracted to Bastien (106). The narrator bears witness to the homoerotics of the foursome in a subtle way, namely pointing to Clifford's nervous reaction to David's body exposure (103). In the 'democratic' atmosphere of the boat, the adults behave in a rather free fashion, touching each others' bodies (112), as they never dared in 'real' life. However, behind these homoerotic drives and the worship of Sparsholt's masculinity (110), there is a much stronger feeling of momentousness. Although Johnny cannot detect the expression on their faces, their body language gave away "a sense of something nice being planned" (111).

Back to the working of memory, the forecast of David's scandal is offset by the flashbacks of Johnny's summer in France. References to the sexual activity between the two boys in Nîmes the year before are subtle again. Drawing again on Proust's keyhole narrating, Bastien's mother notices "that something was going on" (118). This is the closest the narration is to rendering both boys' affair, a few disjointed scenes that trace and elude memory. Back to the present and Cornwall, Bastien proves to be uneasy and elusive, increasingly interested in girls, to Johnny's desperation. Evoking Edward Manners's infatuation with Luc, Johnny starts off a goose-hunt after the French guy. In more senses than one, Bastien is an echo of Luc and David Sparsholt himself, Johnny's fascination being informed by nostalgia, the unfathomable and the elusive. Only occasionally do the sexual undertones of both boys' summer in France come back. When that happens, the present freezes delaying itself and Johnny wants "it to go on for a long time" (150) enjoying procrastination. Hence, the present is moulded by the traces of memory, too vivid to be neglected or overcome.

From the third section onwards *The Sparsholt Affair* is definitely focused on and by Johnny's viewpoint. As Stephanie Bishop argues, he is, "like many of Hollinghurst's leading men, [...] a nervous outsider — an observer of those who move with greater confidence and panache."[659] This idea of non-belonging, being the absent presence that bears witness to others' lives, thus fits the young Sparsholt. Like Nick Guest, he is a guest to his own story which he experiences through others, very particularly the haunting scandal of his father back in the sixties. A young adult in the seventies, he comes across the circle that befriended his father at Oxford. Evert lives in his dead

---

[659] Stephanie Bishop: *"The Sparsholt's Affair." The Monthly,* https://www.themonthly.com.au/iss ue/2017/november/1509454800/stephanie-bishop/sparsholt-affair-alan-hollinghurst,   2017, n.p.

father's huge house, which he has transformed into a transgenerational gay commune. Johnny first meets them while they are holding a meeting of the memoir club where people's names and faces were unkown and unreachable to him (Hollinghurst, 2017: 164). This group of survivors goes on surviving as long as they write and read to each other on their shared past, thus making up a recognisable memory. The memorialising purpose of these meetings goes further yet when one of the members suggests that "someone should write a history of the old Club" (167). That is, it is the memories of memories that reach readers of *The Sparsholt Affair*. The conflict with truth when recalling the past arises in the Memo Club as well. Ivan Goyle, Evert's young lover, introduces Johnny to how the Club works. The third Tuesday of the month they meet, read a memoir and "they have to tell the truth" (173). Thus, they make up a web of truth and memory that defies forgetting and alternative truths, particularly official historiography. This is related to the debate on biofiction in *The Stranger's Child*. There is in *The Sparsholt Affair* no Paul Bryant writing on a dead writer. It is rather a communal biofiction that these characters project in telling their own memoirs. The closest the novel is to Bryant's account of Cecil Valance is when Evert attempts to write his father's memoirs. Once a valued writer, Victor Dax is, as often happens in Hollinghurst's novels, someone of the past, virtually forgotten and not read any longer (188). However, while Bryant fulfils Valance's biofiction, Evert proves unable to conclude Victor's, who comes to be inevitably cited as one of "the great forgotten novelists" (188). The father's forgetting runs parallel to the son's sense of withdrawal and denial of the former. This explains the connecting thread between delay, as mentioned above, and memorising as celebratory and traumatic events. The narrator says about Evert that "the memoir was a game of postponement" (189). Both celebrating his father and denying him while delaying the memoir is a rather complex process akin to traumata. In between the traumatic event and its belated recurrence lies the (im)possibility of putting it into words. This would justify Evert's contradictory desire and resistance to write in the act of postponement.

Memory and how it is gathered in memoirs is not always desirable. Very often in Hollinghurst's fiction, recalling the past is unfathomable and threatening, especially for characters like Johnny. The shadow of his father's affair looms large not only because of the tabloids, as Gerald Fedden's in *The Line of Beauty*. Thus, people know about him before even having met him. This is the case with Francesca (206), the upper-class lesbian socialite who asks the young Sparsholt to father their future daughter Lucy. It is Francesca who firstly mentions Freddie's ignominious memoir, *The Lion Griefs* where, Evert points out, the limits between facts and fiction are blurred (207). The book, though never explained, allegedly gathers Green's memoirs in Oxford in the form of a generation's bio-fiction. Whether the lion of the title is David is never known, although it is probable in view of his grievable career. Be it as it may, Iffy, an old friend of Evert's, warns Johnny about Freddie who has written a diary with the secrets of the whole lot and of which everybody seems to be afraid (207). Drawing on the echoic character of traumata, the past haunts the present and is likely to resurface and destabilise it. However, it is when the past meets the present literally, rather than when Johnny toils "through Freddie's peculiar memoir" (376), that everything makes sense. In bringing his father and Evert back together after half a century, the youth understands their Oxonian affair and its implications. In conjuring memory when it falters, *The*

Sparsholt's Affair delves into a crucial issue in Hollinghurstian fiction. It is remarkable that Johnny brings both men together when Evert's memory is getting worse, as if trying to freeze the liminal moment when remembering is still possible, just before only texts can summon what is gone. Drawing on the paternal-filial undertones the novel is scattered with, Victor's Dax is a case in point. Evert's once popular father is, as happens with Cecil Valance, an example of a second-rate artist. Green's account of his visit to Oxford as a visiting writer is demolishing, but more so is the passage of time and forgetfulness. When Evert intends to write his own memoir, he goes after his father's memorabilia. In the process, he finds out his father's portrait has been removed from his old college to a dark room where it hangs "above the refrigerator" with its name and date of birth and death (330).

Harvey argues that *The Sparsholt Affair* is a novel about "the failure of cultural transmission, about stalled emotion and stymied confidences."[660] I would add it is a novel about losses —that is incidentally the title of the fourth section— and what remains of gay culture, as Hollinghurst himself has conceded.[661] As happens in *The Stranger's Child*, the dialogue and mutual understanding is not always an easy task. However, despite this failure in transmission, there are some points that link generations together, namely the wish to account for their identities, be it in the form of paintings, memoirs, keyhole focalisations/narrations or others. Names are forgotten, revised and occasionally resurfaced. But new and old generations alike share an aporic drive that compels them to represent the unrepresentable. This draws on the structure of the novel, which leapfrogs in time and overlooks major events leaving them in the blackout. *The Sparsholt Affair* gives access to much less than is recalled, as it always happens in biofictions. However, the web profiles of the new generation that, Hollinghurst has labelled as binary (2018), are the response to the accounts Freddie, Evert and the rest give of their lifetimes. This evolution in representational options, from faceless pictures to social networks and dating apps, is conspicuous since Johnny does overtly what in former times was hidden out of secrecy and fear of open shame (371). Also, Lucy's What-Maisie-Knew focalisation of "Losses" renders the changing ways of representing oneself and family lifestyles. The daughter of Johnny, the semen-donor to lesbian couple Francesca and Una, her two mothers, and the granddaughter to Una's aristocratic father, Sir George, and David Sparsholt (307), makes the seven-year-old into the core, so to speak, of new family models. The same holds for extra-family arrangements Lucy comes familiar with. Evert's all-male commune is normalised in its exceptionality when the child calls it the funny men's House of Horrors (312). This is what remains of a gay subculture to the eyes of a late-twentieth-century child. Yet, this sense of loss and survival is not without irony, Lucy's focalisation being crucial. When she asks Evert about him knowing her grandfather David, the situation is hilarious and the effect rather Jamesian: "We used to do things together ... sometimes" (316).

Chapter 5, "Consolations," offsets the losses of chapter 4. However, the chapter does not feature the celebratory tone that would cancel loss completely. Indeed, consolation is closer to mourning as the Freudian coming to terms with what is no more and thus avoid melancholia. Having lost his last lover, Pat, Johnny is a sixty-year-old, reasonably

---

[660] Harvey: "Cartographer," n.p.
[661] Hollinghurst (reader): "Alan Hollinghurst's."

known painter, who is commissioned to paint a portrait of the Miserdens, a new type of elite he despises. His relation with painting as a life-inspiring event helps the protagonist to overcome loss. This he does in physical rather than psychological terms. Like oils on the canvas, he experiences a "molecular change in the material of life itself" (398). The physicality he grants on his mourning process gives way to a crystallisation of loss (398). Unlike other Hollinghurst's heroes, Johnny overcomes the acting-out of trauma and works it through well into the future. He does so getting acquainted with the changing media of self-representation and relationality mentioned above. He sets up a profile, a new version of the classic self-portrait (410), and uses Grindr to have casual sex (411). The faceless of his father's draft by Goyle is thus updated in equally faceless pictures men upload to meet sexual partners; like the one where there is oral sex while staring at the camera and using sexual toys (412) and that he sees on his one-day-affair Michael's phone. Like Alex in *The Spell*, Johnny finds in drugs and the gay club scene the way to overcome bereavement. Having lost almost all, his father included, the pure physicality of the club turns the scenario of his aporic process of self-extinction and self-renewal. In entering the club, "the nudging oneness with all the other half-naked men was entrancing" (427). Drawing again on Alex's example once his young lover abandons him, once introduced to the line of beauty in *The Spell*, Johnny knows his way. In part as an effect of the drugs and on the other hand of his post-bereavement autosuggestion, he feels that sexual acts can be private in a public space (which recalls the numerous examples in Hollinghurst's sex tetralogy) and that he can remain in this homoerotic Arcadia for ever (428). Foreplay as postponement remains crucial to Johnny's experiencing of desire. But there is fulfilment in his desire, though there is lack as well. It is no surprise, drawing on Hollinghurst's penchant for metaphor and momentousness, that David dies when his son experiences resurrection (430). Johnny's rebirth coincides with his staring at himself on mirrors. It is not that mirrors are absent in the rest of the novel. Yet, at the end of the novel, it is no longer a narcissistic drive; specularity has more to do with self-recognition, drawing on Lacan's 'mirror stage', and with the complex paternal-filial bond. The now older Sparsholt sees his last lover's eyes in the mirror (433), but especially his own face, first weary and apprehensive (432), and later as an old man with the "implacable erection of a satyr" (439). However, the 'authentic' specular experience is that of facing his father's corpse. Absent for most of his life, David's present absence as a corpse guides Johnny's grieving performance. Like Charles Nantwich in *The Swimming-pool Library*, David is many things in one, "'War hero,' 'Criminal,' 'Old Gent'" (443). However, Johnny, unlike Will Beckwith, is the son to the criminal/victim/traumatised and not to the perpetrator. Despite the many differences, the end of *The Sparsholt Affair* comes back to the beginning of *The Swimming-pool Library*. It is as if the circle was closed so far. If Will celebrates his *belle époque*, though anticipating a traumatic end (Hollinghurst: 1998a: 3), Johnny's recovered celebration of life with his young lover Zz does not prevent him from the "knowledge that something momentous and terrible was still waiting to be felt" (Hollinghurst, 2017: 431). This seems to be Hollinghurst's heroes' unflinching fate.

Some concluding remarks

Narcissus and Echo are closer than it may seem at first sight. This was a premise of this book that the analysis of Hollinghurst's fiction has proved. His early novels draw on self-narcissistic characters who narrate their own stories of self-discovery. Yet, the traumatic undertones they are scattered with prevent the completion of their *Bildungs-romane*. As his career evolved, the narcissism of autodiagetic narration and the exclusively gay cast, which conveyed a sense of excess of sameness, have changed to explore new ways of specularity. The narcissistic commodifies self-beauty, Will Beckwith being the outmost example. However, Hollinghurst's characters prove, beauty is not without harm, particularly when it is signposted in nostalgic terms. This is what configures the echoic in his novels. Characters may stare at themselves or at each other. However, current traumata uphold nostalgia and its echoic sense of return. All Hollinghurst's novels, with the limited exception of *The Spell*, yearn for something lost. Thus, loss and its subsequent mourning, incidentally melancholia, inform the echoic that complements and progressively replaces the narcissistic. It is in this sense that I consider his last novels more relational than his previous ones. The writer even thought of having *The Swimming-pool Library* narrated by a ghosted protagonist dying of AIDS. Also the narrator of *The Folding Star* is almost a spectral character surrounded by AIDS victims and going after his elusive spectral beloved, who is but a narcissistic projection of himself and his desire. Narcissism evolves in the next two novels; part of the commodity club culture of *The Spell*, or a failed attempt at preservation in a world not his own in the case of the protagonist of *The Line of Beauty*. In the latter, the feeling of return to the origins or to nothingness, which is a gay Arcadia, is more problematic than in the previous texts. It is not only an intertextual return to the past, as Will and Edward experience in coming across Charles Nantwich and Edgar Orst respectively. *The Line of Beauty* is echoic as a whole, for the novel is itself a return to the eighties and the decade's own neo-Victorian revivalism. Thus, Nick's thwarted narcissism —Apollonian I called it in chapter 5— is dismantled by the Dionysian eruption of AIDS. The anti-relational self-contained poetics of AIDS that looms large on what I have called Hollinghurst's (sex) tetralogy is somehow replaced by much more echoic trans-generational narratives in the last two novels. It is not so much the current character's self-centred viewpoint that matters. The relation between different moments and characters is much more interlocked in rather echoic terms, all echoing the others. Cecil Valance and David Sparsholt are focal points echoed throughout. Yet, in their echoing, they are as changed as those who echo them as generations pass. That is why, memory, which is a constant issue in Hollinghurst's fiction, becomes central to understanding the evolution of characters and their relations to each other and the discourses that make up them all; hence, the obsession of most characters in *The Stranger's Child* and *The Sparsholt Affair* to write biographies and memoirs which contend for holding the truth. In the end, the truth of life-writing proves to be as elusive as beauty and trauma.

In being between the celebration of beauty and sex and their traumatic underside, Hollinghurst's fiction is a liminal event, or a series of events. No writer before (and I would say after) him has portrayed gay subculture and sexuality with his prowess and genuineness, which "ma[kes] previous writers of sexually explicit fiction, gay or straight alike, look squeamish and incurious in comparison."[662] The male body is worshipped and sexuality reified, reason why these novels have been sometimes considered limited as well as limiting in their scope. When authors like John Updike argue Hollinghurst's fiction focuses on void self-gratification,[663] it is unfair, to say the least. The problem for this type of criticism is with gay self-gratification. This is particularly the case of *The Spell*, featuring gay club life styles at the turn of the millennium: gay stereotypes, especially studs and naïve ones, many of them leading promiscuous lives. This, which may be limiting in, for example, Updike's view, is not necessarily so. As I already mentioned, drawing on Harvey, (homo)sexuality is the way for the novels to address democratic bonds between men beyond class and race.[664] In Hollinghurst, gay promiscuity is no longer a moral label, but a political one which breaks, albeit transiently, with social differences. In being persecuted and prosecuted irrespective of their status, gay characters have made up bonds which set them away from the norm. They create alternative spaces where naked male bodies find no distinction with one another. Clubs, prisons, public schools and universities, imaginary Arcadias, idealised pasts or voluntary exiles frame their sexual encounters and fantasies. These are all-male scenarios which operate apart from social heteronormative codes and where the intimacy of sexual practices turns a public issue. This celebration, and often commodification, of male beauty and gay sexuality is both reified and problematised. Such problematisation adopts two main forms. Hollinghurst's novels often ironise on characters and situations to come to terms with stereotypes. In this sense, camp proves to be constant in his novels. Gay life styles are theatricalised and ridiculed as well as they are upheld. This aporia is Hollinghurst's response to simplistic criticisms. Gay promiscuity is both a stereotype and the target of irony, but also a sign of the community's subculture. As pointed out above, beauty has a traumatic underside that looms large along the writer's production.

From the premises of trauma theory, this book has delved into how trauma poetics helps to understand gay subculture. Contemporary homosexuality was the effect of a traumatic event, namely Wilde's downfall. More recently, gayness has been redefined by AIDS, a historical trauma that has annihilated a community and menaced its hardly-gained culture. Hence, beauty and sexuality are not only celebrated, but also longed for and problematised when they are lost. Harvey has said *The Sparsholt Affair* is a novel about the failure of cultural transmission.[665] In my view, Hollinghurst's production as a whole is about multifunctional failure, loss and thwarted desire. It is often when pleasure (and social recognition) is about to be fulfilled that an event makes it all vanish. This happens to virtually all Hollinghurst's heroes, which makes almostness a leitmotif. The double temporality of trauma narratives applies to these novels, often

---

[662] Harvey: "Cartographer," n.p.
[663] In ibid.
[664] Ibid.
[665] Ibid.

featuring different generations, the older ones always casting a spell and a traumatic secret over the new ones. The traumatic event is introjected or incorporated, depending on each case. However, the sense of belatedness and the haunting the traumatic event cast on the present prove to be relentless in all the novels. AIDS, imprisonment, social downfall, Nazism, even occasionally homosexuality itself, are main gay traumatic events in Hollinghurst's fiction. They are often latent, unknown by some characters, unrecognised by others. However, their echoes are unremitting and eventually irrepressible. Thus, when a triggering —often a minor event— takes place, the belated trauma resurfaces. This happens in an echoic fashion, the present echoing the past and viceversa; hence the specular structure of many of Hollinghurst's novels and narratives, particularly his early ones. The clash between celebration and trauma turns into an aporic, liminal discourse that characterises these texts. Numerous tropes address this aporia that some characters and narrators utter or intend to utter. Indeed, as some of them argue, as has been recalled along the book, they continue writing, speaking or uttering as long as it is (im)possible to write, speak and utter. Belatedness is often represented in the form of postponement, which grants both pleasure and pain on the one who waits, and also a constant feature of Hollinghurst's fiction. Henry James, one of his major tutelary spirits, is a hypotext continuously updated to meet the traumatic discourse of gay celebration/trauma.

There are three last aspects I would like to address to close this monograph. I have grouped Hollinghurst's novels in a 'teatrology' and a couple of family sagas. Like any other grouping, it is as tentative as inaccurate. Yet, it helps to understand the writer's evolution from the late-eighties to the twenty-first century and makes the structure of the book user-friendly given the complexity of the texts, especially their multiple cross-references and intertextual allusions to multiple, albeit related, texts and cultural discourses and events. In a tentative fashion, it could be argued that whereas what I have called his 'tetralogy' relies on presence and his last two novels in absence. With presence, I make reference to the overwhelming narrative and/or focalising occurrence of a protagonist (or protagonists in *The Spell*) that configure a closed focal point and scenario. It is rather postmodern in more senses than one, especially in its use of irony and self-begetting intertextuality. I do not mean that absence is not also present in the first four novels. There are spectral presences, particularly when it comes to the traumata the heroes are unable to cope with, let alone utter. However, in most cases, the encounter between the heroes and the secrets they have been deprived of eventually takes place and changes it all. After a period of latency, the trauma bursts out. The effect of AIDS looms large in all the 'tetralogy', even if *The Spell* gives it a turn, focusing rather on the celebratory survival after loss. Presence is also related to narcissism. Most of these heroes draw on narcissistic narratives, not only because they are looking at themselves in mirrors, which is a constant feature in Hollinghurst. They are a narcissistic effect of a long gay tradition. The specular effect of this encounter determines these novels' structures and narrative discourses. Being projected on and back from the other (be it James, Firbank, Forster, or other characters) makes these heroes' presence overwhelming and somehow claustrophobic. The last two novels can be labelled as texts of absence. I say that because they turn around an episode that remains in the dark or elusive as time passes. Cecil Valance and Sparsholt, unlike Nantwich, Orst and Nick's scandal at the Feddens', feature episodes which are as crucial as forgotten. It is for this reason that memory, which is an important issue along Hollinghurst's novels, becomes the core of the more recent ones. There is still narcissism to these novels and their heroes. However, such narcissism is diffused as time goes by, memory falters, memoirs contradict each other and the echoic eventually prevails. It is the echoes of memory, of hearsay, of more official historiographic accounts that make up these novels' keyhole discourse and blackout structure.

There seems to be also a shift from the intergenerational to the transgenerational in Hollinghurst's literary discourses. Thus, particularly The *Swimming-pool Library* and *The Folding Star* feature the encounter between the post-gay-liberation generation and its closeted predecessor to represent the problematic relation between both. The novels aim to repair historical injustices and utter the silenced. It is obvious that the new generation of gays is not responsible for the suffering of the old one. However, rehabilitation of former injustices is mandatory to move forward and come to terms with new traumata. In a sense, these texts are pedagogic and they also render the ethical turn characteristic of humanities in the last decades. The problematics of intergenerational bonds is especially conspicuous in *The Spell* where father and son collide and share experiences in the context of the 'post-gay'. *The Stranger's Child* and The *Sparsholt Affair* break once more with prior novels. It is not so much paternal-filial affiliations that matter, but the transmission of traumata, discourses and/or the celebration of beauty transgenerationally. Hence, as I mentioned above, the epic family saga is the genre Hollinghurst makes use of in both texts to address how the transmission of secrets, encrypted or not, is often thwarted. Be it as it may, he insists in exploring the limits of memory as time passes. Finally, both inter and trans-generationality is not only related to family bonds. In fact, in most cases, it is the continuum, if at all, of gay identity and aesthetics that these novels address. In this sense, intertextuality, a major postmodernist trait, is central to Hollinghurst's discourse. As pointed out in the introduction, some articles and the few monographs on the author often focus their attention on it. I have not overlooked intertextuality, for it is mandatory to fully understand his literary project. However, this monograph has explored intertextuality within a wider scope, namely gay genealogy and especially its discourses of trauma and celebration.

The last point I will make reference to is the shift of Hollinghurst's fiction from being mostly focused on gayness to sexual ambiguity. Parallel to this widening in the scope of gender identity and desire representation, there has been a decrease in sexual explicitness, slightly noticeable in *The Line of Beauty* and more conspicuous in the last two novels. *The Swimming-pool Library* is the paradigm of Hollinghurst's early fiction; it features an all-male cast, virtually all gay characters, and it is sexually explicit to the extreme. The novel was an effect of its time, namely the gay liberation movement and the AIDS crisis. That is why it is so concrete, albeit ambitious, in its aspirations. It proves to be homage to silenced gay generations and an attempt to stage their problematic reconciliation with the present. Sexual explicitness is a political issue since gayness was decriminalised only in 1967 and since, with the coming of AIDS, (homo)sexuality was newly criminalised and medicalised. This sense of urgency has been progressively lost. The prowess of sexuality as political vindication changed to a post-gay/AIDS one in *The Spell*, where celebration and self-gratification were somehow ends in themselves. I am not saying celebration cannot be vindicative as well, but it is in a different fashion. Indeed, *The Line of Beauty* returns in part to the spirit of *The*

Swimming-pool Library. However, this was only a temporary move. Hollinghurst's last two novels update James to current concerns, especially its subtlety and ambiguity. Characters are no longer exclusively gay, but also straight, bisexual, asexual and even pansexual. This wide scope of identities and the cultural referents they address make *The Stranger's Child* and *The Sparsholt Affair* more in tune with current trends. Homosexuality is still a sexual/gender identity or position, no longer residual or marginalised. In fact, former gay features like camp have been normalised and become part of mainstream discourses. This process of assimilation, which for some critics, erases former subversiveness can be read otherwise. The fact that other gender identities and sexualities have been incorporated also means that the mainstream has been refashioned. Hence, neither subcultures are so marginal nor the centre is so normative any longer. Has Hollinghurst's discourse softened? Has his discourse lost part of its political force and aesthetic prowess? It is possible although I do not think so. In any case, in the process, his novels have helped redefine heteronormativity, have celebrated beauty and resurfaced traumata.

References

Primary sources

Hollinghurst, Alan. 1980. *The Creative Uses of Homosexuality in the Novels of Forster, Firbank and Hartley*. Unpublished Thesis.
——. 1998a. *The Swimming-pool Library*. London: Vintage.
——. 1998b. *The Folding Star*. London: Vintage.
——. 1999. *The Spell*. London: Vintage.
——. 2000. Introduction to *Ronald Firbank. Three Novels*. London: Penguin.
——. 2001. "I often Laugh when I'm Alone." The Yale Review 89.2, 1-18.
——. 2004. *The Line of Beauty*. London: Picador.
——. 2005. "Introduction to Bruges-la-Morte." In Georges Rodenbach. Bruges-la-Morte. London: Dedalus, pp. 11-19.
——. 2011. *The Stranger's Child*. London: Picador.
——. 2017. *The Sparsholt Affair*. London: Picador.

Secondary Sources

Ackroyd, Peter. 1988. *Hawksmoor*. London: Abacus.
——. 2002. *Albion. The Origins of the English Imagination*. London: Chatto & Windus.
Adams, Stephen. 1980. *The Homosexual as Hero*. Barnes and Noble: New York.
Alderson, David and Linda Anderson (eds) 2000. *Territories of Desire in Queer Culture*. Manchester: Manchester University Press.
Alderson, David. 2016. *Sex, Needs & Queer Culture. From Liberation to the Post-Gay*. London: Zed Books.
Anon. 2001. "Penguin Reviews of *The Spell*." Accessed on 4 September 2007 at: http://search. barnesandnoble.com/booksearch/isbnInquiry.asp?z=y&EAN=978014028.
Anon. 2007. "*Death in Venice*, Thomas Mann." Accessed on 23 January 2007 at: https://www. enotes.com/topics/death-in-venice/critical-essays/death-venice-thomas-mann.
Anon. 2008. "Críticas de 'La Ronda' (1950)." Accessed on 26 September 2008 at: http://www. filmaffinity.com/es/reviews/1/548137. html.
Ayala, Francisco. 2005 (1971). "Introducción" to *Muerte en Venecia*. Madrid: Edhasa, 7-16.
Baker, Nicholson. 1994. "Lost Youth", *The London Review of Books*, 9 June 1994, https:// www.lrb.co.uk/the-paper/v16/n11/nicholson-baker/lost-youth.
Barnaby, Andrew. 2017. *Coming Too Late: Reflections on Freud and Belatedness*. New York: SUNY.
Beckford, William. 1983. *Vathek*. Oxford and New York: Oxford University Press.
Bishop, Stephanie. 2017. "*The Sparsholt Affair*," in *The Monthly*, November 2017.
Bloom, Harold. 1975. *The Anxiety of Influence: A Theory of Poetry*. Oxford: Oxford University Press.
Boyne, John. 2017. "*The Sparsholt Affair* Review: A Blitz of Gay Longing." *Irish Times*, 7 October 2017. https://bit.ly/3o68Iyx.

Bradford. Richard. 2007. *The Novel Now. Contemporary British Fiction*. Oxford: Blackwell Publishing.

Bradley, John. 1996. "Disciples of St Narcissus. In Praise of Alan Hollinghurst." *The Critical Review* 36, 3-18.

Bristow, Joseph. 1995. *Effeminate England. Homoerotic Writing after 1885*. Buckingham: Open University Press.

——. 1992. Sexual Sameness. *Textual Differences in Lesbian and Gay Writing*. London and New York: Routledge.

——. 1997. *Sexuality*. London: The New Critical Idiom.

Brooker, Joseph. 2005. "Neo Lines: Alan Hollinghurst and the Apogee of the Eighties." London: Birkbeck eprints: Accessed on 5 May 2007 at: http://eprints.bbk.ac.uk/archive/00000470.

Brown, Angus. 2016. "The Touch of Reading in Hollinghurst's Prose." In Mendelssohn, Michèle and Dennis Flannery (eds.). *Alan Hollinghurst: Writing under the Influence*. Manchester: Manchester UP, 25-39.

Burton, Peter.1991. *Talking to …*. Exeter: Third House.

Butler, Judith. 2016. *Frames of War. When is Life Grievable?* London and New York: Verso Books.

Callil, Carmen and Colm Tóibín. 1999. *The Modern Library. The 200 Best Novels in English since 1950*. London: Picador.

Calvo, Mónica. 2000. "A Feminine Subject in Postmodernist Chaos: Jeanette Winterson's Political Manifesto in *Oranges Are not the Only Fruit*." *Revista Alicantina de Estudios Ingleses* 13, 21-34.

Campbell, Michael. 1968. *Lord Dismiss Us*. London: Corgi.

Canning, Richard. 2001. *Conversations with Gay Novelists. Gay Fiction Speaks*. New York: Columbia UP.

Cannon, Kelly. 1994. *Henry James and Masculinity. The Man at the Margins*. London: Macmillan.

Caruth, Cathy. 1996. *Unclaimed Experience: Trauma, Narrative, and History*. Baltimore: John Hopkins UP.

Caruth Cathy (ed). 1995. *Trauma: Explorations in Memory*. Baltimore MD and London: John Hopkins UP.

Chambers, Colin and Mike Prior. 1987. *Playwrights' Progress: Patterns of Postwar British Drama*. Oxford: Amber Lane.

Chambers, Ross. 1993. "Messing around Gayness and Loiterature in Alan Hollinghurst's The Swimming-pool Library." In Judith Still and Michael Worton (eds). *Textuality and Sexuality. Reading Theories and Practices*. Manchester: Manchester University Press: 207-217.

Congreve, William. 1994. *The Way of the World*. London: New Mermaids.

Cooper, Brenda. 1999. "Snapshots of Postcolonial Masculinities: Alan Hollinghurst's *The Swimming-pool Library* and Ben Okri's *The Famished Road*," *The Journal of Commonwealth Literature*, 34(1), 135-157.

——. 2000. "A Boat, a Mask, Two Photographers and a Manticore: African Fiction in a Global Context." *Pretexts: Studies in Writing and Culture* 9(1), 63-76.

Cooper, Michael. 1990. "Discipl(in)ing the Master, Mastering the Discipl(in)e: Erotonomies of Discipleship in James' Tales of Literary Life." In Joseph Boone and Michael Cadden (eds). *Engendering Men*. New York and London: Routledge, 66-83.

Corber, Robert J. 1999. "Sentimentalizing Gay History; Mark Merlis, Alan Hollinghurst and the Cold War Persecution of Homosexuals." *Arizona Quarterly* 55(4), 115-141.

Critchley, Julian. 1992. *Some of Us. People who Did Well under Thatcher*. London: John Murray Publishers.

Dellamora, Richard. 1994. *Apocalyptic Overtures, Sexual Politics and the Sense of an Ending*. New Jersey: Rutgers University Press.

D'Emilio, John. 1992. "Capitalism and Gay Identity." In John D'Emilio, *Making Trouble*. New York: Routledge.

de Quincey, Thomas. 1979. *Confessions of an English Opium Eater*. Harmondsworth: Penguin.

Dirda, Michael. 2004. "A Condition of England Novel." Accessed on 19 September 2007 at: https://wapo.st/33q1I88.

Dollimore, Jonathan. 1991. *Sexual Dissidence, Agustine to Wilde, Freud to Foucault*. Oxford: Oxford UP.

——. 2001. *Death, Desire and Loss in Western Culture*. New York and London: Routledge.

Dukes, Thomas. 1996. "Mappings of Secrecy and Disclosure": *The Swimming-pool Library*, the Closet, and the Empire." *Journal of Homosexuality*, 31(39), 95-107.

Dyer, Geoff. 2011. "The Secret Gardener." Accessed on 17 March 2015 at: http://nymag.com/arts/books/reviews/alan-hollinghurst-2011-10/.

Edelman, Lee. 1994. *Homographesis. Essays in Gay Literary and Cultural Theory*. New York and London: Routledge.

Edwards, Tim. 1994. *Erotics and Politics. Gay Male Sexuality, Masculinity and Feminism*. London and New York: Routledge.

Eeckhout, Bart. 2012. "English Architectural Landscapes and Metonymy in Hollinghurst's The Stranger's Child." *CLCWeb: Comparative Literature and Culture* 14.3. Accessed on 19 December 2018 at https://doi.org/10.7771/1481-4374.2042

Elsner, John. 1996. "Naturalism and the Erotics of the Gaze: Imitations of Narcissus." In Natalie Boymer Kampen (ed.). *Sexuality in Ancient Art*. Cambridge: Cambridge UP.

Esteban Muñoz, Jose. 2009. *Cruising Utopia: The Then and There of Queer Futurity*. New York: New York UP.

Evans, Peter and Celestino Deleyto (eds). 1998. *Terms of Endearment. Hollywood Romantic Comedy of the 1980s and 1990s*. Edinburgh: Edinburgh UP.

Fernández, Laura. 2006. "Hollinghurst narra como era la Inglaterra de Margaret Thatcher." Accessed on 6 February 2008 at: http://www.elmundo.es/ 2006/02/14/catalunya/1930020.html.

Firbank, Ronald. 1988. *The Complete Firbank*. London: Picador Classics.

——. 2000. Ronald Firbank. *Three Novels*. London: Penguin.

Fitzgerald, Scott. 1986. *The Great Gatsby*. New York: Macmillan.

Flannery, Dennis. 2005. "The Powers of Apostrophe and the Boundaries of Mourning: Henry James, Alan Hollinghurst, and Toby Litt." *The Henry James Review*, 26(3), 293-305.

Fletcher, John. 1992. "Forster's Self-Erasure: Maurice and the Scene of Masculine Love." In Joseph Bristow (ed). *Sexual Sameness: Textual Differences in Lesbian and Gay Writing*. London: Routledge: 64-90.

Forster, E. M. 1998. *Maurice*. London: Penguin.

——. 1987. *The Life to Come and other Stories*. New York: Norton.

——. 1982. *Where Angels Fear to Tread*. Harmondsworth: Penguin.

——. 1989. *A Passage to India*. Harmondsworth: Penguin.

Foucault, Michel. 1995. *Discipline and Punish. The Birth of Prison*. Trans. Alan Sheridan. New York: Vintage Books.

Freud, Sigmund. 1958. "Mourning and Melancholia." In *Standard Edition of the Complete Psychological Works of Sigmund Freud*, vol. XIV, trans. James Strachey. London: Hogarth Press, 239-258.

Friedländer, Saul. 1993. *Memory, History, and the Extermination of the Jews in Europe*. Bloomington: Indiana University Press.

Frontain, Raymond-Jean. 2002. "Comedy of Manners." In Claude Summers (ed). *The Gay and Lesbian Literary Heritage*. New York and London: Routledge, 161-163.

Genette, Gérard. 1980. *Narrative Discourse: An Essay in Method*, trans. Jane E. Levin. Ithaca: Cornell University Press.

Gide, André. 1977. *If It Die*, trans. Dorothy Bussy. Harmondsworth: Penguin.

——.1973. *The Counterfeiters*, trans. Dorothy Bussy. New York: Vintage Books.

Gifford, Terry. 1999. *Pastoral*. London: The New Critical Idiom.

Gilbert, Geoff. 2016. "Some Properties of Fiction: Value and Fantasy in Hollinghurst's House of Fiction." In Mendelssohn, Michèle and Dennis Flannery (eds.). *Alan Hollinghurst: Writing under the Influence*. Manchester: Manchester UP, 125-140.

Greenblatt, Stephen. 1992. *Shakespearean Negotiations: The Circulation of Social Energy in Renaissance England*. Oxford: Clarendon Press.

Gunnarsdottir Champion, Margarét. 2001. "Art Mirrors the Spectator: The Field of Otherness in The Picture of Dorian Gray." In Ruth Parkin-Gounelas and Effie Yiannopoulou (eds). *The Other Within. Volume I: Literature and Culture*. Thessaloniki: Athanasios A. Altinzis, 249-256.

Gutleben, Christian. 2001. *Nostalgic Postmodernism. The Victorian Tradition and the Contemporary British Novel*. Amsterdam and New York: Rodopi.

Guy-Bray, Stephen. 2002. "Elegy," in Claude Summers (ed). *The Gay and Lesbian Literary Heritage*. New York and London: Routledge, 205-207.

Haggerty, George. 2002. "Thomas Gray." In Claude Summers (ed). *The Gay and Lesbian Literary Heritage*. New York and London: Routledge, 317-318.

Halberstam, Judith. 2005. *In a Queer Time and Place*. New York: New York UP.

Hartley, L. P. 1972. *The Go-Between*. London: Longman.

Harvey, Giles. 2018. "The Cartographer of Sex." *The New York Times Magazine*. 18 March 2018, 26-55.

Harvey, Keith. 2002. "Camp Talk and Citationality: A Queer Tale on 'Authentic' and 'Represented' Utterance." *Journal of Pragmatics* 34: 1145-1165.

Hawkins, Harriet. 1982. "The Audience's Dilemma." In Harriet Hawkins. *Congreve: Comedies. A Selection of Critical Essays*. London: Macmillan, 199-208.

Higgins, Patrick. 1996. *Heterosexual Dictatorship. Male Homosexuality in Post-War Britain*. London: Fourth State.

Hitchins, Henry. 2004. "The Double Curve. Alan Hollinghurst's New Novel Demonstrates the Aesthetic Poverty of Conservatism." *The Times Literary Supplement* (9 April), 21.

Hirst, David L. 1979. *Comedy of Manners*. London: Methuen.

Hogarth, William. 1997. *The Analysis of Beauty*. New Haven and London: Paul Mellon Centre for British Art Yale University Press.

Hollinghurst, Alan (reader). 2018a. "Alan Hollinghurst's *The Sparsholt Affair*." In Talks at Google (video). 3 May 2018. https://www.youtube.com/watch?v=H69iLEK8nUo

Hollinghurst, Alan (reader). 2018b. "Alan Hollinghurst on *The Sparsholt Affair*." In Shakespeare and Company (video). https://www.youtube.com/watch?v=4JQuPJjTNbs

Housman, Alfred E. 1989. *Collected Poems and Selected Prose*. Harmondsworth: Penguin.

Hutcheon, Linda. 1988. *The Poetics of Postmodernism*. History, Theory, Fiction. New York and London: Routledge.

——. 1998. "Irony, Nostalgia, and the Postmodern." Accessed on 24 October 2002 at: file:///C:/Users/Usuario/Downloads/pdfcoffee.com_irony-nostalgia-and-the-postmodern-by-linda-hutcheonpdf-4-pdf-free.pdf.

Isherwood, Christopher. 1991. *A Single Man*. London: Minerva.

Izquierdo, Agustín. 1989. "Introduction" to Georges Rodenbach's *Bruges-la-Morte*. Madrid: Valdemor, 7-12.

James, Henry. 1983. *A Small Boy and Others*. Princeton: Princeton University Press.

——. 1996. "The Altar of the Dead." Accessed on 16 January 2008 at: https://www.gutenberg. org/files/642/642-h/642-h.htm.

——. 1977. *The Spoils of Poynton*. London: Penguin Books.

——. 1987. *The Turn of the Screw*. London: Everyman.

——. 1986. *The Wings of the Dove*. Harmondsworth: Penguin.

——. 2000. *Washington Square*. Oxford: Oxford University Press.

——. 2000. *What Maisie Knew*. London: Wordsworth Classics.

Jeffery-Poulter, Stephen. 1991. *Peers, Queers and Commons*. London: Routledge.

Jolly, Roslyn. 1993. *Henry James. History, Narrative, Fiction*. Oxford: Clarendon Press.

Jones, James. 2002. "Thomas Mann." In Claude Summers (ed). *The Gay and Lesbian Literary Heritage*. New York and London: Routledge, 427-430.

Johnson, Allan. 2014. *Alan Hollinghurst and the Vitality of Influence*. London: Palgrave.

Juárez Hervás, Luisa. 1999. "Desire as Colonizer. A Reading of Homosexuality and Colonialism in Alan Hollinghurst's *The Swimming-pool Library*." In Fernando Galván (ed.). *On Writing (and) Race in Contemporary Britain*. Alcalá: Universidad de Alcalá, 67-72.

Kaplan, Cora. 2007. *Victoriana: Histories, Fictions, Criticism*. Edinburgh: Edinburgh UP.

Keen, Susanne. 2001. *Romances of the Archive in Contemporary British Fiction*. Toronto: Toronto UP.

Keehnen, Owen. 1995. "A Talk with Alan Hollinghurst." Accessed on 22 September 2005 at: http//www.Owen Keehnen Interviews.

Kemp, Peter. 1994. "Aesthetic Obsessions," in *The Times Literary Supplement*, No. 4756, May 27, 19.

Kopelson, Kevin. 1994. *Love's Litany. The Writing of Modern Homoerotics*. Stanford: Stanford UP.

Kristeva, Julia. 1982. *Powers of Horror: An Essay on Abjection*, trans. Leon S. Roudiez. New York: Routledge.

Kushner, Tony. 1992. *Angels in America: A Gay Fantasia on National Themes*. London: Nick Hern Books.

Lacan, Jacques. 1966. "Le Stade du miroir comme formateur de la fonction du Je telle qu'elle nous est rélévée dans l'experiance psychoanalytique." (Communication faite au XVIème congrès international de psychoanalyse à Zürich, 17 juillet 1949), in *Écrits I*. Paris: Seuil, 89-97.

Laing, Olivia. 2017. "Alan Hollinghurst's *The Sparsholt Affair* Feels Like Looking through a Keyhole." *New Statesman*, 3 October 2017. https://www.newstatesman.com/culture/books/ 2017/10/alan-hollinghursts-sparsholt-affair-feels-looking-through-keyhole

Lane, Christopher. 1995. *The Ruling Passion. British Colonial Allegory and the Paradox of Homosexual Desire*. Durham and London: Duke UP.

Lasdun, James. 2017. "*The Sparsholt Affair* by Alan Hollinghurst review – passion and folly, beautifully observed." *The Guardian*, 5 Oct 2017. https://www.theguardian.com/books/ 2017/ oct/05/the-sparsholt-affair-by-alan-hollinghurst-review

Lee, Don. 2004. "Thatcher's London, Sex, Drugs and the Ruling Class." Accessed on 19 September 2007 at: https://bit.ly/3G6z3Tr.

Letissier, Georges. 2007. "Queer, Quaint and Camp: Alan Hollinghurst's Own Return to the English Tradition." *Études Anglaises Contemporaines* 60(2), 198-211.

Lewis, Holly. 2016. *The Politics of Everybody: Feminism, Queer Theory and Marxism at the Intersection*. London: Zed Books.

Liggins, Emma. 2003. "Alan Hollinghurst and Metropolitan Gay Identities," in Daniel Lea and Berthold Schoene (eds). *Posting the Male. Masculinities in Post-War and Contemporary British Literature*. London: Genus, 159-170.

Lilly, Mark. 1993. *Gay Men's Literature in the Twentieth Century*. London: Macmillan.
Llewellyn, Mark. 2007. 'Breaking the Mould? Sarah Waters and the Politics of Genre'. In Heilmann, Ann and Mark Llewellyn (eds.), *Metafiction and Metahistory in Contemporary Women's Fiction*. Houndmills, Basingstoke: Palgrave Macmillan, 195-210.
Lodge, David. 2006. *The Year of Henry James: The Story of the Novel*. London: Harvill Secker.
Lusin, Caroline. 2010. 'Writing Lives and Worlds: English Fictional Biography at the Turn of the 21st Century'. In Nünning, Vera, Ansgar Nünning, and Birgit Neumann (eds.), *Cultural Ways of Worldmaking: Media and Narratives*. Berlin & New York: Walter de Gruyter, 265-283.
Magrinyá, Luis. 2002. "Éxtasis para la madurez," "Babelia." *El País* (29 March): 24.
Mann, Thomas. 1975. *Death in Venice*, trans. H. T. Lowe-Porter. London: Penguin.
Manning, Tony. 1996 "Gay Culture: Who Needs it." In Mark Simpson (ed.). *Anti-Gay*: London: Cassel, 107-118.
Marcus, J. S. 2005. "Fiction in Review. Alan Hollinghurst." *Yale Review* 93. 3: 180-185.
Marín, Juan María. 1992. *La tradición de la comedia inglesa en Joe Orton*. Unpublished Ph. Thesis. Universidad de Zaragoza.
Martínez-Alfaro, María Jesús. 2003. *Narrative Strategies in Charles Palliser's The Quincunx, The Sensationist and Betrayals*. Unpublished Ph. Thesis. Universidad de Zaragoza.
Mathuray, Mark. 2017. *Sex and Sensibility in the novels of Alan Hollinghurst*. London: Palgrave.
Mayne, Andrew. 1985. "Introduction" to *Loot* by Joe Orton. London: Methuen, i-xxxviii.
McLeod, John. 2016. "Race, Empire and *The Swimming-pool Library*." In Mendelssohn, Michèle and Dennis Flannery (eds.). *Alan Hollinghurst: Writing under the Influence*. Manchester: Manchester UP, 60-78.
McNally, Terence. 1995. *Love, Valor, Compassion!* New York: Plume.
Melville, Herman. 1986. *Billy Budd, Sailor and Other Stories*. New York: Viking Penguin.
Mendelsohn, Daniel. 2011. "In gay and crumbling England." Accessed on 9 March 2016 at https://www.nybooks.com/articles/2011/11/10/gay-and-crumbling-england/
Mendelssohn, Michèle and Dennis Flannery (eds.). 2016. *Alan Hollinghurst: Writing under the Influence*. Manchester: Manchester UP.
Miller, Laura. 2018. "Rising to the Sunlit Surface." Accessed on 5 August 2018 at https://slate.com/culture/2018/03/alan-hollinghursts-the-sparsholt-affair-reviewed.html
Mitchell, Donald. 2000. *Britten and Auden in the Thirties*, introd. Alan Hollinghurst. London: Boydell.
Mitchell, Kay. 2016. "Who are you? What the Fuck Are you Doing here?: Queer Debates and Contemporary Connections." In Mendelssohn, Michèle and Dennis Flannery (eds.). *Alan Hollinghurst: Writing under the Influence*. Manchester: Manchester UP, 174-190.
Mort, Frank. 1996. *Cultures of Consumption: Masculinities and Social Space in Late-Twentieth-Century Britain*. London and New York: Routledge.
Moss, Stephen. 2004. "I don't Make Moral Judgments." Accessed on 22 November 2004 at: http://books.guardian.co.uk/bookerprize2004.
Murphy, Stephen. 2004. "Past Irony: Trauma and the Historical Turn in Fragments and *The Swimming-pool Library*." *In Ramifications of Trauma Theory, Literature and History*. Third Series. Manchester: Manchester University Press, 58-75.
Navokov, Vladimir. 1988. *Lolita*. Harmondsworth: Penguin.
Nietzsche, Fiedrich. 2017. *The Birth of Tragedy Out of the Spirit of Music*, trans. Ian Johnston. Accessed on 17 July 2018 at: http://johnstoniatexts.x10host.com/nietzsche/tragedyhtml.html.
Norton, Rictor. 1997. "The Homosexual Pastoral Tradition." Accessed on 7 August 2002 at: http://www.infopt.demon. co.uk/ pastor01.html.

Novak, Amy. 2008. "Who speaks? Who listens? The problem of address in two Nigerian trauma novels." *Studies in the Novel*. vol. 40, no. 1/2, Postcolonial trauma novels, 31-51.

O'Keeffe, Alice. 2011. "Alan Hollinghurst." Acessed on 7 May 2015 at www.thebookseller.com/ profile/alan-hollinghurst.

Onega, Susana. *Peter Ackroyd*. 1998. Plymouth: Writers and Their Work.

——. 1999. *Metafiction and Myth in the Novels of Peter Ackroyd*. Rochester: Camden House.

——. 2006. *Jeanette Winterson*. Manchester: Manchester University Press.

——. 2007. "Ethics, Trauma and the Contemporary British Novel," Seminar on literary theory. 20th Conference of the International Association of University Professors of English (IAUPE). University of Lund (Sweden). August 2007.

Orton, Joe. 1976. *The Complete Plays*. London: Methuen World Classics.

Ovid. *The Metamorphoses*. http://hompi.sogang.ac.kr/anthony/Classics/OvidEcho Narcissus.htm.

Page, Benedicte. 2004. "Inside the Tory Stronghold." *The Bookseller Magazine* (13 February), 30-31.

Penney, James. 2013. *After Queer Theory: The Limits of Sexual Politics*. London: Pluto Press.

Powers, John. 2018. "*The Sparsholt Affair* Confirms Alan Hollinghurst's Status as a Literary Master." Npr Books. 12 March 2018. https://www.npr.org/2018/03/12/592868267/the-spars holt-affair-confirms-alan-hollinghurst-s-status-as-a-literary-master?t=1530086438599.

Proust, Marcel. 1990. *En busca del tiempo perdido*, trans. Pedro Salinas. Madrid: Aguilar.

Quinn, Anthony. 2004. "The Last Good Summer." Accessed on 19 September 2007 at: shorter l.at/govxA.

Ranelagh, John. 1991. *Thatcher's People. An Insider's Account of the Politics, the Power and the Personalities*. London: Harper and Collins.

Raven, Simon. 1969. *Fielding Gray*. London: Panther.

Rennison, Nick. 2005. *Contemporary British Novelists*. London and New York: Routledge.

Rivkin, Julie. 2016. "*The Stranger's Child* and *The Aspern Papers*: Queering Origin Stories and Questioning the Visitable Past." In Mendelssohn, Michèle and Dennis Flannery (eds.). *Alan Hollinghurst: Writing under the Influence*. Manchester: Manchester UP, 79-95.

Rodenbach, Georges. 2005 (1892). *Bruges-la-Morte*. London: Dedalus.

Ronan, Joseph. 2016. "Ostentatiously Discreet: Bisexual Camp in *The Stranger's Child*." In Mendelssohn, Michèle and Dennis Flannery (eds.). *Alan Hollinghurst: Writing under the Influence*. Manchester: Manchester UP, 96-109.

Rothberg, Michael. 2009. *Multidirectional Memory: Remembering the Holocaust in the Age of Decolonization*. Stanford: Stanford UP.

Said, Edward. 1991. *Orientalism*. Harmondsworth: Penguin.

Samuel, Raphael. 1994. *Theatres of Memory*. London: Verso.

Schwab, Gabrielle. 2011. *Haunting Legacies. Violent Histories and Transgenerational Trauma*. New York: Columbia UP.

Sedgwick, Eve. 1985. *Between Men. English Literature and Male Homosocial Desire*. New York: Columbia University Press.

——. 1991. *Epistemology of the Closet*. London: Penguin.

——. 2003. *Touching Feeling: Affect, Pedagogy, Performativity*. Durham: Duke UP.

Seligman, Craig. 1994. "Sex and the Single Man." *The New Yorker*, October 24, 1994, 95.

Shakespeare, William. 1994. *Four Comedies. The Taming of the Shrew, A Midsummer Night's Dream, As You Like It, Twelfth Night*. London: Penguin Classics.

Silva, Stephen da. 1998. "Transvaluing Immaturity: Reverse Discourses of Male Homosexuality in E. M. Forster's Posthumously Published Fiction." *Criticism*, vol. 40, n. 2, 237-272.

Simpson, Mark. 1996. *Anti-Gay*. London: Continuum.

Sinfield, Alan. 1998. *Gay and After*. London: Serpent's Tail.

198   José M. Yebra

——. 2000. "Culture, Consensus and Difference: Angus Wilson to Alan Hollinghurst." In Alastair Davis, and Alan Sinfield (eds). *British Culture of the Postwar. An Introduction to Literature and Society.* London: Routledge, 83-102.

Siropoulos, Vagelis. 2001. "The Dionysian (Gay) Abject: Corporeal Representation in The Birth of Tragedy and Death in Venice." In Ruth Parkin-Gounelas and Effie Yiannopoulou (eds). *The Other Within. Vol. I: Literature and Culture.* Thessaloniki: Athanasios A. Altinzis, 93-103.

Schnitzler, Arthur. 2008. *La Ronde*, trans. Stephen Unwin. London: Nick Hern Books.

Sontag, Susan. 1964. "Notes on Camp." Accessed on 4 December 2002 at: http://pages.zoom.co.uk/leveridge/sontag.html.

——. 2001. *Illness as Metaphor and AIDS and its Metaphors.* New York: Picador.

Stevens, Hugh. 1998. *Henry James and Sexuality.* Cambridge: Cambridge University Press.

Summers, Claude (ed). 2002. *The Gay and Lesbian Literary Heritage.* New York and London: Routledge.

Swchartz, Alexandra. 2018. "A Novel of Sex and Secrecy." *The New Yorker*, 19 March 2018. https://www.newyorker.com/magazine/2018/03/19/a-novel-of-sex-and-secrecy

Tait, Leo. 2011. "*The Stranger's Child* by Alan Hollinghurst review." Accessed on 27 November 2017 at: https://bit.ly/3g4rnGM.

Techiné, André. 2007. "Hymne à la vie, interview d'André Téchiné." Accessed on 4 July 2008 at:http://www.evene.fr/cinema/actualite/interview-andre-techine-temoins-beart-blanc-702php.

Tennyson, Alfred. 1987. *The Poems of Tennyson in Three Volumes.* Harlow: Longman.

Tillyard, Stella. 2005. "Interview, Alan Hollinghurst." *Prospect London* 116, 62-65.

Tóibín, Colm and Carmen Callil. 1999. *The Modern Library. The 200 Best Novels in English since 1950.* London: Picador.

Tóibín, Colm. 2004. *The Master.* London: Picador.

——. 2005. "The Comedy of Being English." *The New York Review of Books.* 52.1. Accessed on 16 January 2008 at: http://www.nybooks.com/articles/17671.

Tonkin, Boyd. 2004. "A Week in Books." Accessed on 7 may 2005 at: http://findarticles.com/p/articles/mi—qn4158/is/ain12817243.

Trollope, Anthony. 1969. *Phineas Finn.* Oxford: Oxford UP.

Walton, James. 2017. "Alan Hollinghurst's New Novel is Dazzling – and Just like all his Others." Accessed on 27 June 2018 at https://www.spectator.co.uk/2017/10/alan-hollinghursts-new-novel-is-dazzling-and-just-like-all-his-others/

Waugh, Evelyn. 1987 (1945). *Brideshead Revisited.* London: Penguin.

Weeks, Jeffrey. 1990. *Coming Out. Homosexual Politics in Britain from the Nineteenth Century to the Present.* Quartet Books: London.

White, Edmund. 1994. *The Burning Library. Writings on Art, Politics and Sexuality 1969-1993.* London: Chatto & Windus.

White, Edmund (ed). 1994. *The Faber Book of Gay Short Fiction.* London: Faber.

Whitehead, Anne. 2004. *Trauma Fiction.* Edinburgh: Edinburgh UP.

Wiegand, David. 2004. "Surface Cracks." Accessed on 28 August 2007 at: https://bit.ly/3AzMtWV.

Wilde, Oscar. 1971. *The Works of Oscar Wilde.* London and Glasgow: Collins.

——. 2018. *The Picture of Dorian Gray.* Accessed on 18 September 2018 at http://www.planetpublish.com/wpcontent/uploads/2011/11/The_Picture_of_Dorian_Gray_NT.pdf

Wilson, James. 1996. "*The Folding Star* Review." *The Michigan Daily.* 5 February. Accessed on 13 April 2007 at https://digital.bentley.umich.edu/midaily/mdp.39015071754951/258.

Winter, Jay. 2006. "Notes on the Memory Boom: War, Remembrance and the Uses of the Past."
    In Bell, Duncan (ed.), *Memory, Trauma and World Politics. Reflections on the Relationship
    between Past and Present*. New York: Palgrave MacMillan, 54-73.
Winterson, Jeanette. 1994. *Arts & Lies: A Piece for Three Voices and a Bawd*. London: Jonathan
    Cape.
——. 1997. *Gut Symmetries*. London: Granta.
Wood, James. 2004. "The Ogee Curve." *The New Republic*, 231(4691), 47-49.
Woods, Gregory. 1998. *A History of Gay Literature. The Male Tradition*. New Haven and
    London: Yale University Press.
Yebra, José M. 2010. "Utopia and Dystopia in Homoerotic Territory in Alan Hollinghurst's *The
    Swimming-pool Library*, *The Folding Star* and *The Spell*." *Odisea*, 11. Universidad de
    Almería, 169-181.
——. 2011. "A Terrible Beauty: Ethics, Aesthetics and the Trauma of Gayness in Alan
    Hollinghurst's *The Line of Beauty*." In Onega, Susana and Jean-Michel Ganteau (eds.).
    Ethics and Trauma in Contemporary British Fiction. Amsterdam and New York: Rodopi,
    175-208.
——. 2013. "Neo-Victorian Biofiction and Trauma Poetics in Colm Tóibín's *The Master*." *Neo-
    Victorian Studies* 6 (1), 41-74.
——. 2015. "Transgenerational and Intergenerational Family Trauma in Colm Tóibín's *The
    Blackwater Lightship* and 'Three Friends.'" *Moderna Sprak* 2015 (2), 122-139.
Žižek, Slavoj. 2005. *Interrogating the Real*. New York: Continuum.